AMERICAN INDIAN POLICY IN THE TWENTIETH CENTURY

AMERICAN INDIAN POLICY IN THE TWENTIETH CENTURY

EDITED BY
VINE DELORIA, JR.

UNIVERSITY OF OKLAHOMA PRESS : NORMAN

West. Amer.

E
93
A44
1985

cla

Library of Congress Cataloging in Publication Data

Main entry under title:

American Indian policy.

   Includes bibliographies and index.
   1. Indians of North America—Government relations—Addresses, es-
says, lectures. 2. Indians of North America—Legal status, laws, etc.—
Addresses, essays, lectures. I. Deloria, Vine.
E93.A44   1985   323.1'197'073   85-1057
ISBN 0-8061-1897-0 (alk. paper)

Essays by Joyotpaul Chaudhuri; Vine Deloria, Jr.; Thomas Holm;
Michael G. Lacy; Daniel McCool; Robert A. Nelson and Joseph F.
Sheley; and David L. Vinje reprinted by permission of *The Social
Science Journal,* Colorado State University.

The paper in this book meets the guidelines for permanence and dur-
ability of the Committee on Production Guidelines for Book Longevity
of the Council on Library Resources, Inc.

7/21/86

Contents

AMERICAN INDIAN POLICY IN THE TWENTIETH CENTURY

Introduction

BY VINE DELORIA, JR.

The study of government policy, at any level, is best done by hindsight. Avowed beliefs of politicians and political parties are often subject to the expediencies of the moment and the road to programmatic hell is well paved, a beautiful boulevard of good intentions. Even the most astute of scholars has a difficult time discerning how policies were formulated and put into effect. Chance and happenstance are more often the determinative factors in our lives than we would be willing to admit. Yet human societies seem always to stumble upward toward a more sublime and humane ordering of their domestic relations. Despite our contemporary shortfalls, there is no question that we live in a better world, that we have more concern for the weak and helpless, and that we are evolving better and more comprehensive ways of handling our human problems.

Federal policy for American Indians shows the same line of progression as do other areas of policy consideration. A century ago Congress blithely and arrogantly dictated what would happen in Indian country and neither the Indians nor the federal agencies that served them had much to say about it. Today hardly a thought is voiced in the area of Indian policy without consultation with a wide variety of Indian people. Policy seems no worse today than it did in earlier eras of American history. But is it worse today than it was yesterday? Although a sizable segment of the American Indian community would argue against

3

the seemingly arbitrary acts of the federal government, these complaints issue from a secure position that allows Indians to hammer unmercifully at those who make policy. Therefore, the *process* of formulating the federal government's posture toward Indians has changed substantially and definitely for the better in almost every instance.

Not only do we possess a keener sense of justice today, we also have a better sense of what is appropriate for communities. A century ago, Congress decreed in the General Allotment Act that all Indians would become farmers and subsequent agreements and statutes allotting tribal lands were enforced with a frightening efficiency. Even on reservations so crowded with trees one could not walk the lands or in barren desert areas, allotment was carried out in defiance of common sense because Congress had so decreed. Today we have many programmatic options available to us within the general rubric of federal Indian policy. Reservations are encouraged to modify national programs to fit their particular needs, and no tribe is expected to carry out a program or policy in defiance of nature and good judgment.

When we come to see federal Indian policy in the broadest and most comprehensive historical setting, we are led to some rather unsettling conclusions. Within the perspective of Indian-white conflict there is no question that the major thrust has been one of dispossession of the natives by those colonizing the continent. The first response in formulating a policy for the United States was the naïve belief that moving the natives westward toward the uninhabitable regions would be sufficient to resolve the question of primacy in political and economic affairs. Within this setting, however, some care was taken to protect the legal rights of the Indians and to preserve both the national identity and the cultural integrity of the tribes. True, missionaries played a critical role in implementing the policy of removal of the tribes west of the Mississippi River. The missionaries also did yeoman work in the translation of the Bible and some political documents of the United States into the native languages, and some missionaries, most prominently Samuel Worcester, went to prison in an effort to help the tribes protect their national status.

When it became apparent that removing Indians from contact with whites would not resolve the problems posed by the presence of two radically opposed ways of life, efforts were made to bring Indians within the scope and operation of the then-dominant social order. Economic integration, through the vesting of a portion of the tribal land estate in individual tribal members, was believed to be the key in bringing Indians within the social and cultural embrace of American society. Debates over the efficacy of this course continued in some quarters until very recently and much of the present configuration of Indian country is a product of this ideology. When viewed with some degree of detachment, the economic integration of Indians into American society has many positive aspects; when examined from the perspective of premature and forced integration of Indians, economics has been a poor vehicle for achieving social reforms within the tribes. It has only produced a small, articulate elite that attempts to broker cultural exchanges.

In Indian affairs, perhaps more than any other area of American political life, policy occurs at two levels of involvement. High-level pronouncements deal with the theory and ideology of social responsibility, and here the pendulum swings back and forth between accepting an onerous and continuing financial responsibility for providing services to Indian communities and abruptly casting Indians into the American mainstream where they can slowly be digested at the bottom of the industrial economic pyramid. This arena is defined by newspapers, politicians, and legislatures. It is usually phrased in pious but well-intentioned ideas that seek spiritual comfort and direction rather than instructions on how to accomplish the task. We find the classic statements of high-level policy in the presidential messages to Congress on Indians, in political party platforms, and in congressional resolutions. We rarely, if ever, find a simple statement dealing with the implementation of policy.

At a much lower level of policy we find the nebulous arena of implementation. Here personal whims, misunderstandings, the security of federal employment, the informal networks of political bureaucracy, and the guerrilla tactics of political activism play an important role in defining what the pretty phrases devised at the higher levels actually mean. Regardless of the posture of any national administration toward Indians and their problems, the lower-level bureaucracy largely determines what the actual policy of the government will be. Implementation of policy rarely resembles anything previously described by the policy makers. This disparity has both positive and negative aspects. The unwieldy bureaucracy takes a long time to adjust to a change in direction and unless there is a zealot like John Collier frantically pushing it along, a federal agency will take years to change its policy orientation. Protection and frustration come in equal amounts in institutional life.

Traditionally we have sought to analyze federal Indian policy in a linear fashion, pretending that one line of ideology is dominant at both levels of policy making. Our chronologies have sought to identify the critical actors and actions that illustrate the determination of the federal government to find a resolution of its Indian problem. While this line of thought helps us interpret the heroes and the villains of the piece, it rarely accounts for the important changes in the configuration of Indian country. As a result we are often left speechless and without a framework for understanding each incoming administration. Our evaluation of federal policy becomes personified in presidents and and congressmen and we can only grade things according to whether we feel they were better or worse than what preceded them. But *better* and *worse* are not the words of art that allow us to seek new directions or to clarify the nature of the problems we face in understanding this subject.

This collection of essays attempts to escape from the dilemma of chronological policy analysis. It views federal Indian policy as a sometimes-connected "bunch" of topical interests that have considerable interplay and that all demand our attention in every generation. *Bunch* is the proper word to describe these various interest areas because they are not neat, clean, and clear areas of concern. Rather they are intangible and emotional aspects of American Indian concerns that are not often reduced to a structural framework within the larger area of policy considerations. We can even conceive of them as those distracting topics that dissidents bring up, to our embarrassment, just when meetings and research seem to be reaching a satisfactory conclusion. They form substantial concerns when viewed alone as if they constituted the primary topic of policy analysis. When we attempt to define a subfield of policy, these ideas linger in our minds and cause great discomfort, and we articulate our best thoughts only to realize that we have merely opened ourselves to the questions these ideas represent. In taking a topical approach, then, we hope to cover the major areas that should be considered before any effort is made to describe federal Indian policy. Perhaps by providing some substantial building blocks we can enable policy analysts to construct a new edifice of understanding for the future.

Joyotpaul Chaudhuri provides both an overview and a critical analysis of federal Indian policy by discussing how certain key legal concepts have forced analysis into predetermined channels. Property, sovereignty, and self-determination are the ideas most prominent in federal Indian policy, according to Chaudhuri, but they must be understood within the context of the larger jurisprudential framework that dictates that concepts used in federal Indian policy are always struggling to escape the dilemma of being contextual, yet speaking of certain fundamental values shared by larger nations with considerably different status and powers than Indian tribes. Chaudhuri concludes that Indian issues have often been a sideshow in the larger American drama despite the fact that serious study of Indians offers an opportunity to examine democratic theory in its most profound local manifestation.

7

Almost all federal policy analysis relies heavily upon the descriptions of an Indian tribe offered by Chief Justice John Marshall in the *Cherokee* cases. Sharon O'Brien takes up the challenge of Marshall, emphasizing the continuing international aspect of American Indian life, and examines how federal Indian policies must be examined in the light of modern developments in international law. One of the major stumbling blocks, the application of decolonization procedures only to noncontiguous colonial possessions, prevents American Indians from realizing the full benefits of liberation and independence movements that motivate aboriginal peoples in other parts of the globe. Nevertheless, O'Brien demonstrates that Indian tribes have made accomplishments comparable to the progress made by peoples now independent of colonial ties. Mostly, she argues, repudiation of the doctrine of plenary congressional powers would do much to eliminate the vacillations in federal Indian policy and establish for the tribes some fundamental human rights now being recognized on the world stage.

Geographical contiguity, as Fred Ragsdale contends, can be seen in the perceptions of the federal court system as a dominant factor in keeping Indians within the purview of the trust doctrine. It also creates innumerable roadblocks when seen at the reservation level in relationships between states and tribes. The American political system is designed to share sovereignty between two different entities in the same geographical area. That is why we have a confederation of states and not a true federal republican form of government. When small reservation tracts of land are located within an area already under two different political jurisdictions and a third entity, the tribe, closely tied to the federal power, is given sovereignty also, immense complications occur.

The temptation always presented to Indian tribes in this situation, Ragsdale notes, is to conform their government and laws to those of the other two, thereby eliminating some areas of conflict and, most of all, gaining a measure of respect because they have incorporated popular procedures of law. But do tribes want their governing bodies to be like Albuquerque's or any other municipal government? Ragsdale does not offer much comfort in noting that while tribes seem determined to cling to outmoded ways of perceiving themselves, as either submerged nations or conquered peoples, their uncritical adoption of Anglo institutions negates the positive benefits they derive from geographical differences. Not only is the situation complicated, it seemingly cannot be resolved as long as reservations occupy a distinct place in the scheme of things and tribes show no inclination to surrender their status in this respect.

Indians, it is said, are often willing participants in the American political process and by their participation they endorse the policies the federal government devises for them. When we look back at important policy changes in American history, there is no question that the Congress, or the president, as the case may be, has sought to get Indian consent for the changes that are made. Michael G. Lacy examines several instances in which major legislative changes were made in the status and property of Indian tribes, seeing in these adjustments in the federal relationship a model of cooptation designed to appear as legitimizing devices to the uninformed public. Cooptation seems a useful device, according to Lacy, when the minority is perceived as a threat, and here *threat* is not simply a manifestation of power or the effort to grasp power but the appearance of gaining some measure of control, no matter how tenuous. Lacy's point is well taken and he illuminates this area of policy formation because he includes, as a fourth member of the policy dyad, the public without whose ignorance and inattention many changes in policy would not be politically possible. We have certainly seen cooptation in its crude sense in the social programs of the sixties and seventies. When we extend the ideology of cooptation to cover major statutes of the past, we find a useful model that answers the vital question of *how* policy is finalized.

It is almost axiomatic that when the Supreme Court is faced with a difficult Indian case, it falls back on an old legal doctrine that piously states that affairs between Indians and the United States are *political* matters not subject to judicial review. In the formative years of American existence Indian tribes did have a political recourse: they could align themselves with foreign nations and they could go to war against the United States, and they did both. These acts were, for their time and for the circumstances of the Indians, the proper political responses to the failure or refusal of the United States to carry out its obligations. With the incorporation of Indian tribes and lands in the domestic affairs of the United States and the passage of the Indian Citizenship Act, Indians were given another political tool—the vote—although they could not use it directly as a means of countering the actions of the federal government. The vote was a more subtle way of influencing white politicians who sought office as Indians grew more sophisticated about exercising the voting franchise.

Daniel McCool presents the first comprehensive effort to analyze Indian voting. There has been surprisingly little written on Indian voting, even though Indians have been citizens for voting purposes since 1924. One difficulty inherent in analyzing Indian voting is simply that of identifying Indian precincts; reservations, particularly large reservations such as the Navajo and Papago, present few difficulties; smaller reservations, the rural off-reservation towns predominantly or significantly Indian, and urban Indians plague us with insuperable problems in determining the presence of Indian voting. Not only is McCool's analysis the first good national study of Indian voting, it demonstrates several realities that even the most experienced observers of the Indian political scene have missed: Indians are rather good at splitting tickets and they most definitely reward their friends and punish their enemies. In short, McCool tells us, Indians are among the most sophisticated of American voters.

Dealing with the federal government, in the milieu of cooptation, is fraught with danger, and we can tell almost immediately where Indians are confronting the tactic of

· cooptation. Traditional Indian political rivalries feature families and clans in fierce but not moral competition. In the case of the Oglala Sioux and the Creeks of Oklahoma, on the other hand, Tom Holm finds the appeal to the old traditionalism and the accusation against the incumbents that they are operating a "white man's government" evidence of a profound struggle to avoid cooptation.

Holm suggests that traditional leadership relied heavily upon community consensus for its directions and points out that modern tribal governments, built upon the premise that a simple majority will prevail, violates long-standing Indian concepts of society and produces a peculiar kind of conflict that is not easily resolved. It is how persons perceive the origin of authority, where it vests, and how it is exercised, Holm relates, that characterizes a new kind of political struggle within tribes that is not likely to ease any time in the future. Federal policy can hardly confront problems of this nature, and when the federal institutional apparatus does attempt to resolve the political problems of tribes, it almost always becomes a partisan supporting those Indians who have cooperated with it in the past. Hence, Holm's analysis reinforces Lacy's suggestion that cooptation is one of the major techniques the federal government uses to control Indians.

Traditionalism is not found solely in tribal policies. Indeed, David L. Vinje points out that traditionalism has considerable impact on economic development plans. Basically the question Indians need to resolve is whether the reservation is to be considered a homeland or a resource. Economic development is possible if the reservation is viewed as a homeland, but only if appropriate technology is used to enhance the resources and advantages already found there. Unfortunately, many federal bureaus that have attempted to help Indians in the past two decades have viewed the reservations primarily as a resource and human services and community considerations have had to take a back seat to expansive development schemes that have generally failed.

Apart from appropriate technology, which is not always available because of the lack of knowledge by both Indians and federal agencies of the state of alternative technology, Vinje suggests that a new pattern for economic development may conceivably be forming. On the Navajo Reservation, economic development problems appear more closely related to third world economic problems than they do to other Indian reservations. The Navajo Reservation is a particular case, however, that is incapable of being duplicated on any other reservation. It has the unique status of being larger in area than some currently recognized third-world countries, adding important elements to Vinje's thesis regarding the future of Indian economic development. Regardless of how we view Indian reservations, the movement in recent times among the disaffected Indians would seem to indicate that Vinje's analysis is not only insightful and perceptive but probably prophetic in a larger sense.

Both tribal government and economic development can be conceived within the larger rubric of tribal sovereignty, and many Indians today prefer to think of their tribes as quasi-independent nations. The immediate local impact of this kind of thinking generally is manifested in a concern that reservation institutions reflect the deliberations of a national attitude. Thus tribal courts and law enforcement, two aspects of internal sovereignty, have become important areas of institutional development in recent years. Robert A. Nelson and Joseph F. Sheley provide an example of the kinds of conflict that can occur when a tribal government attempts to exercise its internal sovereignty after decades of supervision by the Bureau of Indian Affairs.

The response of the Bureau to Indian overtures for more direct control over law enforcement functions has been to weave a much tighter web of regulatory control over those activities that tribes presently control. Gradually the Bureau forces the tribe to compartmentalize its activities, eventually reaching the point where tribal members lose both their bearings and their enthusiasm for assuming responsibility for activities on the reservations. Nelson and Sheley, in the interests of constructive suggestion, propose a form of compromise in which both the Bureau and the tribe can find some benefits. Whether such a compromise would work over the long term in such an explosive area as law enforcement remains to be seen. It is, nevertheless, important to note that only by resolving disputes in this critical area can models be found that might have more universal application.

Finally, in the field of policy we are confronted by instances in which it is obvious that the law was not meant to apply to Indians, but subsequent developments have applied it to Indians and always to their detriment. Mary Wallace and John Petoskey each discuss a subject area in which there is presently a good deal of controversy and litigation. In 1952, Congress attached the McCarren Amendment to pending legislation. This amendment waived sovereign immunity for the United States in certain kinds of state water-rights litigation. Three years later the Supreme Court found that the federal government enjoyed certain reserved rights on public lands that threatened to disrupt state administration of water in the West. Finally, in 1983 the Supreme Court ruled that Indian water rights were also included under the McCarren Amendment and must also be litigated in the state courts. This radical and illogical chain of events has opened up the field of water rights for either intensive litigation or controlled negotiation. Mary Wallace traces the history of litigation on the McCarren Amendment and suggests that the *Winters* doctrine has now taken on a new meaning, the scope of which will be determined in the future.

It is not just recent legislation that is causing problems. In 1978, Congress passed the American Indian Religious Freedom Act in an effort to clarify the status and rights of Indians in practicing their traditional religions. Since the passage of that act, unfortunately, as John Petosky points out, litigation has demonstrated how empty congressional promises can be. Tribes seem to be stalled at the threshold of the establishment clause and there do not seem to be any good examples or analogies that can be used to illustrate

13

the differences between tribal religions and the various denominations of the Christian tradition that have cumulatively influenced the present interpretation of the First Amendment religious freedom.

Each of the essays in this collection separates a definable subject area and attempts to forge new ways of understanding the complexity of Indian affairs. There is, admittedly, considerably more to contemporary Indian life than legal and political notions, and it may be that unforeseen cultural changes may create a new climate in which policy considerations can be seen differently. But history tells us that cultural changes of any magnitude follow structural and institutional changes in the manner in which Indians live. The profound cultural changes Indians have experienced in the past century were partially derived from changes in the role and status of tribal governments caused by actions of the United States. Cultural renewal always seems to rush into the vacuum created by new ways of doing things, and it may be that the developments of the past two decades have created a climate in which traditionalism can reassert itself. That possibility would certainly explain much of the turmoil and discontent that occurs on the reservations today.

The fact remains that many of the policy considerations that tribes must make in the years ahead are going to be initiated by difficulties and successes experienced at the lower levels of policy implementation and not because of sudden changes in policy at the presidential and congressional levels. We have not yet digested the tremendous changes that occurred during the sixties and early seventies, and federal Indian policy has remained fairly constant during the late seventies and early eighties. Hence the essays in this collection can be immensely useful in helping both Indians and non-Indians to understand the hidden difficulties that lie ahead.

1

American Indian Policy: An Overview

BY JOYOTPAUL CHAUDHURI

The field of American Indian law and policy, historically and systematically, has had little to do conceptually with American Indian custom, law, or methods of conflict resolution. American Indian law and policy therefore does not constitute an *ius gentium* in the manner of ancient Roman law whose early ideal was to blend the native tribal law of peoples as they were catapulted into contacts in the expansive dynamics of the Roman Empire. While excellent treatments of Cheyenne, Dakota, and Cherokee[1] and other tribal conceptions of law exist, the scholarship involved has made minimal impact on the evolution of Indian policy up to present times. Rather than being a branch of comparative law, the formal field of American Indian law is a very special, complex, and often contradictory and confusing branch of Anglo-American legal thinking.

The complexity of American Indian law is almost inversely related to the size of the Indian population, which constitutes one of the smallest groups of minorities in America today. The law is extensive in its scope, span, and the constitutive sources. Civil, criminal, property, constitutional, treaty, agreements, water, resource, statutory, and international law all have interacted in Indian law. The law reflects, more intensely than is the case for other minorities, the shifts and changes in attitudes in American politics. This unique intensity is due in part to the ever present *prop-*

erty dimension in American Indian affairs that continues today in environmental, land, and resource questions involving Indians. All the traditional Anglo-American jurisprudential issues of right, property, contract, due process, obligation, title, and sovereignty cry out for clarification most poignantly in the shifts and changes of Indian policy. Together, they constitute the vanishing points of American jurisprudence.[2]

Related to the property issue is the continuous preoccupation with and yet ambiguity in American law with respect to the aboriginal nature of Indian peoples.

As de Tocqueville and others have noted, the preoccupation with law is more present in American culture than is the case for many other cultures. There is a preoccupation with doing things "legally." This preoccupation, however, does not necessarily treat law and morality as synonymous subjects, as the chroniclers of Indian discontent have noted. But Indian affairs does indicate the lacing of diverse activities, even outrageous ones, with the imprimatur of law and accounts for many of the contradictions in Indian policy.

The discussion of Indian law should not be taken to mean that indigenous tribal law has not played a role in the evolution and development of Indian behavior. Quite the contrary is the case. The evolution, adaptation, and persistence of Indian customary relationships, in spite of the overwhelming nature of Anglo-American law, illustrate the great distance between formal legal prescription and Indian behavior. Whether it is the ghost dance tradition and rebellion of the 1880s,[3] or its modern descendants in Indian nationalism, or the quiet insistence that clan relationships can be more important than civil rights,[4] it is apparent that the normative suppositions of Indian "living law" and American Indian "positive" law continue to be quite different. To be sure, Madison's concept of factions is no stranger in Indian tribal politics. However, some of the issues of "traditionalism" versus "progress" in some Indian communities involve intercultural issues and gulfs between the "living law" and American Indian "positive" law.

16

The Sources of American Indian Law

The making of American Indian law has involved many sources. The Constitution, following the previous centralized English model of handling Indian policy, identifies Congress (Article 1, Section 8) as the proper body empowered to regulate commerce with the Indian tribes. Some states in the early years of the Republic bypassed Congress and congressional intent as expressed in the Trade and Intercourse acts. Some of those states like Maine and Massachusetts in the 1870s were involved in litigation and compromises over the implications of state neglect of congressional and constitutional intent.

Until 1871 treaties were often used for defining the relationship between tribes and the United States. However, Congress unilaterally brought treaty-making to an end in 1871 as the result of compromises arising out of a dispute between the Senate's special role in treaties and the special prerogatives of the House in originating appropriation bills. After 1871 "agreements" and executive orders together with ordinary congressional legislation began to take the place of treaties. This in turn gradually began to soften and erode the role of international law and increased the authority of congressional statutes. This tendency, when coupled with the continuous shift toward the positive law orientation in legal education, has resulted in a weak understanding of the intellectual roots of Anglo-American law in important areas of *seisin,* possessory, and aboriginal rights. Instead, in the tradition of positive law, congressional statutes as interpreted by the courts have taken on an importance beyond that of the era of the Cokes and the Jeffersons, when there was no substitute for legal analysis and scholarship.

In addition to the Constitution, statutes, agreements, and orders, administrative rules of executive agencies and, naturally, court decisions are also important sources of law.

Apart from these general sources, the policies of tribal governments and in some cases state statutes can be the source of policy for individual Indian groups or communities. Thus in Oklahoma and in some areas of the Northwest, state policies have operated in lieu of federal policy incrementally and contextually. These state encroachments are subjects of continuing controversy from their beginnings to the present period.

The Subjects of Indian Law

In addition to the sources of Indian law, the field can be examined in terms of its subjects—the various kinds of Indians. There is a bewildering series of cross-cutting categories. To begin, there are various forms of federal recognition. Recognition can be based on the legal nature of the land status of the tribe, as found in treaty-based reservations such as the Pine Ridge Reservation in South Dakota. However, many reservations in Arizona and New Mexico, such as Papago and Hopi, are not treaty reservations but executive order reservations. The permanence of the relationships involving executive order reservations may be somewhat different from the case of the treaty order reservations. A case in point is the continuing Hopi-Navajo disputes in the joint-use area of a reservation created originally by an executive order. Of course, a treaty reservation Indian's rights can also be changed over time, as is the case for many Oklahoma Indians due to the terms of Oklahoma statehood in addition to the consequences of the breakup of tribal lands into allotments in the late 1890s.[5] For example, the inheritance laws of Oklahoma Indians with respect to allotments have features distinct from inheritance laws in other parts of Indian country.

There are also reservations directly created by Congress. Even though Congress in the Indian Reorganization Act of 1934[6] authorized the Secretary of Interior "to proclaim new Indian reservations," various Indian groups had to petition Congress for the recognition of "new" Indian reservations. When Congress creates a new Indian reservation it may add unique features to the rights of the Indians involved. Thus, in 1978 when Congress created a new reservation for the Pascua Yaquis[7] near Tucson, Arizona, it did not extend ordinary law enforcement powers in non-felonious contexts to the tribe but maintained the existing jurisdiction of the state enforcement agencies.

States also can create reservations and recognize tribes as has been the case for Tiguas in Texas and Lumbees in North Carolina prior to the extension of some federal social program benefits to these groups.

There are, in addition to federally recognized Indians, hundreds of bands of Indians in the United States who do not have federally designated trust land. Many of these groups regard themselves as Indians and are able to demonstrate various degrees of evidence of their roots. The Tonto Apaches of Arizona, until formal recognition took place in the 1970s, provides a clear example of Indians exercising possessory rights without formal title.

The largest federally unrecognized group in the country are the Lumbees of Robeson County in southeastern North Carolina.[8] The Lumbees have obtained state recognition and have eligibility for some federal programs but do not as yet have the entitlements of a federal tribe.

Quite the opposite situation involves tribes like the Klamaths of Oregon who were once federally recognized but were "terminated" as tribes in the aftermath of the "termination" era of the 1950s. Similarly the Menominees of Wisconsin were also terminated. Termination as in the case of the Menominees meant the loss of trust status for the land that went on the tax rolls in Wisconsin. It also meant the end of tribal government and Indians as individuals having the same formal individual status as non-Indians. However, the Menominees have won congressional restoration to tribal status.

The last category of Indians are off-reservation Indians. These in turn can be rural or "urban" Indians. Rural off-reservation Indians do not live generally on trust lands but may continue to enjoy certain privileges in their ancestral home reservation depending on location and tribal policy. They may also enjoy certain service benefits as individual

Indians with respect to health care, for instance, depending on policies applying to specific areas. Urban Indians, however, are the largest off-reservation group of Indians in the country numbering close to half the Indian population. They, too, may have some property rights in their ancestral reservation or voting rights in absentia, but these are not subjects that can be readily generalized about since in part they vary on the basis of tribal history as well as tribal policy with respect to absentee voting and definition of membership. With respect to individual rights as Indians (quite apart from basic constitutional rights as Americans), there are many ambiguities about access to a whole host of governmental services.[9] In 1974 by statutory interpretation of congressional intent, the Supreme Court[10] extended in a limited way federal benefits to culturally rooted urban Indians living near reservations. To date this decision has not resulted in a massive impact in the services available to a majority of urban Indians, though some new services have become available in some geographical areas close to reservations, such as Phoenix, Arizona.

Individual Indian Status

In addition to classifications by community such as reservation or off-reservation, there are additional complexities in defining various kinds of individual Indians. The very term "Indian" itself has been a subject of controversy. In the civil rights era of the sixties various attempts were made to substitute other general labels, particularly Native Americans, but that term has not gained universal acceptance among Indians. Some controversial Indian figures[11] have objected to the newer label as not being an improvement over the older American Indian label. The latter term in spite of its shortcomings still has the widest usage for general purposes, though it should be pointed out that the specific tribal identity is the key question in intratribal and intertribal affairs and communication.

Historically, of course, Indians knew they were Indians,

and self-identification is still a matter of great pride as identity is traced through descent, lineage, clan, and acceptance in specific tribes. But the Anglo-American preoccupation with formal definition poses a whole host of problems.

Federal, state and tribal definitions have wide variations. In the federal government alone[12] definitions may vary widely from the Department of Interior, the Indian Health Service, and the Department of Labor. The Department of Interior generally will use the affiliation with a recognized tribe as a starting point. But contextual variations may occur. Thus in some cases a quarter-blood quantum could be used. In other cases the tribal rolls could be used. The tribal rolls may vary widely in their definitions. Thus, in the Southwest tribes can update their rolls. However, in Oklahoma for some of the tribes the rolls have been frozen since the land allotments of the 1890s and one must trace ancestry to an original roll number. However, the tribes in Oklahoma also are updating their membership lists on their own.

When a payment for a land settlement in a court case occurs, a new registration list may be used by the federal government after advertisement. The final registration list for compensation is often much larger than the formal membership roll of the tribe.

The tribes themselves widely vary in their own definitions of tribal membership for voting purposes in general or residence purposes for reservation tribes. Many tribes have used quarter-blood definitions. In the Southwest specific matriarchal or patriarchal descent is used by some tribes as an additional criterion and the U.S. Supreme Court has upheld such "discrimination" as being within the powers of tribes.[13]

The Labor Department is not bound by Interior's definition on who is an Indian. Armed with a solicitor's opinion, Labor can and has extended various earmarked Indian manpower benefits to many Indians not affiliated with formally recognized tribes.

Similarly states and tribes leave latitude on defining anyone who is an Indian. In turn the U.S. Census has used self-definition as the basis of identification in the 1970 and 1980 censuses, which in turn causes problems of comparability with the 1950 census which used a different set of definitions and of course had a different level of operational counting problems. Since census figures are used for many federal programs, these definitions have serious implications for resources. In short, the legal definition of Indianness is complexly *contextual.*

The Limits of Tribal Authority

Beyond the question of definitions of individual Indian status, an even more important question is the question of the nature, extent, and limitations of tribal authority. This question like so many others is affected by cultural presuppositions without the benefit of clear formulations of comparative law. As in other culturally defined questions of Indian policy, the dominant influence is that of Anglo-American legal culture rather than aboriginal perspectives on authority.

In Anglo-American political and legal theory, the questions of authority are intimately intertwined with conflicting perceptions of tribal *sovereignty.* Unfortunately, the untangling of these conflicting perceptions of monistic, pluralistic, and contextual conceptions of sovereignty is usually missing in most arguments. Since most lawyers are trained in the monistic positive law tradition originating with Thomas Hobbes, John Austin, and their descendants, the common perception is that sovereignty is an "entity" that is indivisible—you either have it or you don't—and for the American positivist, it is usually Congress who has it. In turn, contemporary Indian activists argue that tribes have it. Since this essay is not intended to resolve the issue, it will be sufficient to point out that at least two additional conceptions of sovereignty exist. One would be a pluralist conception of a decentralized minimalist sovereignty involving many centers of political authority. A third would be a contextual and Jeffersonian[14] concept of sovereignty where sovereignty can still be "absolute" but would be so in the limited context of specific legal relations, such as aboriginal, undivided, and unceded land rights. The rights would be quite different in ceded and contracted "rights" or legislatively created privileges.

In any case, apart from philosophical issues, the actual case law on sovereignty constitutes a middle-eastern bazaar where practically anything is available to those who are eager and earnest and have the resources for persisting in the adversary system of justice. This has been the way from the beginning of constitutional law as shaped by John Marshall.

The logical inconsistencies involved in the handling of Indian property questions are well illustrated in the jurisprudence of Justice John Marshall who shaped so much of early American jurisprudence. In the *Dartmouth College* case,[15] Justice Marshall dealt with problems of property title in the context of the shift of sovereignty between two political systems, the English and the American, as a result of the force of arms or the American Revolution. Despite the creation of a new political system by force, Marshall proceeded to point out the continuities of law inherent in the idea of the obligation of contracts. English titles were to be respected despite the creation de novo of American institutions.

The three major opinions of Marshall involving Indian sovereignty are in *Cherokee Nation* v. *Georgia* (1831),[16] *Worcester* v. *Georgia* (1832),[17] and *Johnson* v. *McIntosh* (1823).[18] The *Worcester* opinion gives to Indian tribes sovereign treaty-making power analogous to that of England.

> The constitution, by declaring treaties already made, as well as those to be made, to be the supreme law of the land, has adopted and sanctioned the previous treaties with the Indian nations, and consequently admits their rank among those powers who are capable of making treaties. The words "treaty" and "nation" are words of our own language, selected

in our diplomatic and legislative proceedings, by ourselves, having each a definite and well understood meaning. *We have applied them to Indians, as we have applied them to the other nations of the earth. They are applied to all in the same sense.*[19] (Emphasis added.)

The *Worcester* case speaks of Indian nationhood and its accompanying treaty-making power in the strongest possible terms. In the *Cherokee Nation* case, some of the rhetoric sounds thunderingly pro-Indian since the Indians "are acknowledged to have an unquestionable, and, heretofore, unquestioned right to the lands they occupy, and that right shall be extinguished by a voluntary cession to our government." However, Indian sovereignty is diluted by two factors in the *Cherokee* case. First, the Indian nation is denominated as a domestic dependent nation under the dominion of the United States. Second, despite the pro-Cherokee rhetoric, Marshall declined to issue an injunction against the state of Georgia.

The case of *Johnson* v. *McIntosh* shows an entirely different Marshall than is the case in the *Cherokee Nation* and the *Worcester* cases. The opinion in the Johnson case does not speak of the Indian right of voluntary cession of land. Nor does it uphold the property rights of Indians even before the adoption of the Constitution of the United States. Instead, John Marshall denied the legitimacy of land grants made by the Illinois and Piankeshaw tribes in 1773 and 1775, respectively. By beginning with European discovery, then on to English conquest, the American Revolution and ending with U.S. land grants, Marshall concludes that Indians were mere occupants who were incapable of giving or granting land.

Indian inhabitants are to be considered merely as occupants, to be protected, indeed, while in peace, in the possession of their lands, but to be deemed incapable of transferring the absolute title to others. However, this restriction may be opposed to natural right, and to the usages of civilized na-

24

tions, yet if it be indispensable to that system under which the country has been settled, and be adapted to the actual condition of the two people, it may, perhaps, be supported by reason, and certainly cannot be rejected by Courts of Justice.[20]

Marshall's jurisprudence in Indian cases seems inconsistent or at least ambiguous with respect to the nature of Indian property rights. However, we know something about the politics of John Marshall in Indian as well as non-Indian cases. It is his politics rather than "reason" which provides the explanation. The *McIntosh* decision is consistent with Marshall's nationalism and his imperial conceptions of the unitary state. The *Worcester* decision conforms to his Federalist and antistate politics. The *Cherokee* case, like *Marbury* v. *Madison,* is a victory for judicial supremacy by judicial proclamation. Neither instance required any support for the weak judiciary from the hostile and more powerful executive branch, even though popular history mistakenly interpreted Andrew Jackson's political rhetoric as noncompliance. Thus "native title" and tribal sovereignty, while shrouded in the language of law, was displayed appropriately according to the varying necessities of politics. The variance in the meaning of native title has continued to exist in the dominant society's common law system from Marshall's time to the contemporary era. This does not mean that the Anglo legal system has rendered native title and Indian sovereignty meaningless but merely that the history of sovereignty is a somewhat uneven one.

Despite the *Johnson* decision, native title continued to be recognized in the treaty-making process with Indian tribes at least as an instrument of convenience for the disposition of Indian lands. Bilateral agreements dealing with Indian title were ended abruptly in 1871 through a curious and unusual action by the U.S. Congress, as has been previously noted. Angered by some provisions of Indian treaties and also as a tool for clipping the Senate's unique role in treaty ratification, the House added a rider to an appropri-

25

ation bill that there would be no further treaty-making with Indian tribes. The Senate, anxious to pass the appropriation bill, went along with the rider ending treaty-making.

The net effect of the *Johnson, Cherokee,* and *Worcester* cases is to provide three different approaches to questions of tribal authority and sovereignty. In the well-known cycles of U.S. interest in Indian policy, the three cases provide the cornerstone of three different starting points. The *Johnson* case provides the weakest basis of tribal authority. The *Cherokee* case provides a middle-of-the-road position in tribal authority. In this middle path tribes typically win immunities from state taxation and licensing.

The *Worcester* case, by way of contrast, provides the high point of Indian sovereignty wherein tribal authority, in principle at least, is not only protected from state encroachment but certain basic immunities apply with respect to the United States as well. Thus in 1959 the United States Court of Appeals, relying greatly on the *Worcester* decision, said that the First Amendment did not apply to tribes in the same manner as it applied to states, since "Indian tribes are not states. They have a status higher than that of states."[21]

The Burger Court appears to be in a transitional state with respect to tribal sovereignty. Justice Stewart in *United States* v. *Wheeler*[22] emphasized, in the manner of the *Worcester* conception of inherent sovereignty, that in certain criminal cases the tribe acts as an independent sovereign and not as an arm of the federal government. However, Justice Rehnquist often directs attention to the *McIntosh* principle instead. Thus, in 1978 he denied the right of the Suquamish Tribe to have jurisdiction over non-Indians on the reservation. In his analysis he referred to and relied on the *McIntosh* formulation on several occasions and noted that "Indian tribes come under the territorial sovereignty of the United States and their exercise of separate power is constrained so as not to conflict with the interests of this overriding sovereignty."[23]

Even Justice Stewart seems bent in modifying his previous

support of the *Worcester*-like conception of inherent sovereignty as expressed in the *Wheeler* case in the later (1981) case of *Montana et al.* v. *United States et al.*[24] There he argues that the treaty-based authority of the Crows over their reservation does not extend to regulating the hunting rights of non-Indians on acquired land within the reservation boundaries. While the *Oliphant* (or *Suquamish*) case and the *Montana* cases are still straws in the wind, there seems to be declining support for a strong conception of inherent sovereignty and points toward the resurgency of the *McIntosh* principle, thereby illustrating the continuing self-contradictions and fluctuations of Indian policy.

Now we seem to be heading toward the essence of a positivist conception of law as the command of the sovereign Congress unlimited by formal jurisprudential concepts or other "vague omnipresences in the sky" in the tradition of Holmes, Frankfurter, and now Justice Rehnquist.[25]

The ambivalence, confusing intent, and self-contradictory premises that characterize judicial policy also finds its parallel in the history of legislative policy with respect to tribal authority.[26] At times in early American history, Indian policy was the conquest of "hostile" tribes and Indian policy was administered by the War Department. Later in more benign times some issues of "democratic" theory found their way in fragmentary fashion into Indian policy. Thus, both Jeffersonian and Jacksonian intent was directed at the removal of Indians west of the Mississippi. The Jacksonian theme emphasized the use of force. Jefferson emphasized the importance of "consent" although the context was still removal. When Jeffersonian consent was defined in Indian policy the operational meanings were provided not in the context of comparative cultures but in the unilaterally defined English context of implied consent of Hobbes and Locke. Typically a "chief's" mark was indicative of consent for an entire band or tribe, neglecting the examination of the authority structure of the tribe involved. Roger William's more sensitive dealing with Indians in founding Rhode Island remains even today as a remarkable example of an attempt to treat Indian tribal governments as equal partners in the process of obtaining consent. The Williams model of a culturally sensitive extended dialogue, the Jeffersonian model of consent, and the Jacksonian method of unilateral decision making appear to provide three alternative ways of shaping Indian policy.

The removal acts of the 1830s and the Indian allotment acts of the 1880s and 1890s are examples of unilateral policy making sometimes with the claim that it was in the best interest of the Indians involved. The Indian Reorganization Act of 1934, which formally recognized the authority of tribal governments, remains as probably the best example of Jeffersonian consent at work. The act did not systematically incorporate existing Indian conceptions of authority but at least in an Anglo-American sense provided an "individualistic" opportunity to Indian tribes to formulate their own tribal governments and constitutions.

John Collier, the architect of the Indian Reorganization Act, had to compromise many of his own ideas in order to get some recognition of tribal authority. In his personal philosophy, however, there was a kinship with the spirit of Roger Williams with respect to the sensitivity for differing attitudes toward property, authority, and community in the Indian worlds.

The current period of legislative policy is often heralded as the era of self-determination beginning with the passage in 1975 of the Indian Self-Determination and Education Assistance Act.[27] This act in principle gives tribal governments the "authority" to assume contractually the responsibility for various governmental services. There is less to the act than meets the eye, since the authority is circumscribed with bureaucratic necessities, the realities of the histories of tribal resources, and the vagaries of congressional appropriations bills.

Tribes must have administrative permission for engaging in contracts. Further, large numbers of tribes, particularly in Oklahoma, have already lost their tribal resources over which to exercise authority. Of course the southwestern tribes are in a different position from the Oklahoma tribes. However, ultimately the success of "self-determination" is tied in part to the resource allocation to specific Indian programs. If obligations to Indians are regarded as purely discretionary, appropriations bills will reflect the moods of the country and of Congress. The "self" in self-determination remains in large part non-Indian.

Rights of Indians

In addition to the rights of tribes there remains the question of rights of individual Indians. Morally and culturally, rights could be exclusively traced to aboriginally based human rights or to rights as members of sovereign nations. Various Indian groups have claimed *fundamental* rights under international law[28] and as members of tribes.[29] However, in the American political system individual Indian rights largely flow from one of two sources—the common rights of U.S. citizenship or the implications of membership in a recognized tribe.

Until 1924 a generalized rule of Indian citizenship in the U.S. did not exist. As a general principle,[30] Indians were excluded from U.S. citizenship since they were not regarded as being born subject to the jurisdiction of the United States. However, the vast majority of Indians had become citizens by 1924 through various devices including land allotments, collective legislation for specific groups, or other legislation aimed at specific target groups. Then in 1924, Congress decided to close the loopholes of Indian citizenship and passed an Indian Citizenship Act which brought the Indians into the Fourteenth Amendment protection of the rights of citizenship. An Indian was to be regarded as a citizen of the U.S. and the state in which he resided after 1924, in addition to the rights of membership within a tribe. An Indian, therefore, can have three separate sets of rights: federal, state, and tribal.

It should be noted that the Indian Citizenship Act has not yet been without its critics. Some Indian activists have criticized the unilateral proclamation. Even though Indian participation in the U.S. armed forces has been proportionately higher than that of many groups, some Indians, occasionally and unsuccessfully, have sought to question the legitimacy of the draft. On the non-Indian side some states balked at the extension of voting rights to Indians. This was the case in Arizona from 1924 until the early 1950s.

Although in principle Indians had rights against the federal government and the states, the Citizenship Act did not extend the Bill of Rights to situations involving tribal governments. The judiciary in the previously discussed Navajo case declined to extend the Bill of Rights in the context of tribal governments. Then in 1968 the situation was changed by Congress when it passed what has come to be known as the 1968 Indian Civil Rights Act.[31]

Students of the law are keenly aware that the nationalization of the Bill of Rights and its application to the states has a complex history and one that is still in process. However, at least the Fourteenth Amendment was ratified by the states. No such ratification was sought from the tribes in the context of the Indian Civil Rights Act. The "rights" were extended unilaterally by Congress thereby again raising many questions of the role and meaning of "consent" in democratic theory.

While Indian tribes are not immune from the excesses of authority and power, many issues have been raised about both the legitimacy and the cultural implications and impact of the 1968 Civil Rights Act. The legitimacy issue is simple. In the case of general civil rights, at least, the states had a role in passing the Fourteenth Amendment. Indian civil rights flow from no such participation.

The cultural impact is even more significant. The intrinsic individualism of the Bill of Rights could endanger the remaining aspects of selfhood as conceived by specific Indian tribes. This was precisely the issue in the *Santa Clara* case where tracing membership patrilineally was regarded initially as being sexist in character. The Supreme Court declined to interfere with the Santa Clara conception of membership and did not extend Fourteenth Amendment standards to tribal definition of membership. However, it should be noted that the Court depended largely on statutory interpretations of congressional intent. Moreover, the 1968 Civil Rights Bill on purpose did not transfer all the Fourteenth Amendment rights to the tribal context. The establishment clause, the 12-person jury, and the grand jury mechanisms are notable examples of exclusion.

Thus while Congress and the courts have shown some sensitivity to cultural factors in the writing and application of the 1968 Act, the very manner of passage and the contents of the Act may have a long-run, unilaterally created assimilative effect on Indian diversities.

Conclusion

The history, content, and persistence of Indian tribal and intertribal activism[32] illustrates the complex nexus of normative questions that are involved. The issues are not merely those of civil rights. On the contrary, some of the most intense Indian protest occurred in the 1970s when the civil rights movement was waning. Rather than the last hurrah of civil rights, Indian issues involve much deeper issues of democratic theory, of consent, of international law, and of cultural survival as well as those of civil rights.

The American response to these aboriginal issues has been probably more benign than is the case for aboriginal rights in many other political systems with aboriginal populations. However, American ideals of the consent of the governed and the importance of legitimacy over force highlights the need for careful and sustained moral and policy analysis of United States-Indian relationships. Yet as this essay has shown, both judicial and legislative policy making demonstrate little systematic thought. In the executive branch also after the mid-seventies little architectural work has occurred in program development. Indian policy has been again shunted aside. Nor should this be surprising given their relative powerlessness in the larger society.

31

Indian policy has often been a sideshow in a larger American drama, despite that the issues involved are at the core in democratic theory as well as jurisprudence.

NOTES

1. For examples see John Phillip Reid, *A Law of Blood—The Primitive Law of the Cherokee Nation* (New York: New York University Press, 1970); Ella Deloria, *Speaking of Indians* (New York: Friendship Press, 1944); E. Adamson Hoebel and Karl Llewellyn, *The Cheyenne Way: Conflict and Case Law in Primitive Jurisprudence* (Norman: University of Oklahoma Press, 1961); and Michael E. Melody, "On Cosmological Government: White Buffalo Calf Woman among the Lakota." Paper delivered at American Political Science Association, New York City, 1978.

2. Joyotpaul Chaudhuri, "Native American Title and Public Policy: The Vanishing Point of American Jurisprudence." Paper presented at International Studies Association, Toronto, Canada, February 1976.

3. James Mooney, *The Ghost Dance Religion and the Sioux Outbreak of 1890,* Bureau of American Ethnology 14th Annual Report, Part 2 (Government Printing Office, Washington, 1896). See also Vine Deloria, *Behind the Trail of Broken Treaties* (New York: Dell Publishing Co., 1974).

4. See *Santa Clara Pueblo* v. *Julia Martinez* 56 L. Ed. 2d. 106 (1978).

5. See *The American Indian Treaties Series* (8 vols.; Washington, D.C.: Institute for the Development of Indian Law).

6. 48 Stat. 984 (1934).

7. 92 Stat. 712 (1978).

8. See Adolph L. Dial and David K. Eliades, *The Only Land I Know: A History of the Lumbee Indians* (San Francisco: Indian Historian Press, 1975).

9. See Joyotpaul Chaudhuri, *Urban Indians of Arizona* (Tucson: University of Arizona Press, 1974). Also, Allan L. Sorkin, *The Urban American Indian* (Lexington: D. C. Heath, 1978).

10. Morton, *Secretary of the Interior* v. *Ruiz et ux.* 415 U.S. 199 (1973).

11. Russel Means of the American Indian Movement in a panel "discussion" at the 1981 annual meeting of the Western Social Science Association, San Diego, expressed this objection.

12. For a listing of federal and state definitions, see U.S. Department of Commerce *Federal and State Indian Reservations and Indian Trust Areas* (U.S. Government Printing Office. 1974) (0311-0076 Stock).

13. *Santa Clara Pueblo* v. *Julia Martinez.*

14. For a Jeffersonian concept of rights see Joyotpaul Chaudhuri, ed., *The Non-Lockean Roots of American Democratic Thought* (Tucson: University of Arizona Press, 1977).

15. *Dartmouth College* v. *Woodward,* 4 Wheaton 518 (1819).

16. *Cherokee Nation* v. *Georgia,* U.S. 1 (1831).

17. *Worcester* v. *Georgia,* 31 U.S. 515 (1832).

18. *Johnson* v. *McIntosh,* 21 U.S. 543 (1823).

19. *Worcester* v. *Georgia,* p. 559.

20. *Johnson* v. *McIntosh,* p. 591.

21. *Native American Church* v. *Navajo Tribal Council,* (1959) 272 F. 2d 131.

22. *United States* v. *Wheeler,* (1978) 435 U.S. 313.

23. Ibid.

24. *Montana* v. *United States, et al* (1981) No. 79-1128.

25. The best scholarly support for Indian sovereignty is still found in Cohen's classic formulation: "those powers which are lawfully vested in an Indian tribe are not, in general powers granted by express acts of Congress, but rather inherent powers of a limited sovereignty which has never been extinguished." Felix Cohen, *Handbook of Federal Indian Law* (Albuquerque: University of New Mexico Press, 1971), p. 122. Reissue of 1942 edition. Two current casebooks on Indian law are Monroe Price, *Law and the American Indian* (Indianapolis: The Bobbs-Merrill Co., 1973), and David H. Getches, Daniel M. Rosenfelt and Charles F. Wilkinson, *Cases and Materials on Federal Indian Laws* (St. Paul: West Publishing Co., 1979).

26. For an overview of legislative history see Vine Deloria, "Native Americans: The American Indian Today," in Richard D. Lambert and Alan W. Heston, ed. *ANNALS* (March 1981). Vol. 454.

27. 88 Stat. 2203 (Pub. L. 93-680).

28. See Deloria, "Behind the Trail of Broken Treaties: An Indian Declaration of Independence."

29. See *B.I.A., I'm Not Your Indian Any More* (Rooseveltown, New York: Akwesasne Notes, 1974).

30. *Elk* v. *Wilkins,* 112 U.S. 94 (1884).

31. 82 Stat. 73 (Title II—Rights of Indians; Civil Rights Act of 1968. Pub. L. 90-284).

32. See Vine Deloria, *Custer Died For Your Sins* (New York: Avon Books, 1969). Also, Rachel Ann Bonney, "Forms of Supratribal Indian Interaction in the United States." Ph.D. dissertation (Anthropology), University of Arizona, 1975.

33

2

Federal Indian Policies and the International Protection of Human Rights

The rights of indigenous peoples first became a question of international law in the late fifteenth century. When the European nations began exploring the Americas, no principles existed by which they could lay claim to the lands or ascertain the rights of native inhabitants. To fill the void and to minimize hostility between nations with competing claims, European legalists quickly formulated the concepts of discovery, effective occupation, just war, and native rights.[1] Indeed, controversy about the rights of indigenous populations had a profound impact on the development of international law in the sixteenth century. Today, four centuries later, the issue of aboriginal rights is once again a subject of concern, study, and debate in the international community.

For the past three decades, international governmental and nongovernmental organizations have been working to formulate human rights standards applicable to the special needs of the world's indigenous peoples. These organizations have convened several conferences and have made considerable progress toward the formulation of standards designed to protect indigenous peoples. This essay reviews the current status of aboriginal rights protection in the international arena and evaluates American Indian policies of the federal government over the past thirty years in the light of existing and proposed international standards of aboriginal rights protection.

The International Protection of Aboriginal Rights:
An Overview

For the past several centuries, international law has held that a state's treatment of the individuals within its borders was within the exclusive concern of its own domestic law. The first major departure from this principle occurred following World War I when, through peace treaties and the League of Nations, the international community imposed an obligation on certain countries to accord their minority populations a minimum standard of fair treatment. Revelations of the horrors of Nazi Germany during World War II put to rest the notion that a nation's treatment of its citizenry was a matter of purely domestic concern. The United Nations Charter, adopted in 1945, reflected a more realistic viewpoint, including in Article I the goal of achieving "international cooperation . . . in promoting and encouraging respect for human rights and for fundamental freedoms for all without distinction as to race, sex, language or religion." The charter assigned responsibility for the development of human rights standards to the Economic and Social Council (ECOSOC), with directions to establish a Human Rights Commission. The commission in turn established the Sub-Commission on the Prevention of Discrimination and the Protection of Minorities.

Since its inception, the United Nations (UN) and its affiliated bodies, such as the International Labor Organization (ILO) and UNESCO, have formulated more than twenty-two general and a large number of more specialized human rights conventions. These documents cover a wide range of topics, including the basic rights of all individuals in the political, economic, and social sphere, the rights of women, children, and workers, and protection against genocide, racial discrimination, and slavery. Some of the other basic United Nations documents also contain provisions applicable to indigenous peoples, notably the Universal Declaration of Human Rights, 1949 (see especially articles 1 and 2); Convention of the Crime of Genocide, 1948; Supplementary Convention on the Abolition of Slavery, 1956; International Convention on the Elimination of All Forms of Racial Discrimination, 1965; International Covenant on Civil and Political Rights, 1966 (see especially articles 1 and 27): Optional Protocol to the International Covenant on Civil and Political Rights, 1966; International Covenant on Economic, Social and Cultural Rights, 1966; and UNESCO Declaration on the Principles of International Cultural Cooperation, 1966. Despite the inclusion of some provisions applicable to indigenous peoples, these documents generally reflect the UN's individualistic and egalitarian perspective on human rights.

Only a few of the early International Labor Organization conventions specifically address the issue of indigenous populations. The ILO's interest in indigenous populations dates from 1921. Between 1936 and 1957, the ILO drafted a number of conventions dealing with indigenous peoples, especially in the area of labor.[2] The most important of these documents is the 1957 Convention 107 on the protection of Indigenous and Other Tribal and Semi-Tribal Populations in Independent Countries and the recommendation on the same subject. The convention was an outgrowth of a major ILO study on indigenous populations undertaken in the early 1950s. Both the study and the convention sought to improve the living and working conditions of the Indian peoples of the Andes in order to facilitate their integration into the economic, social, and political fabric of their respective national communities.

With the exception of provisions relating to the recognition of indigenous law (articles 7, 8, and 13) and provisions concerning the rights of indigenous peoples to retain their land base (articles 11 and 12), the convention is regarded as inadequate to provide the necessary protections and has received less than full support by native peoples. The convention is predicated on the concept of individual rights and offers protections against discrimination so as to allow for individual assimilation into the dominant society. But the right of self-determination for specific groups of people, including the right to retain traditional lands, culture, language, and religion are the goals of aboriginal peoples; individual assimilation as defined by the convention represents the very antithesis of their objectives. By 1973, however, as a response to various indigenous movements, the ILO rejected integration as the only goal of indigenous policy and expressed its interest in revising Convention 107 to reflect the rights of indigenous peoples to "maintain their separate identity and way of life."[3]

In 1960 the General Assembly passed the Declaration on the Granting of Independence to Colonial Countries and Territories, which stated that "all peoples had a right to self-determination." Despite the argument by some states that the provisions of the convention and the work of the Decolonization Committee should apply to "peoples" in contiguous or enclave areas, the UN, bowing to pressure from Latin America, Africa, and the United States, to date has applied the convention only to noncontiguous or overseas colonial possessions.[4] This application has basically avoided the fundamental goal of indigenous peoples for social, cultural, and religious protection.

Finally, in the mid-1960s the UN turned its attention to the problems of minority rights and racial discrimination. In 1965 the UN hosted a Seminar on Multinational Society in Yugoslavia. The UN's willingness to consider the rights of minorities is reflected in Article 27 of both international covenants. Throughout the 1970s, the UN, as part of its Decade to Combat Racism, hosted a number of conferences and initated a series of studies on the subject. From two of these reports came proposals that the UN specifically recognize and address the needs of indigenous peoples. The 1978 UN Conference on Racism recommended that states recognize, among other rights, the rights of indigenous peoples to "freely express their ethnic, cultural and other characteristics; to have an official status and to form their own representative organizations; to maintain and use their own language, and to carry on their own traditional economic structure."[5]

An earlier 1970 study on racial discrimination had called for the UN to initiate a "complete and comprehensive study" of discrimination against indigenous peoples.[6] A year later, ECOSOC, acting on this proposal, passed Resolution 1580(L) which authorized the sub-commission to undertake a comprehensive study of discrimination against indigenous populations and to suggest necessary national and international measures to eliminate such discrimination. This study, thirteen years in the making and scheduled for dissemination in 1984, covers three broad areas: the work of international organizations and the current status of international human rights law as it relates to indigenous populations; the status of rights and discrimination problems encountered by aboriginal peoples in the thirty-seven nations determined to have native peoples; and the specific problems of indigenous peoples in the areas of housing, education, language, culture, employment, ownership of land, political rights, religious rights, and equality in the administration of justice. The study will also contain a set of conclusions, proposals, and recommendations.

One of the Study's Special Rapporteur's early recommendations has already been implemented. In 1982, ECOSOC, acting on the sub-commission's proposal, established a permanent five-member Working Group on Indigenous Populations. The Working Group meets yearly to review developments and to monitor the evolution of standards for the promotion and protection of human rights of indigenous peoples. Observers anticipate that this Group will provide a UN draft on the rights of indigenous populations. With a view to heightening awareness of the special problems and rights of aboriginal peoples and in recognition of the need for a UN declaration of indigenous rights, a number of international and regional conferences have convened to consider the plight of indigenous populations. In 1977 the first international conference on indigenous peoples was held within the UN system. Sponsored by the Non-Governmental Organization Sub-Committee on Racism, Racial Discrimination, Apartheid and Decolonization of the Special NGO Committee on Human Rights, the International NGO Conference on Discrimination Against Indigenous Populations in the Americas formulated a program of action and made recommendations to UN bodies and national governments.[7] Bardados II, a conference of indigenous representatives and anthropologists was held the same year in the West Indies. It evolved from an earlier conference of anthropologists sponsored by the University of Berne, Switzerland, and the World Council of Churches. Barbados II subsequently adopted a Declaration of Barbados deploring the physical, cultural, and legal domination of American Indians.

Human rights violations experienced by Indians of the Andes region were the focus of a seminar sponsored by the International Commission of Jurists and the Latin American Council for Law and Development in Bogota, Columbia, in September, 1979. A year later, the Work Group Indian Project of the Netherlands hosted the Fourth Russell Tribunal on the Rights of Indians of the Americas. The tribunal considered and decided fourteen cases of violations of the rights of American Indians and issued a set of recommendations, a final statement, and proclamation.

In 1981 the Special NGO Committee on Human Rights and NGO Sub-Committee on Racism, Racial Discrimination, Apartheid and Decolonization sponsored an International NGO Conference on Indigenous Peoples and the Land in Geneva, Switzerland. The conference adopted resolutions on indigenous land rights, international agreements and treaty rights, land reforms, transnational corporations, and nuclear armament.

The same year UNESCO, in cooperation with the Latin American School of Social Sciences, convened a Conference of Specialists on Ethnocide and Ethnodevelopment in Latin America in Costa Rica. The conference drafted the San Jose Declaration of 1981, which emphasized the cultural aspects of ethnocide and the right of ethnic groups to exist and develop.

A number of international and national organizations established to promote and protect the rights of indigenous populations sponsored and attended many of these conferences. The UN's Economic and Social Council has granted consultative status to several of these groups, formed exclusively by aboriginal peoples in the last ten years. Consultative status gives an organization the authority to attend UN meetings, to provide UN bodies with documentation, and to speak in open session. Among those receiving consultative status are the World Council of Indigenous Peoples, the Inuit Circumpolar Conference, the Indian Law Resource Center, Four Circles Direction, Congress of American Indian Movements of South America and the International Indian Treaty Council. In addition to these groups, several other nongovernmental organizations such as the Indian Council of South America, the Australian National Conference of Aborigines, Survival International, Cultural Survival, the Anthropology Resource Center, the Anti-Slavery Society for the Protection of Human Rights, the International Work Group of Indigenous Affairs, the Documentation and Information Center for Indigenous Affairs in the Amazon Region, and the Indigenous Population Documentation Research and Information Center are active in researching, publishing, and promoting the cause of aboriginal peoples.

One of the central goals of these conferences and organizations has been to promote the adoption of a new international declaration on the rights of aboriginal peoples. Toward this end, all conferences have issued a number of principles and declarations. In general, all reports stress that the following minimum rights of indigenous peoples must be recognized:

(1) Indigenous peoples shall qualify as peoples possessing a right of self-determination;

(2) Indigenous peoples and groups shall be entitled freely and independently to practice, develop, and perpetuate their own religions, languages, cultures, traditions, social systems, and ways of life;

(3) Indigenous peoples shall not be deprived of their rights or claims to land, property or natural resources without their free and informed consent.[8]

United States Indian Policies and Human Rights Standards

Although the United States has not ratified any of the major human rights documents, it has consistently presented itself as the most prominent proponent and defender of human rights. The nation points with pride to the leadership of Woodrow Wilson, who, in his Fourteen Points speech to Congress, put forth the thesis that all peoples have a right to self-determination, and to Franklin Roosevelt, who declared that all of humanity should possess the "four freedoms." In 1977, then President Carter, in an address to the UN, announced the United States' commitment to continue the struggle for human rights and to deal with its "own national inadequacies." The United States' treatment of its Indian population is one of the "national human rights inadequacies" to which Carter referred. The following section evaluates the United States' progress over the past thirty years in according American Indian nations their right to self-determination, land, and culture.

Self-Determination

As we have seen, the strongest international affirmation of the principle of self-determination is found in the first article of both the United Nations International Covenant on Civil and Political Rights and the International Covenant on Economic, Social and Cultural Rights: "All peoples have the right to self-determination. By virtue of the right they freely determine their political status and freely pursue their economic, social and cultural development."[9]

The right of self-determination is the most important right sought by indigenous peoples. Self-determination allows a group to determine its own future by determining its own form of government, laws, and policies. The United States' recognition of tribal rights to self-determination has vacillated over the past one hundred and fifty years between acknowledgment of the principle and attempts to eradicate tribal existence.

The European powers and the early United States government originally dealt with the Indian nations through the treaty process as international sovereigns. By 1831, though, tribes were no longer regarded as international sovereigns and were characterized by Chief Justice John Marshall as "domestic dependent nations." The Indian nations, Marshall emphasized, were a "distinct political community, having territorial boundaries within which their authority is exclusive."[10]

Despite this important decision by the Supreme Court affirming tribal rights of self-determination, the United States implemented a series of policies over the next century and a half to divest Indian nations of their sovereignty, land, and culture. In 1871, Congress ended the making of treaties with Indian nations, thereby laying the groundwork to deal with tribal members as individuals. The 1871 act was followed by laws establishing Indian schools, tribal police forces, and court systems, all of which emulated Anglo-American traditions and sought to assimilate the Indian quickly. In 1887, Congress passed the Dawes Act, the most assimilationist measure of all. Heralded by Theodore Roosevelt as a "mighty pulverizing engine to break up the tribal mass,"[11] the Dawes Act subdivided the reservations and allotted tribal land to individual tribal members in 40- or 160-acre parcels, with the federal government purchasing the remaining lands of the tribe. By 1934, as a result of this policy, two-thirds of the tribal lands had passed into white ownership.

Government policy appeared to shift during the 1930s when Bureau of Indian Affairs Commissioner John Collier convinced Congress to restore and promote tribal rights to self-determination. The Indian Reorganization Act of 1934 halted further allotments of Indian lands and established tribal governments and courts. Many critics charge, however, that rather than allowing the establishment of governments that reflected Indian values and traditions, the Bureau of Indian Affairs drafted tribal constitutions that were tailored to Anglo-American standards. By the early 1950s, the forces for assimilation had again gathered strength and Congress adopted a new Indian policy—termination. This policy involved the unilateral termination of the United States' relationship with the tribes, with the ultimate goals of assimilating all Indian people by breaking down cultural and tribal bonds. By 1961, Congress had terminated its relationship with 109 bands and tribes.

Termination was an unmitigated failure and in the early 1970s, government policy again changed. Acquiescing to the reality that "Indian people will never surrender their desire to control their relationship both among themselves and with non-Indian governments, organizations and persons," President Richard Nixon announced a new era of self-determination.[12] "The time [had] come to break decisively with the past and to create the conditions for a new era in which the Indian future is determined by Indian acts and Indian decisions."[13]

The government's commitment to allowing tribes a meaningful exercise of self-determination can be evaluated from a number of perspectives. This section considers two questions. Does the federal government allow all tribes to exercise their right of self-determination? Have federal policies in recent years inhibited or expanded the exercise of tribal self-government?

The right of self-determination is a right that should apply to all Indian tribes. Article I of the ILO convention, for example, states that its provisions are applicable to members of all tribal or semitribal populations, regardless of their legal status in their respective countries. The United States, however, recognizes only certain tribes—those that are "federally recognized"—as having a right of self-determination. Terminated tribes and nonfederally recognized tribes, which make up almost one-third of all indigenous peoples in the United States, have no federally recognized rights of self-determination.

Federally recognized tribes have either concluded treaties with the federal government or otherwise have received official recognition of their status. These tribes are eligible for Bureau of Indian Affairs' services; they have recognized and identifiable rights and are allowed to exercise some powers of government. Terminated tribes are those with whom the federal government has severed its political relationship. The claim of these tribes to sovereignty and to self-determination is no longer acknowledged by the federal government and its members are no longer eligible for BIA services.[14] Of the bands and tribes that were terminated in the 1950s, Congress has restored less than ten to federal status. Unrecognized tribes are groups who through accidents of history have never established a formal political relationship with the United States. Approximately two hundred Indian tribes do not exist as legal entities in the eyes of the federal government; they have no recognized land base and they receive few, if any, federal services.

In 1978, however, the Bureau of Indian Affairs, through the Federal Acknowledgment Program, took steps to rectify this inequity. The Federal Acknowledgment Program establishes a procedure whereby Indian tribes may apply for federal recognition. Under the guidelines established in 1978, a tribe must submit a petition with documentation that proves the existence and operation of some form of tribal governmental authority from historical times until the present. By 1983 more than seventy tribes had started this long and complicated petition process. So far, five Indian groups have received federal recognition through this process.

In practical terms, self-determination is a question of jurisdiction: Who has the authority to make and enforce laws governing the Indian group? Tribal self-determination can be evaluated by determining how much authority tribes have in regulating actions that occur within their territorial boundaries. Chief Justice John Marshall ruled in 1832 that Indian nations constituted "a distinct independent political community, having territorial boundaries within which their authority is exclusive."[15] By the end of the nineteenth century, the Supreme Court had drastically altered Marshall's ruling. The federal courts, relying on the commerce clause, ruled that federal ownership of Indian lands brought jurisdictional authority and declared Indians to be wards of the federal government.[16] The result of these decisions was a declaration that Congress possessed plenary (total) control over tribes. The only limitations on this control were "such considerations of justice as would control a Christian people in their treatment of an ignorance and dependent race."[17]

Indian tribes began to reassert tribal rights and sovereignty in the twentieth century. The reserved rights doctrine, which held that tribes retained all of their sovereign powers unless expressly removed by Congress, to some extent tempered the plenary doctrine. In addition, the courts ruled that the Fifth Amendment protected treaty lands. Most important, the idea that the government functioned primarily as a guardian began to lose force. Guardianship began to evolve into a trust relationship that emphasized tribal rights and corresponding government obligations to protect tribal resources.[18]

In 1954, during the termination era and over tribal objections, Congress passed Public Law 280—a law which granted six states concurrent criminal and civil jurisdiction over Indian reservations. Prior to Public Law 280, tribal sovereignty and the federal-tribal relationship had precluded states from the regulation of Indian affairs. Whereas Public Law 280 affected only certain tribes, albeit the majority, the Indian Civil Rights Act, passed in 1968, and the 1978 *Oliphant* v. *Suquamish Tribe*[19] decision affected the authority of all tribes to maintain safety and order in a manner compatible with cultural traditions. Intended to protect Indians from arbitrary actions by their tribal councils, the Indian Civil Rights Act extended most Bill of Rights guarantees to tribal members vis-á-vis their governments; it authorized federal courts to review writs of habeas corpus involving Indians, and it limited tribal courts from imposing fines of greater than six months in jail or $500.

Though conceding that the Indian Civil Rights Act was

well intentioned by Congress, many tribal leaders opposed the Act's passage on several grounds. Critics emphasized that the alien philosophy of individualism inherent in the Bill of Rights was incompatible with, and therefore inimical to, many cultural traditions. The concept of one-person, one-vote had no relevance for the Pueblo theocracies, for example. Protections against self-incrimination undermined societies emphasizing full and honest discussions in dispute settlements. Indeed, the general adversary system of justice used by the United States conflicted with traditional systems of arbitration. Most important, by allowing appeals to federal court in cases involving writs of habeas corpus, the act removed the tribe's authority to function as a final arbiter in criminal cases involving imprisonment. And finally, the act's imposed sentencing limitations reduced tribal authority to maintain proper order.

Ten years later, the Supreme Court's *Oliphant* decision further diminished tribal sovereignty significantly by prohibiting tribal criminal jurisdiction over non-Indians, thereby impairing tribal ability to maintain order within reservation boundaries. The Suquamish Tribe had arrested two non-Indian men on charges of resisting arrest, assaulting an officer, recklessly endangering another person, and injuring tribal property during the Suquamish annual Chief Seattle Days celebration. The defendants, suing under a writ of habeas corpus, argued that the tribe possessed no criminal jurisdiction over non-Indians. The Supreme Court agreed, ruling that the tribe's exercise of criminal authority over non-Indians was inconsistent with its "dependent status."[20]

The decision, which many Indians felt to be a contrived piece of legal reasoning, supported its argument with selected historical data and exhibited a cultural bias supposedly outmoded in today's enlightened age. The Court acknowledged that Congress had never expressly removed tribal criminal jurisdiction over non-Indians, but it also argued that Congress had never legally recognized this kind of tribal jurisdiction. This reasoning directly contravened the reserved rights doctrine. To support their findings the

Justices cited the following passage from an 1834 report: "With the exception of two or three tribes . . . the Indian tribes are without laws."[21] The same 1834 report, however, had also clearly stated that an exercise of federal criminal jurisdiction in Indian country had been extended to the federal government by the tribes as a "courtesy, not a right."[22] Finally, the Justices, quoting from an earlier case, made the point that to allow non-Indians to be judged by Indians would result in non-Indians being judged by "a standard made by others and not for them. . . . It tries them, not by their peers, not by the custom of their people, nor the laws of their lands but by . . . a different race, according to the laws of a social state of which they have an imperfect conception."[23] The Justices failed to explain why the reverse was not also true—why Indians did not experience a similar disadvantage when subjected to procedures and judgments of Anglo law.

The erosion of tribal powers in the exercise of civil and criminal jurisdiction has been somewhat balanced by progress in obtaining more control over the administration of their tribal programs and services. In 1975, responding to "a strong expression of the Indian people for self-determination," because the "federal domination of the Indian service programs has served to retard rather than enhance the progress of Indian people," Congress passed the Indian Self-determination and Education Assistance Act.[24] The act gives all tribes an opportunity to assume control of governmental programs and services formerly provided by the BIA, including housing, community development, and law enforcement. Today, more than 50 percent of all BIA programs are administered by the tribes themselves. While the act is an important milestone, the manner in which it has been implemented has received criticism. Tribal leaders and a General Accounting Office study charge that BIA resistance, red tape, delays in contract approvals, a lack of appeal process for denied applications, inadequate funding, and the dictation of program priorities have prevented tribes from obtaining full control over the administration of their programs. Many tribes fear that if they take advantage of the self-determination act, Congress, under its plenary authority, again will withdraw its recognition of Indian sovereignty and terminate its relationship with the tribes. Such fears, despite federal protestations to the contrary, are not without some plausibility. Many of the tribes chosen for termination in the 1950s had a high degree of stability and self-sufficiency.

The existence of the plenary doctrine remains incompatible with any meaningful exercise of tribal self-sufficiency. To date, the doctrine has not been limited in any significant manner, nor have the courts ever found any statute dealing with the Indians to be unconstitutional or beyond the scope of the federal government's authority. Consequently, the Indian nations live under the constant threat of having their treaties abrogated, their governing powers extinguished, and their lands confiscated.

Land

The importance of a territorial land base to Indian society cannot be overemphasized. For most indigenous societies the land is a unifying force—the land represents a home, a livelihood, a religion. As white settlements grew, reservations signified safety against an encroaching and alien culture.

Two articles of the ILO convention speak directly to the rights of indigenous peoples to retain their native lands and to necessary compensation in the event of their removal:

The right of the population, collective or individual . . . over the lands [they] have traditionally occupied shall be recognized. (Article 11)

The populations concerned shall not be removed without their free consent . . . except in accordance with national laws . . . for reasons relating to national security, or in the interest of national economic development or of the health of the said population.

When in such case removal . . . is necessary as an exceptional measure, they shall be provided with lands of quality at least equal to lands previously occupied by them. (Article 12)[25]

At first glance, these provisions appear more applicable to a country like Brazil, which is currently removing its indigenous populations from their traditional lands, than to the United States, which completed its removal process in the last century. The United States, however, is violating the above norms as a result of its legal and legislative history regarding Indian property rights.

In 1823, Chief Justice Marshall ruled that the doctrine of discovery vested ultimate title to the lands of the New World in discovering powers.[26] Discovery, according to Marsall, had reduced Indian title to a right of occupancy, but it was a right that was "as sacred as the fee simple, absolute title held by the whites."[27]

The government soon shattered the promised inviolability of the Indians' occupancy rights. Beginning in the 1830s, the government instituted a policy of mass deportation by moving eastern tribes west of the Mississippi River. The Indians carried a congressional promise with them on the Trail of Tears that the United States would "forever secure and guaranty to them, their heirs or successors the country so exchanged with them."[28] That promise evaporated in the mid-1800s when the lure of cheap land attracted hordes of white settlers to the western territories. Faced with a choice between the settlers' demands for land and its promise to the Indians, the government took the predictable course. Often with the use of military action, it forced many tribes to cede their lands in exchange for money and a promise of exclusive control over smaller areas called reservations. By 1880 the government had located most tribes on reservations. By 1940, tribes possessed only 2.3 percent of the country's land mass as a result of the allotment process under the Dawes Act.

Tribes currently own approximately fifty-two million acres of recognized or trust title land. *Recognized title* means that the government acknowledges some form of possessory right to exist in the tribe. Tribes without recognized title are said to possess *aboriginal title*. The distinction between recognized and aboriginal title is important. Recognized lands (usually confirmed by treaty or legislation) are held in trust by the government for the tribes occupancy and benefit. If the federal government should sell or mismanage these lands, it is obligated under the Fifth Amendment due process clause to compensate the tribe. There is nothing, however, to prevent Congress from taking treaty held lands. Under domestic law, Congress has the authority to extinguish recognized title and to abrogate Indian treaties.[29] This continued abrogation of Indian treaties remains a violation of the international legal principle, *pacta sunt sevanda* (treaties must be upheld).

Tribes with aboriginal title have even less protection and generally receive no compensation for the taking of their lands. Federal authority to acquire aboriginal title goes beyond the power of eminent domain that covers other property-owning citizens. Before the government can take land by eminent domain it must prove that the taking is for a "public purpose" and it must pay adequate compensation. Aboriginal lands may be taken at any time and for any reason; "public purpose" does not have to be shown.[30]

The question of compensation was not clearly settled by the courts until 1955 when in *Tee-Hit-Ton Indians* v. *United States*[31] the Supreme Court ruled the federal government was not liable for the harvesting of the Tee-Hit-Tons timber because the government had never recognized the tribe's ownership of the area. Most experts agree that the Court's reason for denying tribal compensation had no basis in legal reasoning but rather rested on financial considerations. Justice Reed indicated in a footnote that the estimated interest alone in pending aboriginal land cases was $9 billion.[32]

Before 1946, tribes had to obtain special legislation from Congress allowing them to sue for lost or mismanaged lands. In 1946, Congress established the Indian Claims Commission as a vehicle for settling claims arising from both recognized and unrecognized title. The impetus for the act was both humanitarian and self-serving—a prelude to settling past debts as a complement to the termination policy.[33] The commission was originally authorized to hear suits for a period of five years, but tribal suits were so numerous that Congress extended the commission's life four times. Even after thirty years, the commission had adjudicated only 40 percent of the claims filed and Congress moved the remaining cases to the Court of Claims.

The government's method of claim settlement left much to be desired. The commission was intolerably slow in settling suits. Tribes had to bear the burden of proof against a formidable opponent, the Lands Division of the Justice Department, in unfamiliar adversary proceedings. If tribes successfully presented their case, the commission determined the awards conservatively. Compensation was not based on current market value, but on the land's value at the time of the taking, an amount usually averaging less than $1 an acre. No compensation was given for land if more than one tribe used the area. With few exceptions, the act did not allow for interest to be awarded. After the commission determined the land's value at the time of taking, the government subtracted the cost of preparing the case and the tribe had to pay 10 percent of its award as attorney's fee. The tribes also had to deduct offsets, "gratuities given by the government to the claiming tribe after the date the claim arose."[34] Hence, the government charged Indians for goods and services they never requested and in many cases never wanted.

Most critical, neither the Indian Claims Commission Act nor any other federal legislation gives tribes the option to regain their lost lands or to acquire new land.[35] Article 12 of the ILO convention clearly states that a government is obligated to offer tribes land of equal value if it has forced them from their traditional lands. That at least twenty-two Indian nations (including several groups of the Lakota Nation, which are rejecting a $122 million award for its sacred Black Hills) are objecting to monetary awards made by the commission illustrates that many tribes still hold to the value enunciated by a chief of the Blackfoot Tribe:

Our land is more valuable than your money. It will last forever. It will not even perish by the flames of fire. . . . We cannot sell the lives of men and animals; therefore we cannot sell this land. It was put here by the Great Spirit and we cannot sell it because it does not belong to us.[36]

Culture

The right to develop and preserve one's culture is stated most clearly in two international documents. The UNESCO Declaration of the Principles of International Cultural Cooperation (1966), Article 1, states that:

1. Each culture has a dignity and value which must be preserved.
2. Every people has the right and the duty to develop its culture.
3. In their rich variety and diversity, and in the reciprocal influences they exert on one another, all cultures form part of the common heritage belonging to all mankind.

Article 27 of the International Covenant on Civil and Political Rights provides that: "In those states in which ethnic, religious or linguistic minorities exist, persons belonging to such minorities shall not be denied the right, in community with other members of their group, to enjoy their own culture, to profess and practice their own religion, or to use their own languages."

The historical federal attitude toward Indian culture is best expressed by the following line taken from testimony before Congress in 1871: "We see nothing about Indian nationality or Indian civilization which should make its preservation a matter of so much anxiety to the Congress or to the people of the United States."[37]This judgment about Indian culture produced government policies and programs that divided communal tribal lands, forcibly placed children in boarding schools and forbade them to speak their Indian languages, and sought to destroy traditional Indian religions. By 1900, one-half of all Indian languages had become extinct. Now, however, government policies no longer aim to eradicate Indian culture. Whether they are adequately designed to preserve and encourage the development of Indian culture remains an open question. This section examines two spheres of life important to the maintenance of a culture—religion and the protection of the family unit.

Religion historically played an important role in Indian-white relations. Bringing Indians the fruits of civilization, which included Christianity, was seen as an adequate exchange for expropriating vast areas of land through bribery, threats, and fraudulent land transactions. The government's determination to eradicate Indian religion reached its height in the 1890s with the spread of the Ghost Dance religion. Built around a prophesy that the world would return to the state it had enjoyed before the coming of the white man and that Indian ancestors and vanished game would reappear, the religious movement offered hope to a population decimated by disease and starvation and imprisoned on reservations. The government saw the religion as a unifying anti-white force among Indians and forcibly sought to prevent its practice. In 1890 the army massacred three hundred Sioux, mostly women and children, at Wounded Knee, South Dakota. In 1892 the BIA promulgated the Indian Religious Crimes regulation, which made it a crime to engage in any form of Indian dancing or feasting. Any violation of this rule carried a minimum of ten days in jail or ten days without rations. This administrative rule continued in force until 1921.

It was not until 1978 that Congress took positive steps to ensure that American Indians were guaranteed a minimal level of religious freedom. Recognizing that "the religious practices of the American Indian (as well as Native Alaskan and Hawaiian) are an integral part of their culture, tradition and heritage . . . [and] are indispensable and irreplaceable. . . ." Congress passed the Indian Religious Freedom Act.[38] Committing itself "to protect and preserve for Native Americans their inherent right of freedom to believe, express, and exercise the traditional religions," the act directs federal agencies to evaluate policies and procedures that may deprive Indians of access to sacred sites on federal lands or that prevent the performance of traditional ceremonies and the possession of sacred objects.

Though the act significantly improves the government's traditional posture, Indian religious rights remain inadequately protected. The law only directs federal agencies to review their policies and procedures for possible interferences with religious practices. The act has no enforcement section; thus it does not mandate that Congress alter policies if they are found to be obstructionist. Thus far, the act has achieved some objectives, but it has proven useless in solving major problems. For example, the Cherokee Nation, the second largest tribe in the United Sates, considers the central area of Tennessee to be its sacred birthplace. The floodwaters of the controversial Tellico Dam placed this entire area under water, forever denying the Cherokees access to their sacred capital, their religious grounds, and the burial place of their ancestors. The courts rejected without comment a motion by the tribe, based on the Indian Religious Freedom Act, for an injunction to prevent the dam's completion.[39] The Navajos lost a similar fight with the U.S. Forest Service to prevent the further expansion of the Arizona Snow Bowl on the San Francisco Peaks, an area of great spiritual significance within their religion.[40]

The impact of the Indian Religious Freedom Act is weak at the federal level and virtually nonexistent at the state level. Although some progress has been made, states remain free to deny tribes access to religious sites and to deny Indian prisoners in state correctional institutions the right to hold religious ceremonies.[41] State schools have denied Indian children excused absences for attending religious ceremonies and have forced them to cut their braids, a symbol with religious meaning for many tribes.[42] State and private museums continue to exhibit sacred objects, such as Iroquois false faces, and to deny religious leaders possession of sacred objects.[43]

In 1978, Congress passed the Indian Child Welfare Act that also purported to take into account tribal culture and values.[44] Unlike the Indian Religious Freedom Act, which represents merely a policy statement without implementation or enforcement procedures, the Indian Child Welfare Act provides specific procedures for implementing the Act's objectives.

For years, tribes had attempted to reverse state child custody proceedings which had, by 1977, taken 25 to 35 percent of all Indian children from their homes. According to a nationwide survey by the Association of American Indian Affairs, state officials placed Indian children in foster homes in South Dakota at a rate twenty-two times higher than that for non-Indians; in Maine, the rate was nineteen times higher; in Minnesota, seventeen times higher. In California, where the adoption rate for Indians was eight times that for the general population, officials placed Indian children in non-Indian homes 93 percent of the time.[45]

The decision to remove a child from its family was usually made at the discretion of non-Indian state employees, who had little understanding of Indian culture. Once the courts decided to remove the child, guidelines restricting placement with family members and requirements for certain living standards effectively precluded many Indian families from consideration as adoptive or foster parents. The child was therefore taken from its family, its tribe, and its culture, a practice in direct opposition to Indian traditions and cultural values emphasizing the extended family. This practice certainly violated Article 23 of the Covenant on Political and Civil Rights, which states, "the family is the natural and fundamental group unit of society and is entitled to protections by society and the state." The placement of nearly one-third of all Indian children in non-Indian homes also represented a violation of the Genocide Convention which defines genocide as including "forcibly transferring the children of a group to another group."[46]

"Recognizing that there is no resource that is more vital to the continued existence and integrity of Indian tribes than their children," the 1978 Indian Child Welfare Act asserted that tribes shall have exclusive jurisdictional rights over state in child custody proceedings involving their children.[47] The act provides for the transfer of state court proceedings to tribal jurisdictions, the resumption of jurisdictional control over child custody proceedings to Public Law 280 tribes, and the appropriation of tribal grants for the operation of Indian child and family service programs. The act stands as a major step toward bringing federal policies into compliance with human rights standards.

Conclusion

This article has examined the federal government's posture toward Indian self-determination, its acknowledgment of Indian property rights, and its willingness to allow Indian cultural freedom as a measurement of the United States' conformity to existing and proposed standards of aboriginal protection. On balance, the federal government's record in these areas is mixed. To conform with existing standards of indigenous rights, the United States must accord the right of self-determination to all Indian nations, including those classified as terminated and unrecognized tribes. A full and speedy implementation of the Federal Acknowledgment Program and an omnibus restoration bill for terminated tribes would rectify this serious deficiency. The government 'must repudiate the legal fiction of aboriginal title and grant those tribes with aboriginal title the same rights and protections that are accorded to recognized title. The federal government must also institute procedures whereby tribes can obtain land in lieu of money for lands illegally taken.

In its dealings with recognized tribes, the government does appear to be moving toward a cautious affirmation of Indian self-determination and cultural rights. The 1975 Indian Self-Determination Act and the 1978 Indian Child Welfare Act represent important progress in moving federal Indian policies closer to compliance with international standards of human rights. Meaningful tribal control will only occur, however, if Congress adequately funds these programs and if Congress grants tribes the latitude to establish programs according to their own needs, standards, and priorities. The Indian Civil Rights Act, Public Law 280, and the *Oliphant* decision prevent tribes from fulfilling their governmental function and must be revised. On a more fundamental level, true self-determination is unattainable without the repudiation of the plenary doctrine. The federal government must clearly recognize the moral and legal rights of tribes to self-determination and must clearly affirm the special relationship tribes possess with the United States as a result of inherent tribal sovereignty.

NOTES

1. Vitorio, Francisco, *De Jure Belli Reflectiones, Classics of International Law* (New York: Oceana Publications, 1964).

2. Convention No. 50 on the Recruiting of Indigenous Workers (1936), Convention No. 64 on Contracts of Employment (Indigenous Workers), and Recommendation No. 48 on the same subject, Convention No. 65 on Penal Sanctions (Indigenous Workers) and Recommendation No. 59 on Labor Inspectorates (Indigenous Workers). And see the 1953 book published by the ILO, *Indigenous Peoples: Living and Working Conditions of Aboriginal Populations in Independent Countries.*

3. ILO Conference Report on equality of opportunity in employment in the American region, Symposium held in Panama City, October, 1973.

4. See, however, UN General Assembly Resolution 2625 in the 1970 Principles of International Law Concerning Friendly Relations and Cooperation Among States.

5. "Report of the World Conference to Combat Racism and Racial Discrimination," A/Conf. 92/40, 1979.

6. "Special Study on Racial Discrimination in the Political, Economic, Social and Cultural Spheres," 1970.

7. "The Declaration of Principles for the Defense of the Indigenous Nations and Peoples of the Western Hemispheres," 1977.

8. Taken from "Principles for Guiding the Deliberations of the Working Group on Indigenous Populations," Indian Law Resource Center, 1983.

9. In 1970 the International Court of Justice in the Greco-Bulgarian case defined a people as:

A group of persons living in a given country or locality, having a race, religion, language and traditions of their own and united by the identity of race, religion, language and tradition in a sentiment of solidarity, with a view of preserving their traditions, maintaining their form of worship, insuring the instruction of upbringing of their children in accordance with the spirit and traditions of their faith and rendering mutual assistance to each other. P.D.I.J. ser. B, No. 17, at 21.

See also Declaration on Principles of International Law Concerning Friendly Relations and Co-operation Among States of 1970; Declaration on the Granting of Independence to Colonial Countries and Peoples (1960); articles 1 and 55 of the Charter of the United Nations: article 21 of the Universal Declaration of Human Rights; Declaration on the Inadmissibility of Intervention in Domestic Affairs and Protection of their Independence and Sovereignty, G.A. Res. 2131 (1965); and Resolution 637 (VII) of 1952: "State members of the United Nations shall uphold the principles of self-determination of all peoples and nations."

Or see the Helsinki Agreement to which the United States is a signatory: Final Act of the Conference on Security and Co-operation in Europe, section VII of the Declaration of Principles Guiding Relations between Participating States: "The participating States on whose territory national minorities exist will respect the rights of persons belonging to such minorities to equality before the law, will afford them the full opportunity for the actual enjoyment of human rights and fundamental freedoms and will, in this manner, protect their legitimate interests in this sphere." See also International Court of Justice Advisory Opinion on Western Sahara, (1975) ICJ Rep. 12 in which the Court ruled that the local nomadic population had legal rights in relation to the land and the right of self-determination.

10. Cherokee Nation v. Georgia 30 U.S. (5 Pet.) 1 (1831).

11. Roosevelt, Theodore, *Messages and Papers of the Presidents*, vol. XV, p. 6672.

12. Publ. L. No. 93-638, codified at 25 U.S.C. §450, §2(2).

13. Message From the President of the United States Transmitting Recommendations for Indian Policy. H.R. Doc. No. 363, 91st Cong., 2d Sess. (1970).

14. Tribes were ostensibly given an opportunity to vote for or against termination. In case after case, however, tribes were either misinformed or misled about the full effects of termination. See, Charles Wilkinson and Eric Biggs, "The Evolution of the Termination Policy," *American Indian Law Review*, Vol. V, No. 1 (1977), 139-84.

15. Worcester v. Georgia, 31 U.S. (6 Pet.) 515, 556 (1832).

16. See, for example, United States v. Holliday, 70 U.S. (3 Wall) 407 (1865). For cases dealing with the United States' role as guardian, see Cherokee Nation v. Hitchcock 187 U.S. 294 (1902); United States v. Kagama 118 U.S. 375 (1886).

17. Beecher v. Weatherby, 45 U.S. 517 (1877) quoted in Lone Wolf v. Hitchcock 187 U.S. 553, 565 (1903).

18. Seminole Nation v. United States, 316 U.S. 286 (1942); United States v. Creek Nation, 295 U.S. 10 (1935); Manchester Band of Pomo

Indians v. United States, 363 F. Supp. 1238 (N.D. Colo. 1973); Menominee Tribe v. United States, 59 F. Supp. 135 (Ct. Cl. 1944).

19. 435 U.S. 191 (1978).

20. *Id.*

21. *Id.* at 197.

22. H.R. No. 474, 23rd Cong., 1st Sess. p. 13.

23. Ex Parte Crow Dog, 109 U.S. 566 (1899).

24. *Id.*, note 12.

25. See also Article 17(2) of UN Charter: "No one shall be arbitrarily deprived of his property," and International Covenant on Political and Civil Rights and International Covenant on Economic, Social and Cultural Right, Article (1(2); "All peoples may for their own ends, freely dispose of their natural wealth and resources. . . . In no case may a people be deprived of its own means of subsistence."

26. Johnson v. McIntosh, 21 U.S. (8 Wheat.) 543 (1823).

27. Mitchel v. United States 34 U.S. (9 Pet.) 711, 745 (1835).

28. Act of May 28, 1830, 4 Stat. 411.

29. See for example, Lone Wolf v. Hitchcock, 187 U.S. 553 (1903).

30. Indian Law Resource Center, "Report on the Presentation of Human Rights Complaints by Indian Nations to the United Nations Commission on Human Rights," (March 1980) p. 8-10.

31. 348 U.S. 272 (1955).

32. *Id.*, at 283 n. 27.

33. 25 U.S.C.A. §§70-70v. See David Getches, Daniel Rosenfelt, Charles Wilkinson, *Federal Indian Law* (St. Paul, Minnesota: West Publishing Co., 1979), p. 152-53.

34. United States Indian Claims Commission, *Final Report*, August 13, 1946-September 30, 1978 (Washington, D.C.: U.S. Government Printing Office, 1979), p. 9.

35. On two occasions in recent years Congress has returned tribal lands. In 1970, Congress returned Blue Lake to the Taos Pueblo and in 1974 similar legislation returned Mount Adams. The Indian Reorganization Act halted further allotments on Indian lands and authorized the Secretary of the Interior to acquire additional lands for reservations. Between 1934 and 1974, the government purchased 595,157 acres for approximately $6 million. During the same period, however, the federal government took 1,811,010 acres of Indian lands to be used primarily for water projects benefitting non-Indians. American Indian Policy Review Commission: Final Report (U.S. Government Printing Office, 1977), p. 310.

36. T. C. McLuhan, compiler, *Touch the Earth* (New York: Simon and Schuster, 1971), p. 53.

37. Rep. No. 336, 41 Cong., 3d Sess., 10-11 (1871).

38. Pub. L. No. 95-341, 92 Stat. 469, codified at 42 U.S.C. 1966.

39. Sequoyah v. TVA, 620 & 2d 1159, cer't den 449 U.S. 953 (1980).

40. Navajo Medicinemen's Association and Hopi Tribe v. Block.

National Indian Law Library. Catalogue: An Index to Legal Materials and Resources, looseleaf service, Native American Rights Fund, Boulder, Colorado (1982), p. B-378, #003977.

Navajo medicine men also lost their struggle to worship in private at Rainbow Bridge, a traditional site in Utah. Badoni v. Higginson, 638 F. 2d 172, cer't. den 101 SCt 3099 (1981).

41. Native American Rights Fund, *Announcements* (Boulder, Colorado, Winter 1979), p. 8-9.

42. *Id.* See also New Rider v. Board of Education, 480 F. 2d 693 (10th Cir. 1973), cer't. den 414 U.S. 1097 (1973). Although the New Rider case was decided prior to the passage of the Indian Religious Freedom Act, see *Gazette Journal*, Reno, Nevada, Sunday, October 11, 1981-5A for an article describing a Nevada court's upholding of a school's expulsion of a Paiute Indian student for violating the school's dress code by refusing to cut his braids.

43. National Indian Youth Council, *Americans Before Columbus*, special edition, (Albuquerque, New Mexico, 1981), p. 4, 7.

44. Pub. L. 90-608 2(4), 92 Stat. 3069.

45. Task Force Report on Federal, State and Tribal Jurisdiction, Final Report to the American Indian Policy Review Commission (1976).

46. One of the most serious charges levied against the United States in the violation of tribal rights from a family perspective is the forced sterilization of Indian women. In 1976 a GAO study of four Indian Hospital Service facilities found that thousands of Indian women had been sterilized without their informed consent between 1973 and 1976.

47. *Id.*, at note 44.

3

The Deception of Geography

BY FRED L. RAGSDALE, JR.

Indian tribes are facing a crisis. The irony of this crisis, compared to the problems tribes have faced in the past, is that the crisis has arisen from tribal *success*. The success stems from the reaffirmation of tribal power to control many aspects of behavior on reservations. The threat flows from the failure of many Indian leaders and their advisers to understand fully the social and legal restraints of the reaffirmed power. As a consequence, too often in the exercise of power the entire status of a tribe is put at risk. In the past, most dangers confronting tribal governments have occurred as a result of specific federal policies. Most of these policies have represented either a wish to assimilate or to facilitate the assimilation of Indians into American society. But at their heart was the transferring of Indian assets to non-Indians.

The fluctuations in federal Indian policy are the usual gist of most studies of tribal government in America. To a great extent, there has been an overemphasis on official policies and not enough attention devoted to the actual status of tribes. For the most part, tribal status has remained relatively stable, unlike the rights of individual Indians or the power of a specific tribe, both of which have changed considerably.

To a great degree, contemporary federal Indian law is modern law beginning in 1959. This division is contrary to contemporary wisdom since one of the putative attractions

63

of Indian law to non-Indians is its reliance on the earliest cases to resolve complex contemporary problems. Though it is true that the roots of contemporary Indian law are in the great decisions of America's greatest jurist, John Marshall, the vast majority of decisions that control tribal behavior are relatively recent.

The success that threatens tribes results from the modern Supreme Court's acceptance of the most fundamental findings of Marshall's Court and its willingness to incorporate the changes in law and society that have since occurred, while at the same time preserving the essence of tribal self-government. As a result, tribes have successfully crossed the historical chasm that exists between the concept of the United States as a struggling new democracy to the contemporary United States which is the superpower of the world. The successful bridging of this historical gap, instead of resolving many long-standing issues, has made the old issues more complicated and created new problems. The paradox of success bringing destruction is not unique; many of the world's great novels embody the same theme. The rise and fall of nations as a result of the original foundation being unable to support the superstructure of success is a common theory of history, and after Edward Gibbon, an idea of general currency.[1]

The Spain to which Columbus returned after his first voyage in 1492 was self-satisfied with its position as the most powerful nation in Europe. Its conquest of the final Moorish garrison at Granada and its expulsion of the Jews meant, at least psychologically, that Spain could control its own destiny for the first time in a thousand years. After Columbus returned with the news of his discovery, Spain and the rest of Europe were forced to confront the questions posed by the presence of the inhabitants of this new world. The intellectual problem was enormous. How this new world would fit into the known world was a serious problem, for not only was it Terra Nova, it was inhabited. The answer was that each country made decisions about the nature of the Indians according to the needs of its internal society and not against some template of international law or even natural law, although both doctrines were used to justify the final posture each nation eventually adopted. The choices made then greatly affect modern Indian law.

Although the relationship between the Spanish and the Indians was a more complicated relationship than is generally acknowledged, recent scholarship indicates that some of the Pueblo Indians became skilled in Spanish colonial law. The theoretical basis of the relationship between the Spanish crown and the aboriginals was citizenship. Spain chose to fit Indians and their property into one of the existing pigeonholes of Spanish jurisprudence. As a matter of law, the Spanish did not recognize Indian tribes as separate or even dependent governments. That Spanish law treated Indians in this manner was viewed primarily as a historical curiosity after *United States* v. *Sandoval,*[2] when the United States Supreme Court held that Pueblo Indians were like other Indians, and that their land, even though held in fee simple rather than in trust, was subject to the same protection as other Indians. Recent litigation in New Mexico regarding the extent of Pueblo Indian water rights raises the issue again. Particularly, are Pueblo Indians covered by the *Winters* reserved water-rights doctrine?[3] This issue will be decided at the district court level in the near future,[4] but the reemergence of the distinction between English and Spanish treatment after many years emphasizes the importance of understanding the legal history of Indians.

The English, and later the British after the Act of Union, treated Indian tribes as nations, as manifested by the treaty process. The treaties were agreements signed between equal nations offering mutual obligations. The English adopted this posture because English jurisprudence separated sovereignty from property. Many of the early royal grants of land were grants of both sovereignty and title, that is, the grantee had both governmental and property rights. In contrast, because the Spanish feared importation of the feudal system into the New World, it chose not to grant governmental powers to its grantees. In the entire period of Spanish domination, only Hernando Cortez received both. The English took such a separation of rights so seriously that they at times purchased back the governmental rights from the original grantee, and in one instance, the price was greater than the grantee's original price for the land and the sovereignty. Because the British chose to treat Indians as citizens of a foreign sovereign, the question of the status of their land and person could be addressed without having to decide their rights within the framework of common law.

When the United States government sought to address the question of the status of Indian tribes in the context of its judicial system, it had to choose between the British view of tribes as nations and the Spanish view of Indians as citizens. During the Revolution, the United States adopted the British policy of dealing with Indians through treaties and also observed the line drawn by the Proclamation of 1763 as the border of Indian country after the Revolution. It was not clear whether this policy would continue when the inevitable conflicts between tribes and states had to be formally addressed, however. The final choice was the result of many different factors: the control of western expansion, the debate over federalism, the fear of state power, and the building of the Supreme Court's power. Yet, the decisions that John Marshall wrote—*Johnson & Graham's Lessee* v. *McIntosh*,[5] *Cherokee Nation* v. *Georgia*,[5] and *Worcester* v. *Georgia*[7]—firmly followed the British policy of treating Indian tribes as nations. The histories of these three landmark cases are well known; it is only necessary to review the holdings because they have great meaning for understanding contemporary issues.

In *Johnson,* the Supreme Court had to decide who had better title, a grantee from a private purchaser of land who obtained his title from an Indian tribe, or a grantee whose title derived from the United States after the United States had purchased the land from the tribe. The issue raised the fundamental question of what the Indians could sell. Marshall held for the grantee whose title had derived from the

United States. After discussing the history of the conquest of the New World, he determined that the Indians had a land tenure heretofore unknown in Anglo-American law—aboriginal title or a right of occupancy subject only to defeasance by the United States and no one else. Indians were like tenants in apartments owned and managed by the United States. Eventually, the Court held that the powers of the landlord were almost unlimited.

The next two cases are really the same; both presented the Court with the same legal issue: the place of Indians in the American system of law. In *Cherokee Nation,* the tribe challenged the authority of the state of Georgia to enforce a series of restrictive laws that affected the Cherokee lands. The tribe sued under the original jurisdiction clause of the United States Constitution, which allows the Supreme Court to act as a court of first jurisdiction or as a trial court to hear a limited range of cases. The tribe claimed that such jurisdiction was correct because the tribe was a foreign nation within the meaning of the Constitution. The Supreme Court has the power to determine its own jurisdiction, but the Court did not invoke this power in *Cherokee Nation.* In other words, because of the posture it adopted, the Court was without power to determine the constitutionality of Georgia's laws.

In explaining why the Court lacked jurisdiction, Marshall said that the relationship between the United States and the Indian tribes was like no other on earth and that Indian tribes, though not nations in the the constitutional sense, were domestic dependent nations, a category not known before in international law. Marshall analogized that this relationship resembled that of a guardian to its ward.

The next one hundred and fifty years of Indian law were consumed with argument attempting to discern the meaning of this analogy. Marshall's description of the unique relationship was transmuted into an absolute legal doctrine, and as a consequence Indians were treated as legal wards for the next century. The wardship theory was used to justify all of the discriminatory laws of the federal government and practices of the states. Ironically, modern law concentrates on the same phrase except to argue the legal boundaries of the trust responsibility.

Worcester raised the same substantive issue as *Cherokee Nation,* the constitutionality of the Georgia laws. This time the Court found it had jurisdiction because the case was on appeal by writ of error by an individual, Samuel Worcester, a non-Indian missionary who had come to Georgia with fellow churchmen to teach the Cherokees. As in *Johnson* the Court reviewed the historical process, but instead of finding that relatively minor activities by European adventurers invoked the rules of conquest and discovery, the Court decided that tribes had significant rights. Since Indian tribes were domestic dependent nations, their relationship and status were a function of federal law; as a result, any law of Georgia applied on the reservation was void as being repugnant to the United States Constitution. This case is a cornerstone of Indian law and is cited repeatedly, as it should be, but it is no longer the universe of law affecting the status of tribes. *Worcester*'s holding can be characterized as follows: the United States has a plenary legislative power over tribes, but all powers not explicitly removed from the tribe reside with the tribe, and as a consequence, the state has no power. It was not until 1959 that this version was accepted and became important for contemporary Indian law.

"Indian country" is a romantic phrase that evokes nostalgia for the Old West as depicted in the movies. Indian country once meant exactly that, the country of Indians, a place where Indians lived and where the trade and intercourse acts controlled. It was a geographical definition with clear-cut jurisdictional overtones. It could be marked on a map with some accuracy. In 1882 the Supreme Court decided *United States* v. *McBratney,*[8] a case that changed Indian country from a geographical concept to something else—exactly what else is a difficult question. Today, except when used for questions of federal criminal jurisdiction, "Indian country" is about as provisional as "Marlboro country," that is, it is an image, or a state of mind, or a sociological phenomenon to many. Indian country is an incredibly complex jurisdictional issue disguised in a colorful phrase.

McBratney is bland, however, and as a consequence the decision has been largely ignored; until recently it seemed, to use Justice Cardozo's metaphor, to sit for another case as a "derelict on the waters of law." The facts of the case belie its complexity. One non-Indian murdered another non-Indian on the Ute Reservation in Colorado. The defendant challenged the jurisdiction of the United States to try him for the crime. The Supreme Court agreed with the defendant and held that the state had the jurisdiction to try the case because Colorado entered the Union on the same footing as the original thirteen colonies. The problem with this reasoning is that it is valid only if there is some source for the power in the original colonies to try causes arising on an Indian reservation. *Worcester* indicated there was none.

The bankruptcy of the opinion became abundantly clear when, in 1946, the same fact situation arose in New York, an original colony. In *New York ex rel. Ray* v. *Martin,*[9] the court again held state jurisdiction to be valid, citing *McBratney* for the proposition and thus forming a perfect tautology. If *Worcester* stood for the proposition that the state had no power on the reservation except that which the United States had authorized, then there was no foundation for power in any of the states and therefore none for the exercise of power by Colorado in 1882 nor by New York in 1946.

In 1959 the Supreme Court heard *Williams* v. *Lee,*[10] which reaffirmed the notions of residual sovereignty laid down in *Worcester.* Unfortunately, like *McBratney, Williams* is not well understood. Like *McBratney,* the case arose arose from simple facts. A Navajo purchased goods on the Navajo Reservation from a federally licensed trading post owned by a non-Indian. When the Navajo was unable to pay for the goods, he was served a summons by an

Arizona sheriff while away from the Navajo Reservation and ordered to appear in the Arizona court. The Arizona court held that since Congress had not prohibited states from exercising this kind of transitory jurisdiction over Indians, the state had jurisdiction to adjudicate this debt and to do so would not infringe on the tribe's right of self-government.

The Court noted that *Worcester* was still good law but that things had changed in the intervening 127 years. "Over the years, the Court had modified these principles in cases where the rights of the Indians would not be jeopardized . . . ." As support for this proposition, the Court cited *New York ex rel. Ray* v. *Martin*,[11] which had followed *McBratney*, and *Felix* v. *Patrick*,[12] which allowed Indians access to state courts as a constitutional right. The Court then formulated a rule that attempted to integrate the entire 127 years of state-tribal relationships following *Worcester*. "Essentially, absent governing Acts of Congress, the question has *always* been whether the state action infringed on the right of reservation Indians to make their own laws and be ruled by them" (emphasis added). Perhaps the euphoria of victory has obscured the *always*. Either many have consciously or unconsciously misunderstood *Worcester*, or the Court was obscuring the truth. Before discussing this enigma, it will be useful to understand why the Court ruled this way and why *Williams* is such a difficult case for both lawyers and laymen to understand.

The Court recognized the following: (1) that formal Indian policy had changed; (2) that the Indian Reorganization Act of 1934 sought to strengthen tribal government; (3) that the Department of the Interior had encouraged tribal courts, and (4) that Congress had passed comprehensive regulations over Indian tribes while acting on the assumption that states had no power in these areas of internal affairs. It was not accidental that the Navajos had made major revisions in their tribal structure that fit the Court's concept of a "perfect" Indian tribe. *Williams* was not the end product of a disgruntled Navajo unable to pay his debts.

Instead, it was the initial battle in the war to resurrect tribal government and to wrest it from the hands of the Bureau of Indian Affairs and keep it free from the states.

The tribe had previously adopted codes, had taken over the Bureau's Court of Indian Offenses and established a Navajo Court of Indian Offenses, and had upgraded the qualifications of its personnel. All of these were done in order to present to the Court a picture of a society capable of handling the demands of the twentieth century. But it was a movie set. The changes were made not because of an internal Navajo demand for new institutions but as a result of outside stimuli. The court and the codes were Potemkin villages. The Navajos knew that unless there was an appearance of progress, "progress" defined as Navajos appearing similar to contemporary Anglo society, they would eventually come under the rule of the state.

From the perspective of tribes, the difficulty with the *Williams* opinion was that it had not rejected state power on the basis of territorial jurisdiction but instead on other not fully understood grounds. It would have been a much different ruling if the Court had said that the state lacked the power to decide this case because it arose in Navajo territory and therefore was within the exclusive province of the tribe. To decide the jurisdictional issue on the idea of infringement meant that something more than mere geography was required to uphold tribal self-government. While the words were clear, "infringe on the right," the Court was silent concerning what specific actions would constitute infringement by the state. Though tribal power was upheld, the limits of tribal power remained a difficult and unanswered question.

In addition to the vexing issue of infringement, the holding created a situation unknown in American law. The Court had held that Arizona was without *subject matter jurisdiction.* In law, subject matter jurisdiction is a court's authority to hear a particular type of case. Every court's power to hear cases is dependent upon a grant from some ultimate authority. This authority may be the state constitution, the state's laws, the United States Constitution or federal laws, or perhaps even from the consent of the people. Regardless of the source of power, it limits the types of cases. As a general rule, state courts are courts of general jurisdiction. This means that except for distinctions between levels of trial courts, state courts have the power to hear most common law and statutory causes of action. The litigant usually needs only to plead a cause of action, for example, the conduct of defendant injured me, and this is sufficient to raise the subject matter issue. It may be that the court cannot hear this particular case because it does not have personal jurisdiction over the parties. This, however, is an inquiry separate from the issue of subject matter jurisdiction.

In contrast, federal courts are courts of limited jurisdiction. This limitation means that a litigant must plead some authority, a federal statute or the Constitution of the United States, which authorizes the federal court to hear the case. The authorization must be specific. To illustrate, one only need recall the famous case of *Ex parte Crow Dog,*[13] where the United States Supreme Court held that the Federal District Court for Dakota Territory lacked the power to try an Indian for the murder of another Indian on the reservation because Congress had never given that court that power.

In the *Williams* case there was personal jurisdiction because both parties were before the court. The holding was that the Arizona court lacked subject matter jurisdiction, however. In other words, that court could not hear this kind of case. If the same facts had happened in London, England, the same people, the same debt, and identical service of the summons, then unquestionably Arizona would have had subject matter jurisdiction. There would still be the issue of whose law, Britain's or Arizona's, should be applied in determining the validity of the obligation, but there would be no question of the court's power to apply either law. If the facts of this case had occurred anywhere other than on an Indian reservation, there would have been subject matter jurisdiction over the debt.

The *Williams* case did not consider which law, the state's or the Navajo tribe's, was applicable; it simply preserved subject matter jurisdiction for Indian tribes. That the exercise of Arizona law would infringe on tribal self-government was sufficient. That *Williams* seemed to change the reading of *Worcester* seemed of little consequence, or at least the change was not taken very seriously. It should have been. Where *Worcester* had represented the principle that the state had no power, it appeared from *Williams* that the state now had some power on the reservation. The border of the reservation was no longer a geographical boundary that marked the limits of the state's power, but was instead a semipermeable membrane that allowed power to flow one way. The connection between *McBratney* and *Williams* was not as clearly apparent as it should have been. *Williams* and *McBratney* require that the teachings of *Worcester* be reexamined.

The effect of *Williams* on Indian tribes was much more than a reassertion that tribal self-government was as American as apple pie. It was also an incentive to tribes to exercise long-dormant powers of self-government; *Williams* brought confidence.

Tribes had the green light to develop the social infrastructure of a modern society. It appeared that the basic police and taxing powers of government were available to the tribes, and non-Indians and nonmembers were as subject to this power as a tribal member. As long as the tribe could show some nexus to self-government, the limits of tribal self-government appeared to be nonexistent. To many experts on Indian law, the major remaining question was criminal jurisdiction by tribes over non-Indians. Why this issue seemed important is still unclear, but its resolution was thought to be vital for tribal development. Many tribal leaders believed that unless their communities had the power to punish, their laws would seem less real. Even though tribal power in criminal affairs was limited by Congress to punishment of a maximum of six months in jail or a $500 fine or both, these sanctions, with the addition of exile or banishment, gave the tribes the authority to regulate most

73

conduct that disrupted their communities. Tribal codes were enacted or amended to include jurisdiction over non-Indians at an almost feverish pace.

Unfortunately, priorities for tribes are not dictated by needs but are determined by available federal monies. If there was money available, some tribes thought there should be a code. Codes were believed to be necessary to give the tribal courts subject matter jurisdiction and avoid the constrictions of the Indian Civil Rights Act and the notice issue. Whether an actual code was necessary is questionable, but no one really cared. As long as tribes could ritually grant their courts proper subject matter jurisdiction, then it was assumed by most that the tribes had the inherent authority of residual sovereignty to exercise this power.

Indian reservations are deceptive when viewed on a map. On maps, great areas of land are delineated as reservations, which gives the impression that Indians own much more land than they do. All maps show are the boundaries of reservations, not the ownership of the land. The reservation is theoretically the limit of tribal power; it is a jurisdictional description rather than a property description.

The Suquamish reservation, Port Madison, is not unusual in that the majority of land is owned by non-Indians. This condition is fairly common in those parts of the nation where allotment acts were vigorously applied. The unusual aspect of Port Madison is that there were approximately three thousand inhabitants of whom only fifty were tribal members. It is this group of fifty Indians that was to test the limits of residual tribal sovereignty. Eventually, the statute was challenged, and the tribe's position was upheld by the Ninth Circuit Court of Appeals.[14] The opinion is pure *Worcester.* Since there was no federal law removing this power from the tribe, the power was still in the tribe. The court's analysis of the relevant statutes and treaties appeared to make the opinion logically precise and therefore difficult to overturn by the Supreme Court on any point of law.

The Ninth Circuit Court of Appeals opinion gave great

hope to tribes; it appeared that tribal self-government was going to be more geographically oriented than pessimists had predicted. But the optimists underestimated the ingenuity of Justice Rehnquist. Rehnquist used the very foundation of Indian law, *Worcester,* to reverse the Ninth Circuit.[15] He found that there were really two restrictions on tribal power rather than one. In addition to being restricted by affirmative acts of Congress, tribal power was also restricted by political status. When Marshall denominated the Cherokee Nation as a domestic dependent nation, he listed some of the elements of that status. The Cherokees held their land in aboriginal title; they lacked the capacity to engage in foreign affairs; they retained the power of internal government subject only to the United States; they could alienate their land only to the United States; and they enjoyed a special protectorate relationship with the United States. These elements distinguish a domestic dependent nation from an independent nation.

It was widely assumed that the idea of a domestic dependent nation was understood after *Worcester.* Political status was important in determining the relationship between the states and the tribes or between the Indians and the United States, but it was surely not an issue in defining contemporary tribal powers. In order to strike down the power of the tribe, Rehnquist returned to the original analytical process that Marshall had used. Rehnquist thought that the question of power was an issue of political status; tribes had lost powers not only as the result of positive law, as the Ninth Circuit had announced, but also because of political status. Indian tribes lacked criminal jurisdiction over non-Indians because it was inconsistent with their political status. The moment a tribe lost its independent status, it also lost the power discovered by the Supreme Court in 1979, criminal jurisdiction over non-Indians.

Oliphant is important, then, not only for its substantive holding, but for its reintroduction of political status as a means of limiting tribal power without affirmative acts of

Congress. Political status as a principle of law makes clear the holdings in *McBratney* and *Williams.* The state had jurisdiction over the non-Indian murder in *McBratney* because to give the tribe jurisdiction would be inconsistent with its political status. Since the reservation is within the state, the state's power, according to *Williams,* is valid on the reservation as long as it does not infringe on the tribe's right of self-government. And, of course, state jurisdiction could not be an infringement because the tribe had lost its jurisdiction over non-Indian criminal offenses at the moment of domestic dependent nationhood. According to Rehnquist, *McBratney* was no longer a whole-cloth opinion but rather an opinion Marshall himself would have rendered if given the opportunity.

Williams is more difficult to understand unless one remembers that not all aspects of domestic dependent nationhood are negative. *Williams* indicates that a positive attribute of political status is the right to be free from state judicial process while on the reservation. This right of nationhood is not the result of an affirmative congressional act, but flows from the political status of the tribe. Service of process is the act of informing someone that he is subject to a court's jurisdiction. It can be accomplished a number of ways. The constitutional issue is usually one of adequate notice. Service of process on Indian reservations by the state is permissible when the litigation is between two non-Indians or between an Indian plaintiff and a non-Indian defendant. Indeed, the service issue was the precursor of the *McBratney* case in allowing state incursions onto the reservation, except that the issue there was one of geography: Was the reservation within the boundaries of the state for service of process? But, when the issue is service on an Indian on the reservation, the authorities are split and those states that have held such process valid are now backtracking.

Service does not raise the jurisdictional issue in normal terms. Its function is notice. A person can be served by a court and there still must be an independent ground for subject matter jurisdiction. To allow Indians to be served on a reservation would not give the state any more substantive power than it already has. But it is part of the judicial process, albeit the least unintrusive part, and the right is freedom from the judicial process. This makes sense if one thinks about *Williams* and the path not taken.

As noted earlier, if the exact case had happened in London or in California, the Arizona court would have to decide what law to apply. The study of the conflict of laws is an overly complicated law professors' game, but it is not without theoretical basis. The Supreme Court could not have used a conflicts analysis for a number of reasons. Navajo, or more explicitly, tribal Indian law, is hard to discover. Because the party alleging that a foreign law applies must plead and prove that law, it would require that all Indian litigants be able to provide evidence sufficient in a court of law concerning the applicable tribal Indian law. This requirement is a great burden, particularly if the tribal law is not written.

A more difficult barrier than the choice-of-law question is the forum issue. The forum is the court that will hear the case. Each forum applies its own procedure or rules of conduct, and more important, each forum decides which law is applicable. In determining which is the applicable law between two states, there are two constitutional constraints—the due process clause of the Fourteenth Amendment and the full faith and credit clause of Article IV. Although the full faith and credit clause has lost some of its vitality in forcing jurisdictions to choose between particular state laws, this loss is hardly noticeable in an age of increasing state uniformity. Between an Indian tribe and the state, however, there is no similar relationship. Contrary to popular belief, no true full faith and credit exists between tribes and states except under the Indian Child Welfare Act,[16] which is a federal statute that forces both parties to obey or suffer a federal court order.

All of the full faith and credit clause cases involving Indian tribes deal with the obligation of the state. No decision has held that a tribe must grant full faith and credit to either the laws or the judgments of a state. Unless the system is mandatory for both parties, it is nothing more than comity. It is ironic that those who wish to expand tribal sovereignty support full faith and credit on the mistaken assumption that it is a manifestation of sovereignty. In reality, full faith and credit can result in a loss of power because it means that in some instances the tribe will have to do what it does not wish to do. Nevertheless, because there is no relationship between the state and the tribe, there is no way to ensure that Indian rights would be protected in a state forum. The only way to ensure that result would be through federal law.

Although many decry what they perceive as poor treatment of Indians by the courts, in truth the judiciary has been the sole friend of Indian tribes among the branches of the federal government. The courts have been trying to find a means of defining the place of tribes in the contemporary political framework, a difficult task. A multitude of factors must be considered and too often Indians and their advisers are ignorant of the real problems. Complex issues are often addressed, at least temporarily, by resorting to simplistic answers based on geography. But the geography is simply one of many factors that must be considered in the tribal decision-making process. Deciding who has what power on a reservation is an extremely complex legal task, and tribes are greatly disserved when the answers given are the result of misunderstood and misapplied principles.

To complicate the situation further, tribes are not only isolated geographically, they are isolated from the usual norms of behavior that would guide cities and states in making decisions about their relationships with Indian tribes or reservations. The lack of norms means that tribes must make many far-reaching decisions without much understanding of the political milieu surrounding them. The idea of political status as a complex balance, as expressed in *Williams* and its progeny, is lost. Too often, tribes are considered as being either sovereign nations or conquered peoples. This binary approach means that neither tribes nor the governments with whom they have relationships can ever really understand the true nature of the issues in question.

Tribal leaders often speak of tribes as independent sovereigns, unless it serves their purpose in dealing with the BIA to emphasize the latter's guardianship responsibilities. Until tribal leaders understand the complexity of the governmental relationships, difficult problems will continue to be solved by piecemeal litigation, probably the most expensive and least effective manner of handling these problems. The more tribes try to stretch the reach of their governments, the more likely they will lose. There should be a more careful analysis of the interests at stake before tribes try to expand their governmental powers to their theoretical limits.

The only real resource that a tribe has is its power as a government. Of course, there are some tribes with enormous natural resources, but few, if any, have the experience or sophistication to develop those resources and move the tribal population significantly up the economic scale. Manipulating the federal government is the path to development urged by too many people, including the Bureau of Indian Affairs. The Reagan administration's policy of attracting more private enterprise on the reservation attempts to speak to Indian problems. But how will an economic base be built on a reservation? As has occurred, it will probably be through tax holidays, attractive land leases, bingo, horse racing, cheapened natural resources, and cheaper labor, all manipulations of government which shift existing resources but which fail to create new wealth.

It is useful to note that the state of West Virginia, which is about the size of the Navajo Reservation, has all of the attributes that most tribes would like to have: universities, developed natural resources, unquestioned taxing powers, zoning power, regulatory power. West Virginia had an unemployment rate of 21 percent early in 1983, so it is apparent that mere power is not enough. The unbridled exercise of tribal powers will endanger the future of tribes. This danger stems from not really understanding the factors the Supreme Court considers when it makes decisions on tribal power. Geography is only a prerequisite for tribal power, and yet the border is often the only factor considered.

The lessons of *Worcester, McBratney,* and *Williams* are that the tribes' relationships with the United States and the individual states are complicated. Decisions concerning government conduct must be made with this known degree of complexity in mind. Tribes have only concentrated on one side of the governmental equation in the litigation of the past twenty-five years. Does the tribe or the state have the right to tax cigarettes sold on the reservation? Does the tribe have the right to impose a severance tax on its oil and gas? Does the state have the power to tax Indians on the reservation? The list is virtually endless. In few, if any, of these cases, has the question of the government's obligation been raised. Who pays for the destitute victim of lung cancer? Who provides the services to the taxed? Who cleans up the waste from the manufacturing plant? Who pays for the costs of a changing society? The questions are usually answered when the Court fills in the blank, but the obligation question never is. It is time for the tribes to consider more fully the complete equation of their proposed conduct.

The Navajos changed their governmental structure for a purpose—to win a landmark case. Many tribes are adopting codes merely to have a tribal code, and the resulting documents may have little relationship to the existing law. Copying a municipal ordinance, crossing out the name of the town, and substituting the tribe's name is not good law reform and tribes doing this are taking a risk. Before passage of the Indian Civil Rights Act of 1968, two cases were decided that held that the Yakima Tribal Council and the Fort Belknap Tribal Court were arms of the federal government and therefore were subject to the same constitutional restrictions as a federal agency.[17] These decisions were mooted with the passage of the act. Nevertheless, because the jurisdiction of the act was interpreted by the Supreme Court to extend only to habeas corpus petitions, a federal court could revive this line of reasoning in order to protect an individual from what it believes to be unconstitutional treatment. The more closely a tribal governmental procedure resembles an Anglo procedure, the easier it will be to make the analogy. If the aggrieved individual is a non-Indian, it would not take much reasoning to conclude that state and civil jurisdiction prevails.

This essay is not meant to be a comprehensive outline of Indian law and policy. The cases and their facts were simplified to make the theory behind the holdings clearer. It is necessary to illustrate how complex even the most fundamental principles of Indian law are, and unless Indians understand the "easy" principles, making decisions on the hard issues is almost impossible. Contemporary Indian leaders have an obligation to the present and to the future of their people, and this commitment can only be met by knowledge. Tribes are under pressure to develop, and this pressure comes from both the government and within, but leaders should tread carefully. In the final analysis, the headlong flight to be "like Albuquerque" has greater risks than ever imagined and every victory that a tribe wins brings other tribes closer to the abyss.

NOTES

1. Gibbon, *Decline and Fall of the Roman Empire,* Modern Library Series (New York, N.Y., 1932).

2. 231 U.S. 28 (1913).

3. Winters v. United States, 207 U.S. 564 (1908) (United States reserved water rights for the Indians by implication when the reservations were created).

4. State of New Mexico v. Armodt, State v. Armodt, Civ. No. 6639 (D.N.M. 1974).

5. 21 U.S. (8 Wheat.) 543 (1823).

6. 30 U.S. (5 Pet.) 1 (1831).

7. 31 U.S. (6 Pet.) 515 (1832).

8. 104 U.S. 621 (1882).
9. 326 U.S. 496 (1946).
10. 358 U.S. 217 (1959).
11. 326 U.S. 496 (1946).
12. 145 U.S. 317 (1892).
13. 109 U.S. 556 (1883).
14. Oliphant v. Schlie, 544 F.2d 1007 (9th Cir. 1976).
15. Oliphant v. Suquamish Indian Tribe, 435 U.S. 191 (1978).
16. Pub. L. 95-608 25 U.S.C. §§1901-1963 (1978).
17. Colliflower v. Garland, 342 F.2d 369 (9th Cir. 1965). Settler v. Yakima Tribal Court, 419 F.2d 486 (9th Cir. 1969), *cert. denied,* 398 U.S. 903 (1970).

4

The United States and American Indians: Political Relations

BY MICHAEL G. LACY

Native Americans have had two centuries of diverse political interaction with the United States government. One aspect of that history is the increasing political inclusion of tribes and individuals into the institutions of the American state. As a way of making sense of that process and its results, this paper presents a reconceptualization of the notion of cooptation,[1] which is then used to frame the analysis of four specific inclusion policies the United States has pursued in managing its relations with Indians. Based on the findings of that investigation, the article concludes by extending and clarifying the new model of cooptation.

The Concept of Cooptation

As defined here, cooptation occurs if, in a system of power, the power holder intentionally extends some form of political participation to actors who pose a threat.[2] Notice that this definition of cooptation differs markedly from popular usage, which typically identifies cooptation with one of its possible results, the neutralization of a threat to the power holder. My conceptualization excludes such results from the definition. Thus, conditions under which cooptation is successful in stabilizing the regime are not defined away, but are left open as a possible question for theorizing.[3] As an empirical matter, inclusion of threatening actors does not necessarily stabilize the system. Neither should it be taken for granted that despite the results, the power holder necessarily coopts with the intention of defusing resistance. As in some of the cases discussed below, the motivation for cooptation might be the genuine desire to expand self-determination. While cooptation requires intention on the part of the power holder to the extent that it is s/he who offers and arranges expanded political participation, malevolency of intent is not a definitional element.

Philip Selznick's classic work on formal organization contains the most familiar formulation of cooptation.[4] Selznick defines cooptation as the "process of absorbing new elements into the leadership of an organization as a means of averting threats [from the environment] to its stability or existence."[5] My objection to Selznick's model derives from the restrictive field (formal organization) within which he uses the term. The crucial distinction in cooptation ought to be between the power holder and resistant elements, not between organization and environment, as Selznick conceptualized it. Selznick's choice of boundaries also flirts with reification, as though the organization were an anonymous organism adapting to its environment, as though the whole organization (elevator-operators up to executives) adapted to threats. Scholars in the Selznick tradition have produced conceptual absurdities by using the organization-environment perspective. For example, Thompson and Allen view cooptation as a form of *cooperation* between parties of more or less equal power![6] In my view, cooptation ceases to be of interest when the question of power is eliminated.

However, not all power-oriented formulations of cooptation are satisfactory. For example, Gamson's definition emphasizes the confrontation of the power holder with resistant actors,[7] but he implicitly restricts its scope to cases in which the threat confronting the power holder is severe and openly acknowledged. Another power-oriented approach to cooptation, which might be called the "political socialization" model, is excessively inclusive in scope.[8] In this view, cooptation denotes whatever techniques the power holder uses to commit people to the regime. This covers a fantastic array of diverse processes. Another objection to the political socialization model is its tendency to obscure the importance of *threat*. Unlike most other conceptualizations of cooptation, the political socialization approach does not stress what is unusual about cooptation: that the power holder moves to include persons who are in some sense "hostile" rather than "friendly."

In the current model, *threat* becomes a defining element of cooptation.[9] An expansion of political participation cannot be termed cooptation unless the actors brought into participation represent a potential or actual source of resistance. The threat confronted by the coopting power holder might be an organized opposition, with a counter-ideology, leadership, and a consciousness of opposition to the power holder, or a threat might be a community of interest, an unorganized aggregate of actors sharing a latent interest. Another typical situation of threat is found when a power holder expands power, either extensively (territorially) or intensively (in scope).

While I emphasize threat as the unique aspect of cooptation, previous models have tended to stress the neutralization of resistance as the defining element. The threat model brackets this issue and focuses instead on the expansion of political participation and the existence of threat as defining factors. Political participation here denotes not only actual policy determination, but also, for example, maneuvers like the extension of citizenship, employment in a government bureaucracy, or membership on citizen advisory committees. In judging whether or not a political process might be analyzed as cooptation, the question of the meaningfulness of participation is therefore momentarily set aside. However, if cooptation is to have any critical content, this bracketing must cease at a later point in the analysis, a consideration the threat model embodies under the heading of *legitimacy* and *filtering* payoffs. These two concepts focus on the neutralization of resistance that *may* result from cooptation.

Legitimacy payoffs occur when political inclusion serves as evidence that the system is actually democratic, is committed to self-determination of the threatening actors, is genuinely oriented to the interests of the people, etc. *Filtering* payoffs are somewhat more complicated, as two different processes come under this concept. Generally, filtering refers to the defusing of a threat group that may happen when its resistance is directed into the official structure of participation. One aspect of filtering may be called *blunting,* which denotes to the effect of structures of political participation (e.g., government bureaucracies) that allow minimal influence over policy and slight impact on the power holder. Channeling, another aspect of filtering, occurs when members of a threat group, having accepted officially provided political participation, cease resistance via other means and confine their activities to those possible within the official structure.

This ends the introduction to the threat model of cooptation. I have not made a complete explication and justification of it here but have only presented sufficient material to permit the understanding of its application to the case of American Indians.

Cooptation in U.S. Government-American Indian Relations

The examples of cooptation to be considered took place between the United States government and American Indians. Specific expansions of participation (that is, cooptation) occurred during the 1960s and 1970s, but the background of these events as well as other instances of cooptation are found in the earlier political history of the Indian in the United States.

The Background of Indian Cooptation

In keeping with the concepts of the model, the first thing to understand is the nature of the Indian's place within the American power system. Originally, the structural position of the Indian in the U.S. was as a member of a tribe, an independent, relatively sovereign group that the colonizing

American system confronted as an obstacle. In its relations with Indians, the American government pursued until 1871 a basic policy of treaty making with individual tribes. Though this practice may rarely have been one of free contracts between equals, and was often prefaced by war, it nevertheless indicated something about the position of Native Americans until then. They appeared to the government not as recalcitrant citizens, but as members of alien nations within the expanding system. Even with the advent of the reservation system in the middle 1800s, Indians retained considerable sovereignty, as the government allowed the tribes on the reservations to manage their own internal affairs, thus maintaining up through the 1860s a policy of dealing "with Indian tribes largely as self-governing units."[10] However, starting at about 1870, U.S. government policy aimed directly toward assimilating Indians into the American system instead of treating them as members of separate nations within the nation. Congress took a major step in this trend in 1871 when it forbade further treaty making between the government and tribes.[11] Continuing in that vein, the Dawes Act of 1887 established the allotment system under which the government deeded land to individual Indians rather than to the traditional tribal structures.[12] The allotment plan, in its attempt to make Indians into freeholding farmers, particularly attempted to assimilate the Indian into white civilization. Generally, the trend of government Indian policy during the 1870s and the 1880s was to

> further minimize the functions of tribal leaders and tribal institutions and to continually strengthen the position of the government representative and his subordinates, and to improve the effectiveness of their programs to break down traditional patterns within the Indian communities.[13]

This historical material demonstrates the original form of the Indian threat: Indians were marginal subjects during an extensive (territorial) expansion of power. Indians are a polar case here, since they were not even citizens of the expanding American system but were instead members of alien systems (tribes) dwelling within the same geographic territory.

Having set the formal side of Indian political history, let us consider the content of the Indian threat, the more immediate background of the cases of cooptation. The most important substantive aspect of the Indian threat derives from the state's ideological commitment to "fair-play," democratic self-determination, and legal-rational norms of conduct in governing its subjects. When Indians are denied legally sanctioned rights, the state can be trapped by its ideology of democracy. When Indians raise objection to their treatment, American ideology can be called into question if the government does not give at least the appearance of adhering to its norms of procedure.

The government's ideological and to some extent actual commitment to legal-rational procedure has made possible the Indian as a *legal* threat. Indians have long used the courts of the United States to pursue, with some success, their various interests and legally guaranteed (e.g., treaty) rights. As early as the 1830s, Indians attempted to defend their sovereignty in a suit before the Supreme Court, arguing that state laws were not applicable to them.[14] In a slightly later case, a Christian missionary to the Cherokees raised the same issue by deliberately disobeying state law while on a reservation.[15] The Supreme Court of the United States ruled that Georgia laws were not applicable on the reservation. The Cherokees had a measure of sovereignty acknowledged in their treaties with the U.S., which recognized the tribe as a power with sufficient autonomy to make treaties with the United States. However, even a cursory acquaintance with American Indian history shows that the principles embodied in these decisions have not been honored or enforced. The significance of these cases is: (1) that they are early examples of the Indian's use of the courts as a technique of resistance and hence an early display of their ability to mount a legal threat; and (2) that these decisions established a legal recognition of Indian tribes as alien sovereign nations, albeit dependent ones, existing within the power system of the United States. As indicated above, the government often attempted to avoid recognizing Indians as members of tribal nations (at least after 1871) and tried to assimilate them. Nevertheless, the legal precedents articulated in these decisions, though rarely honored, remained as a potential basis on which Indians, given a legal-rational political system, could resist the state.

During the nineteenth and twentieth centuries, tribes frequently and successfully have sued for damages claiming breach of treaty rights. For example, since the 1800s, Indians in Oregon and Washington have periodically sued (proceeding as far as the Supreme Court) to protect fishing rights guaranteed by treaty.[16] After 1924, when the Congress passed a bill strengthening Indian title to their lands, a series of lawsuits resulted in the eviction of three thousand whites by one Indian tribe.[17] Litigation has intensified since then, with suits being far too numerous to cover completely. From 1945 to 1975, awards to Indians by the Indian Claims Commission alone amounted to a half-billion dollars.[18] As of Deloria's writing,[19] some one hundred suits brought by Indian tribes were pending against U.S. federal employees and agencies.

The point to be gleaned from this recitation of Indians' potential and actual chances to sue is *not* that their legal rights are adequately defended through these means. Rather, it is only that within a formally democratic political system, the existence of such legal precedents makes Indians a continual legal threat. Furthermore, they have frequently taken advantage of these chances through actual legal action. Whether they win cases or not, Indians can create trouble and expense for the government, as when, for example, the government must mediate between the legal claims of Indians and the demands of powerful whites. In a situation like the recent one in the state of Maine, the federal government occupies the unenviable position of balancing what are legally justified claims of Indians against the demands of white "owners" of the land, who in numbers and economic resources are more influential than the Indians.[20] If the government recognizes the legitimacy of Indian claims but declines to honor them, it must violate the American ideological tradition of the sanctity and stability of legal-rational procedure. The Indians can trap the state in its own ideology, thus precipitating a loss of legitimacy on the part of the state.

There are two other aspects of the Indian threat; one is the economic exploitation of Indians, the other is the rise of Indian protest organizations in the 1960s. Native Americans have a colonial status; even when they technically own their lands, they frequently lose the profits to outsiders. On the Pine Ridge Reservation, for example, Indian farmers and ranchers use less than 1 percent of the land, while non-Indians use more than 50 percent of it, thereby realizing large profits.[21] Of the $170 million earned through agriculture on Indian reservations in 1968, only about one-third went to the Indians themselves.[22] Even more gross exploitation occurs with mineral wealth. The profitability of Indian lands coupled with Indians' relative exclusion from these benefits further contributes to the Indian threat, if one assumes that this exploitation can be maintained only through the power of law backed by the use of force. Such exploitation also has made Indians an object of sympathy for non-Indian liberal and radical elements within the U.S. as well as radicalizing Indians themselves.

This scenario happened in the 1960s. Deloria mentions the desires of radical groups to include Indians as another exploited minority within their united front, a move that met with rather mixed reaction among Indians, who saw themselves as members of alien nations, not as oppressed citizens of the United States. Native Americans did, however, begin to adopt protest tactics in the 1960s, using public demonstrations as a means to dramatize their situation. Urban Indians living away from reservations formed protest organizations such as the American Indian Movement (AIM). Indians participated in the Poor People's March on Washington in 1968.[23] In general, the 1960s saw an increase in Indian protest movements that cooperated to some extent among themselves and with other dissidents.

The main source of the Indian threat has been litigation. Together with economic exploitation and protest organizations, this has been the content of the Indian threat. Such actions are the general background of threat to which the state has had to adapt, and as such, are the key factor underlying the cooptation of Indians.

Specific Examples of the Cooptation of Indians

The first case of Indian cooptation is quite simple. In 1924, President Coolidge signed a bill giving citizenship to all Indians, though nearly two-thirds already were such.[24] The citizenship decree was the political form of the assimilation program that had begun with the unsuccessful allotment policy of the Dawes Act. The Citizenship Act was a case of cooptation, as citizenship is the formal minimum of political participation in a bourgeois-democratic state. This Act illustrates the *blunting* aspect of the *filtering* payoff to cooptation. Since the Indian population at the time (1924) numbered only a few hundred thousand, they could hardly have affected national elections. The Citizenship Act stipulated that gaining the status of citizen was not to be construed as affecting Indians' rights to tribal lands or other property,[25] a caveat probably motivated by a desire that citizenship not eliminate any Indian rights. Neither, however, did this aspect of the citizenship decree eliminate the trust status of Indian lands, under which the Bureau of Indian Affairs retained final control of the lands as trustee for its Native American charges. The extension of citizenship did not give Indians any significant control over their lives or property. Indians' status as citizens has actually been used to support their dependent position. When confronted with the demands of an Indian protest movement to restore the right of treaty making, the state used the Citizenship Act as one of its lines of argument in claiming that Indians could not have this prerogative, as only foreign nations and foreign citizens could make treaties with the United States.[26] Citizenship was thus a blunted form of participation.

The citizenship cooptation has had limited success as a means of increasing Indian support for the state. Many Indians did not wish to be citizens, a situation that remains today. Citizenship was unilaterally "imposed" by the government.[27] The Iroquois, for example, never recognized their U.S. citizenship, going to the extent of feeling it necessary to declare war separately on the Axis during World War Two, as the decision of the U.S. had validity only for *United States* citizens. Any legitimacy payoff due to the Citizenship Act was realized with someone other than Native Americans. Schusky sees the origin of the drive for Indian citizenship as stemming from a stirring of "the national conscience," particularly among easterners who saw Indians as earning citizenship through the civilizing influence of farm ownership and labor during the allotment period.[28] It would have been among such people that any legitimacy payoff would be gained.

In 1933, John Collier, who had a personal history as a worker for genuine reform of Indian policy, became Commissioner of Indian Affairs for the government. Collier first began the explicit practice (known as "Indian preference") of bringing Indians into the government's Indian Service; by 1933, one-third of the classified employees in the service were Indians.[29] He was also the chief force behind the Indian Reorganization Act of 1934, another cooptation of Indians. This piece of legislation reversed the policy of breaking up tribal landholdings and governments by giving more self-government to Indians. The IRA reconstituted tribal governments as political communities that could govern their citizens and deal with the federal government. The IRA is a global form of cooptation; the newly organized tribes were expanded forms of political participation.

The IRA gives the appearance of being a genuine transfer of power to tribes; reorganizing them would seem to expand Indian self-determination. In fact, it provides another example of a filtering payoff to cooptation. As Schusky

92

emphasizes, most tribal politics have concerned property. Under the reservation policy the government deeded land to tribes in a trust status according to which the Bureau of Indian Affairs, as a guardian overseeing its ward's affairs, was ultimately responsible for the use made of the property. As a consequence, tribal constitutions (established under the IRA) frequently contain the phrase "subject to the approval of the Secretary of the Interior."[30] Tribal governments do not have final authority over expenditures of their money or over the use of their land. If the BIA disagrees with a tribal council's decision on property or expenditures, the Bureau can overturn it. As a result, "Indians are apathetic about their local government, and tribes' officers are without influence in their communities."[31] Thus, the IRA accomplished filtering by allowing Indians a blunted structure of participation: "self-determination" subject to veto of the power holder. If Schusky is right in his assessment of Indians' attitudes toward tribal government (and I have seen no evidence to the contrary), the legitimacy payoff of the IRA failed. Indians do not see the tribe as organized under the IRA as their own democratic, legitimate government, but as an alien force, "The Tribe," coercing them and interfering with their lives, much as some "urban working class people look at the police force and city government."[32]

The IRA illustrates another filtering payoff from cooptation, namely the *channeling* effect. When the state confronts a plurality of unorganized but resistant actors, such as Indians unattached to the tribe, there are many possible sources of conflict. In the limiting case, each actor could engage in resistance. While the prospect of facing unorganized resistance might appear more palatable to a power holder, there is also an advantage in confronting an organized source of resistance: predictability. In the case of the IRA, the preceding allotment policy encouraged the atomization of Indians, whereas reorganization created formal, public tribal organizations. The government could now have more rationalized dealings with Indians; reorganized tribes could also serve as organizations to channel resistance through one public organization rather than through several (potential) movements. As a specific example, the U.S. government could make land settlements legally through a single entity, the tribe, rather than through allotments to numerous Indians. The IRA channeled Indian-U.S. government relations through the medium of the tribe.

The next cases of Indian cooptation (after Indian preference and the IRA) began in the 1960s during the Johnson presidency. The government started a general policy that Tyler calls "self-determination through Indian leadership,"[33] but which I view as the cooptive expansion of participation to a threatening group. President Johnson initiated this era in 1968 with the creation of the National Council on Indian Opportunity (NCIO). The NCIO is an advisory council established by Johnson's executive order.[34] He stipulated that members of this council were to be the Cabinet Department secretaries of Interior; Agriculture; Commerce; Labor; Health, Education and Welfare; Housing and Urban Development; the Director of the Office of Economic Opportunity; the vice-president as chair; and six Indian leaders appointed by the president. The council's mandate was to "review Federal programs for Indians, make broad policy recommendations, and ensure that programs reflect the needs and desires of the Indian people."[35] The NCIO is a case of cooptation in the strict sense used here; an advisory council is a form of political participation.

During the Nixon administration, the Indian members of the NCIO made a statement which Josephy sees as a reaction to the failure of the Nixon regime to act on Indian policy.[36] In the statement, the Indian members demonstrated some awareness of the potential justificatory functions (i.e., legitimacy payoff to the state) of the NCIO. They alluded to the "symbolic importance" of their participation, and claimed that their meeting with the vice-president and Cabinet would help to "alleviate some of the cynicism and despair rife among" Indians.[37] Beyond this, they argued that action and commitments by federal members of the council were necessary if Indians were to have a favorable view of it. They gave a series of concrete suggestions, some of which called for the establishment of special positions for Indians in Cabinet departments, and others of which concerned education, economics, urban Indians, legal services, land rights, housing, and agriculture. In a *Special Message to Congress* several months later, Nixon made a series of legislative recommendations that attended to nearly all of the suggestions made by the NCIO.[38] Shortly afterwards, Nixon also appointed eight new Indian leaders to the NCIO to replace former members whose terms had expired and to add two additional members.[39]

Indian reaction to Nixon's legislative proposals was mixed, despite the fact that the proposals reflected closely the NCIO's suggestions. Tyler reports a typical Indian response to the prospective legislation: "We've heard this kind of thing before; now we'll sit back and wait to see the results."[40]

Their skepticism was well-founded, as Congress failed to act on all but a small part of the legislation. According to Tyler, some scholars attribute the legislation's failure to pass to the actual importance the Nixon administration placed on it, others point to the conflict among congressional committees, and some claim that the legislation had little strong support among Indians and that this discouraged action by Congress.[41] Whatever the reason, the legislation instigated originally by the NCIO did not pass. This indicates something about the blunted nature of the participation offered in the form of the NCIO. However, a mildly dissenting view is given by Josephy,[42] who says that some Indians, such as tribal officials, felt that the NCIO was sympathetic to their problems, and Josephy himself thinks that the NCIO was in a position to influence federal agencies and policy. The background of the Indian members of the NCIO under Nixon, given by Josephy, provides indirect evidence about its potential impact on the state.[43] Seven were tribal officials, one was also a state legislator, and one (LaDonna Harris) was the wife of a U.S. senator. These people may have been staunch Indian advocates, but their backgrounds do not type them as radicals. The very fact that participants were appointed by the president points to the blunting possible in the NCIO. In sum, though, the NCIO presents a somewhat mixed picture for the assessment of filtering payoffs. Its direct association with the vice-president and Nixon's adoption of its legislative proposals are evidence that it at least increased Native Americans' access to the state. On the other hand, the failure of the legislative program indicates blunting, in that concrete Indian interests could not be *directly* advanced through the NCIO. The excess of government representatives over Indians (eight to six) ensured that the state could always veto any problematic moves of the Indians, if need be. And finally, the NCIO as a whole had no real authority, other than the mandate to make suggestions and recommendations. To summarize, the NCIO was set up in such a way that filtering of any maneuvers by Indians was always possible, even if the state did not always take advantage of this.

As for a legitimacy payoff, the government's establishment of the NCIO was probably oriented to the problem of justifying Indian policy and engendering greater support for the government among Indians and their sympathizers. Lyndon Johnson's speech announcing the creation of the NCIO was titled "The Forgotten American" and began with a flowery tribute to the Indian followed by the recitation of a litany of Indian problems of the past and present.[44] Though the justificatory effect of the NCIO may have been of interest to the state, there is little evidence that it took place. The NCIO had virtually no impact on Indian public opinion. A reading of numerous Indian newspapers for the periods surrounding Johnson's creation and Nixon's expansion of the NCIO shows little mention of it.[45] Only a few had articles on it, and in none was it praised or criticized strongly. Since there was almost no reaction to the NCIO, it could hardly have accomplished much of a legitimacy payoff for the government among Indians.

A discussion of the 1933 Indian preference policy has been postponed until now, as there have been more recent developments in this form of cooptation. During the Nixon administration, this policy, established under Collier's leadership in the 1930s, was reaffirmed and expanded. Previously, this forerunner of affirmative action had been applied to favor Indians in filling employment opportunities in the Bureau of Indian Affairs, but a 1971 study by the BIA determined that it "had only been applied in the case of initial employment and reinstatement . . . [but] not in the case of training opportunities or promotion."[46] In September, 1971, Commissioner Bruce of the BIA recommended the extension of Indian preference to all BIA employment situations, and in June of 1972 the Interior secretary approved the change.

Indian preference amounts to a general policy of cooptation by encouraging participation of Indians in an administrative arm of the state. At this point let us look at the quality of Indian political participation in the BIA and examine it for filtering and legitimacy payoffs. Tyler claims that more than 50 percent of BIA employees were Indian at the time of his writing, but he admits that only a small percentage of them occupied higher-level positions.[47] Cahn and Hearne quote an Indian as seeing the BIA as "skimming off the top of the potential Indian leadership by incorporating 'good' Indians into the system."[48] That some Indians view BIA participation as cooptation in the pejorative sense can be seen in the following quote from Mildred Ballenger, an Indian tribal official: "The potential leaders of our tribe really have but about two choices: . . . [to leave the Indian community for employment elsewhere], or join the white-oriented group by getting a job with the Indian Bureau. . . ."[49] This suggests that Indian participants in the BIA, while nominally representative of a threatening group, are actually drawn from among those Indians most likely to be sympathetic to the government viewpoint. This shows a situation similar to the NCIO: the people selected are relatively assimilated, and therefore are unlikely to be radical Indian advocates. This serves to blunt Indian preference participation in the BIA.

Another more serious blunting of Indian participation in the BIA is due to the position of the BIA within the state's administrative structure. The Bureau is not situated so as to effectively help or represent Indians. Being in the Department of the Interior is one of the BIA's chief liabilities, from the perspective of Indians. The BIA has amicable connections with natural resource business interests. There are also agencies within Interior, such as the Bureau of Mines and the Bureau of Land Management, that frequently fight against Indian interests. The BIA typically loses in those conflicts.[50] Even Tyler, in his history published by the BIA, admits that there is an inherent "conflict of interest" within Interior because of its involvement in land and natural resource policy as well as its role in representing Indians.[51] Cahn and Hearne claim that even the Interior secretary himself could not give priority to Indian interests (if he wanted to), as other influentials with whom he must interact are not at all supportive of the Indian cause.[52] Alvin Josephy criticizes the BIA even more severely. Citing a study by Leon Osview, Josephy indicts the BIA for having an internal organizational structure that impedes change. Specifically, any innovation suggested by a local BIA operative must be approved by a host of higher-level personnel within the BIA. The emphasis is on "echelons of administrators and absentee specialists higher up."[53] The administrative practices of the BIA thus deemphasize and subordinate action by local BIA personnel.

The Indian preference policy illustrates well a successful filtering outcome, as Indians exert little power through the BIA. The inefficiencies of the BIA, its location within Interior, the marginality of Indian problems within a Cabinet department focused primarily on other issues, the centralization of power in the BIA, and the typically low status occupied by Indians in the BIA all contribute to the blunting of Indian impact on the state. To exaggerate, one might describe a typical BIA-employed Indian as a powerless individual within a relatively powerless bureau that is only part of a larger department subject to control by the president and Congress. The BIA's attraction of potential Native American leaders into its employ channels as well as filters the Indian threat. Within the BIA, educated, competent Indians work for an organization in which they can do little; alternatively, they might have chosen to expend their efforts helping Indians as leaders of various kinds of resistance.

In terms of the legitimacy payoff, the preference policy did little to increase the acceptance among Indians of the state and its policies. The Bureau's unpopularity among Indians comes not from its lack of Indian personnel, but from its inefficacy in helping Indians and from the excessive control it exerts over them. Thus, a legitimacy payoff could not be realized among Indians through the establishment of preference policies. Despite a lack of direct evidence, I would offer the conjecture that Indian preference could, however, serve to justify Indian policy to non-Indians. If Indians are portrayed as the controllers of the BIA, its failures can be attributed to them rather than to the president, Congress, or other representatives of the state, thus displacing responsibility for Indian problems onto the victims.

Conclusion

In its relations with American Indians the United States government has used techniques that may be analyzed as cooptation. Indians have continually been a threat to which the American state has had to adapt. The Indian nations within the United States, in their status as aboriginal and sovereign states within the system, were a formal threat to American political unity. As time has passed, the most potent aspect of the Indian threat has been legal, as Indians have used legal procedures and precedents to win lawsuits against the government. Cultural and political assimilation has been a goal toward which the government has striven in its attempts to neutralize the threat; actions that may be termed cooptation have also been used with success. The Citizenship Act, the Indian Reorganization Act, the National Council on Indian Opportunity, and the Indian preference policy of the BIA are all cases of cooptation with successful filtering payoffs (largely through blunted participation), but legitimacy payoffs have not been so evident.

The way in which filtering took place in these cases suggests a clarification of that concept. In judging whether a cooptive form of participation results in a filtering payoff, the analysis cannot be confined to the attempt to demonstrate that impact was less after cooptation occurred. An actual lessening of resistance could only happen in the most extreme cases of cooptation, as when, hypothetically, an Indian protest leader takes a position in the BIA at the invitation of the government. It is more accurate to say that filtering payoffs occur not just when resistance is actually lessened, but also when dissidents are not able to use their participation to exert influence on the power holder, despite the appearance of giving in on the part of the state. In the filtering payoff the power holder is more likely to *preserve* control rather than *extend* it. In this more limited sense, filtering was definitely successful in all the cases of cooptation of Indians.

Judging the success of legitimacy payoffs is more difficult. Here, there was misplaced emphasis in the original model, as it concentrated on the justificatory potential of cooptation among the cooptees and their constituents but neglected to mention legitimacy payoffs among other actors. This introduces the idea of the relevance of third parties in many instances of cooptation. Certainly gains in legitimacy may be made among threat groups to whom political participation has been extended, but in none of the cases of Indian cooptation was there unequivocal evidence for increases in Indian support for the state based on the various extensions of participation. If anything, the evidence suggests no effect, and in the operations of the BIA, the IRA, and the Citizenship Act, cooptation probably decreased the legitimacy of the United States government among Indians. For the legitimacy payoff in Indian cooptation, one might look to a non-Indian audience to see if the government's cooptive Indian policies were received favorably among it.

In terms of the original threat model of cooptation, it therefore would be wise to add another theoretic actor, an *audience,* to the dyad of coopting power holder and co-opted threat group.[54] The audience's role is to be a possible locus for legitimacy payoffs. The power holder's cooptive maneuvers may be oriented to legitimacy with an audience, who may present a more severe threat than the group nominally represented by the coopted participant. This could explain, for example, the power holder's rationale when cooptation achieves neither filtering nor legitimacy payoffs with the threat group. In the Indian case under consideration, further work might focus on the state's orientation toward a non-Indian audience.

NOTES

*An early version of this article was presented at the Midwest Sociological Society Meetings, Minneapolis, Minnesota, April 1976. I would like to thank Sakari Sariola for stimulating my interest in the concept of cooptation, and for careful criticism of my work on the topic. Robert J. Antonio also made numerous substantive suggestions that greatly improved my thinking on cooptation.

1. A complete discussion of the concept of cooptation and previous work on it appears in Michael G. Lacy, "Cooptation: Analysis of a Neglected Social Process," M.A. Thesis, University of Kansas, 1977.

2. "Power holder" here means either specific powerful persons or a collective actor, such as the state.

3. A pithy critique of previous work on cooptation, James L. Price's "Continuity in Social Research: TVA and the Grass Roots," *The Sociological Review,* vol. 1, no. 2 (Fall 1958), pp. 65-68, also points to the error of including this question in the definition of cooptation.

4. Philip Selznick, *TVA and the Grass Roots: A Study in the Sociology of Formal Organization* (Berkeley: University of California Press, 1949).

5. Ibid., p. 13.

6. See James D. Thompson, *Organizations in Action: Social Science Bases of Administrative Theory* (New York: McGraw-Hill, 1967), p. 75, and Michael Patrick Allen, "The Structure of Interorganizational Elite Cooptation: Interlocking Corporate Directorates," *American Sociological Review,* vol. 39, no. 3 (June 1974), pp. 393-406.

7. William A. Gamson, *Power and Discontent* (Homewood, Ill.: Dor-

sey Press, 1968), p. 135. In a later work, *Strategy of Social Protest* (Homewood, Illinois: Dorsey Press, 1975), p. 29, Gamson operationalizes cooptation in a way that makes its definition dependent upon its results, thereby making the same mistake as in the popular usage alluded to earlier.

8. Representative of this view are William Domhoff, *Who Rules America* (Englewood Cliffs, N.J.: Prentice-Hall, 1967), and Scott Greer and Peter Orleans, "Political Sociology," in *Handbook of Modern Sociology,* edited by Robert E.L. Faris, pp. 808-51 (Chicago: Rand-McNally, 1964).

9. There is precedent in emphasizing threat in defining cooptation, as it is at least implicit in all previous use of the concept. For example, in the traditional elite-recruitment model of cooptation, a conceptualization otherwise quite different than my "threat" model, the cooptive recruitment of personnel would be unnecessary unless the power holders were threatened by uncontrolled changes in their membership. Representatives of the elite-recruitment concept of cooptation include Karl Loewenstein, *Kooptation und Zuwahl: Über die Autonome Bildung Priviligierter Gruppen* (Frankfurt am Main, West Germany: Alfred Metzner Verlag, 1973), and Frederick J. Fleron, "Cooptation as a Mechanism of Adaptation to Change," *Polity,* vol. 2, no. 2 (Winter 1969), pp. 176-201.

In Gamson's *Power and Discontent,* and in Selznick's *TVA and the Grass Roots* specific types of threat are seen to lead to cooptation, but the range of threats considered is too narrow. Even in Thompson's *Organizations in Action,* p. 35, which apparently removes threat by sidestepping the issue of power, threat is implicitly admitted under the rubric of "uncertainty." Finally, the political socialization model also implies the existence of threat, because it considers the needs of a dominant group in managing the potential resistance of subordinate subgroups and individuals.

10. S. Lyman Tyler, *A History of Indian Policy* (Washington, D.C.: Bureau of Indian Affairs, 1973).

11. Ibid., p. 91.

12. Ibid.

13. Ibid.

14. This is the case of *Cherokee Nation* v. *State of Georgia* (1831) which appears in Wilcomb E. Washburn, ed., *The American Indian and the United States: A Documentary History,* vol. 4 (New York: Random House, 1973), pp. 2588-2602.

15. *Worcester* v. *State of Georgia, Ibid.,* pp. 2603-2648.

16. See Vine Deloria, Jr., *Behind the Trail of Broken Treaties: An Indian Declaration of Independence* (New York: Delacorte Press, 1974), pp. 14-15.

17. Ibid., p. 17.

18. Indian Claims Commission, *Annual Report* (Washington, D.C.: Indian Claims Commission, 1975). Mimeo.

19. Deloria, *Behind the Trail,* p. 253.

20. Edgar Cahn and David W. Hearne, *Our Brother's Keeper: The Indian in White America* (New York: New American Library, 1970), p. 82.

22. Ernest L. Schusky, *The Right to be Indian* (San Francisco: American Indian Educational Publishers, 1970), p vi.

23. For details on these and other Native American protest activities of the 1960s, see Deloria, *Behind the Trail,* p. 23.

24. Tyler, *History of Indian Policy,* p. 110.

25. Schusky, *The Right to Be Indian,* p. 21.

26. Deloria, *Behind the Trail,* pp. xi-xii.

27. Schusky, *The Right to Be Indian,* p. 21.

28. Ibid., p. 23.

29. Tyler, *History of Indian Policy,* p. 128.

30. Schusky, *The Right to Be Indian,* pp. 13, 48.

31. Ibid, p. 14.

32. Ibid., p. 44.

33. Tyler, *History of Indian Policy,* p. 217. Although Tyler's work is quite useful and generally unbiased and accurate, this is an appropriate point to note that his monograph was sponsored by the Bureau of Indian Affairs.

34. Lyndon Johnson, "The Forgotten American: The President's Message to the Congress on Goals and Programs for the American Indian," *Weekly Compilation of Presidential Documents,* vol. 4, no. 10 (March 6, 1968), pp. 438-48.

35. Ibid., p. 440.

36. Alvin Josephy, Jr., *Red Power: The American Indians' Fight for Freedom* (New York: American Heritage, 1971), p. 204.

37. National Council on Indian Opportunity, "Statement of the Indian Members of the National Council on Indian Opportunity," in Josephy (ed.), *Red Power,* p. 205.

38. See Tyler, *History of Indian Policy,* pp. 221-22.

39. Richard M. Nixon, "NCIO Presidential Announcement," *Weekly Compilation of Presidential Documents,* vol. 6, no. 36 (September 7, 1970), p. 1132.

40. Tyler, *History of Indian Policy,* p. 222.

41. Ibid., p. 255.

42. Josephy, *Red Power,* p. 204.

43. Ibid.

44. Johnson, "The Forgotten American," p. 438.

45. My evidence here comes from searching a microfilm collection of numerous American Indian newspapers, *Contemporary Newspapers of the North American Indian,* compiled by Bell and Howell microfilms in cooperation with the American Indian Press Association and the Huntington Free Library of the Museum of the American Indian (Washington, D.C., and Bronx, New York, no date of compilation).

46. Tyler, *History of Indian Policy,* p. 225.

47. Ibid.
48. Cahn and Hearne, *Our Brother's Keeper,* p. 129.
49. Ballenger's statement is quoted in Cahn and Hearne, p. 128.
50. See ibid., p. 158, on these points.
51. Tyler, *History of Indian Policy,* p. 254.
52. Cahn and Hearne, *Our Brother's Keeper,* pp. 160-161.
53. Josephy, *Red Power,* pp. 128-129.
54. See Lacy, "Cooptation" (cited above at note 1), for an elaboration of the role of the audience in cooptation.

5

Indian Voting

BY DANIEL McCOOL

One of the most important developments in American political history has been the gradual and often painfully slow extension of the right to vote. Although originally only propertied white adult males could vote, subsequent constitutional and statutory amendments expanded the electorate, but like most previously unfranchised groups, the Indians' right to vote was won only after a long struggle.

The first part of this paper examines that struggle and presents evidence of how American Indians have utilized their right to participate in the electoral process. The second part discusses arguments that were used to justify denying voting rights to Indians. A third part reviews the existing literature on Indian voter turnout and partisanship and presents data on Indian voting in Arizona from 1948 to 1980. Finally, the impact and importance of Indian voting is discussed and suggestions for further research are offered.

Justifications for the Denial of Indian Voting Rights

Although the United States Constitution now prohibits voting discrimination, it leaves to the states the authority to select the "times, places, and manner" of holding elections. Thus each state has established requirements for voter registration. Some state voting requirements have presented problems for Indian tribes, which are immune from most areas of state law. Does this limited immunity mean Indians need not meet state voting requirements? Or does it mean that the tribes must obey election laws passed by state governments—governments that the United States Supreme Court once described as the Indians' "deadliest enemies"?[1] For a hundred and fifty years the courts, the state legislatures, and the Congress have grappled with these questions. The struggle for voting rights mirrors the larger clash of Indian and Anglo cultures; Monroe Price writes that "the history of the extension of the franchise to Indians contains within it the whole panoply of shifting attitudes towards Indians in American society."[2] Throughout that history the pragmatic Anglo has devised a number of strategies that have been used to prevent Indians from voting. They can be classified into three broad categories: constitutional ambiguity, political and economic factors, and cultural and racial discrimination.

Constitutional Ambiguity

The United States Constitution as well as state constitutions contain references to Indians that are vague and ill-defined. This ambiguity has offered a fertile medium to those who would limit Indian access to the polls. The first constitutional question to arise concerned the citizenship of Indians. The Fourteenth Amendment extended citizenship to "all persons born or naturalized in the United States, and subject to the jurisdiction thereof," but a federal district court ruled in 1871 that this amendment did not apply to Indians, who were not "born subject to its [the United States government] jurisdiction—that is, in its power and obedience. . . ."[3]

Since citizenship is one of the criteria for voting, this ruling effectively precluded all Indians unable to prove that they were born under United States jurisdiction from registering to vote. When John Elk, an Indian who had taken up residence among non-Indians, attempted to vote in Nebraska in 1880 the Supreme Court ruled that he was not a citizen because he was born a member of a tribe that was not completely subject to the jurisdiction of the United States. The Court reasoned that the Fifteenth Amendment, which extends the right to vote to all citizens regardless of race, did not apply in his case because Elk was not a citizen within the meaning of the Fourteenth Amendment. That Elk had "completely surrendered himself to the jurisdiction of the United States" and abandoned all tribal ties was irrelevant because the United States had not "accepted his surrender" by issuing a formal naturalization.[4]

Although John Elk was never naturalized, many other Indians were. Through a succession of laws that extended citizenship to individuals or tribes, nearly two-thirds of all Indians were granted citizenship by 1924. United States citizenship was then unilaterally extended to all Indians by the 1924 Citizenship Act.[5]

Even though the question of United States citizenship was settled in 1924, some states still refused to recognize Indians as citizens of the state in which they resided. These states argued that because Indians were subject to federal but not state jurisdiction, then Indian reservations could not be part of the state in which they were located. They relied upon cases such as *United States* v. *Kagama*: "The Indians owe no allegiance to a state within which their reservation may be established, and the state gives them no protection."[6] In 1917 the Minnesota Supreme Court denied Indians the right to vote, reasoning they were not citizens of the state because they were "under a sort of guardianship of the federal government with which the state cannot interfere."[7] The passage of the 1924 Citizenship Act did not quell such claims, but they were not upheld in court. In 1927 a federal district court held that "an Indian, becoming a citizen of the United States and residing in a state, is held to be a citizen of that State."[8] The Arizona Supreme Court reached a similar conclusion the following year: "We have no hesitancy in holding, therefore, that all Indian reservations in Arizona are within the political and governmental, as well as geographical, boundaries of the state. . . . Plaintiffs, therefore, under stipulation of the facts, are residents of the State of Arizona."[9] Twenty years later a federal district court had to once again reiterate the same principle and declare that the Indian pueblos in New Mexico were a part of that state and therefore Indians were state residents.[10]

Despite these holdings, Indians still experienced difficulties in establishing state residency. In Utah in 1956 the state attorney general issued an opinion concerning an 1897 state law that withheld residency from anyone who lived on an "Indian or military reservation" unless that person had previously established residency in an off-reservation Utah county. The attorney general concluded that this proviso prevented reservation Indians from voting.[11] This opinion overruled a previous opinion[12] and gave Utah the distinction of being the last state in the Union to permit Indians to vote. The attorney general's interpretation of the law was upheld by the Utah Supreme Court, which reasoned that Indians should be barred from voting because they were "not as conversant with nor as interested in government as other citizens" and were still subject to special federal protection from state authority.[13] The Utah legislature immediately amended the law, rendering the Utah Supreme Court's decision moot.

Nevertheless, opponents of Indian voting rights continued to try to disfranchise Indians on the basis of state residency. In New Mexico in 1962 an unsuccessful non-Indian candidate for office challenged the validity of Indian voting rights, claiming Indians were not state residents (a heavy Navajo vote helped elect his opponent). The state supreme court again reiterated the right of Indians—as state residents—to vote.[14]

A second area of constitutional ambiguity that has been interpreted to the detriment of Indian voting is the guardianship clause that appears in most state constitutions. In 1920, Indians in North Dakota were refused the right to vote in a county election. The state argued that the North Dakota constitution, which states that "no person under guardianship" shall be qualified to vote, applied to Indians because they were under the guardianship of the federal government. The state cited the well-known case of *Cherokee Nation* v. *Georgia* where the Supreme Court stated that the Indian's relationship to the federal government "resembles that of a ward to his guardian."[15] The Supreme Court of North Dakota dismissed the state's contention and permitted Indians to vote in the election.[16]

In Arizona, which also has a guardianship clause in the state constitution, the case law developed in a somewhat different fashion. In 1928 two Pima Indians attempted to register to vote in the first presidential election held after the 1924 Citizenship Act had granted them citizenship. Their request for registration was denied, with the registrar claiming the Indians were under the guardianship of the federal government and therefore not residents of the state of Arizona. According to the Arizona state constitution, "No person under guardianship, non compos mentis, or insane shall be qualified to vote in any election . . . ."[17]

The Indians lost in the lower courts and appealed to the Arizona Supreme Court in the case of *Porter* v. *Hall.*[18] It appeared that the Pimans had a strong case since the Arizona Enabling Act stipulated that the state constitution would "make no distinction in civil or political rights on account of race or color. . . . That said state shall never enact any law restricting or abridging the right of suffrage on account of race, color, or previous condition of servitude . . . ."[19] Despite this language the court still applied the guardianship proviso to Indians:

It is the undisputed law, laid down by the Supreme Court of the United States innumerable times, from the famous case of *Cherokee Nation* v. *Georgia*, 5 Pet. 1, 8 L. Ed. 25, to the present time, that all Indians are wards of the federal government and as such are entitled to the care and protection due from a guardian to his ward.[20]

The court then concluded that Indians in the state of Arizona were "within the meaning of our constitutional provision, 'persons under guardianship,' and not entitled to vote."[21]

In a strongly worded dissent, Justice Ross pointed out that Chief Justice John Marshall, in his opinion in *Cherokee Nation* v. *Georgia*, stated that the Indian's "relation to the United States *resembles* that of a ward to his guardian...."[22] Justice Ross argued that the "guardianship" clause in the Arizona constitution referred to an actual legal guardianship imposed upon an individual by the courts and not just a resemblance to such a relationship. He concluded that "as the laws are now written it seems to me [Indians] are entitled to register and vote."[23]

The *Porter* ruling was not appealed to the United States Supreme Court, probably because of the prohibitive costs involved. Soon after the outcome of the case was announced, the Arizona attorney general's office ruled that the *Porter* decision would be applied, not only to reservation Indians but also to any individual Indian who moved off the reservation and severed his official tribal relationship.[24] For twenty years the case was allowed to stand unchallenged.

During that twenty years American Indians were called upon to fight in World War II. Approximately twenty-five thousand Indians served in the armed forces during that war,[25] and when they returned home they began to insist on the right to vote. In 1947 the President's Committee on Civil Rights declared the *Porter* case to be discriminatory and explained that: "Protest against these legal bans on Indian suffrage in the Southwest have gained force with the return of Indian veterans to those states."[26]

The year following the release of the Committee on Civil Rights' report, two Mohave-Apache Indians attempted to register to vote in Arizona but were refused. They filed suit and again the Arizona Supreme Court had an opportunity to interpret the meaning of the "persons under guardianship" clause in the case of *Harrison* v. *Laveen*.[27] This time the court took a different view. Citing Ross's dissent in the *Porter* case, Justice Udall's majority opinion stated that the guardianship clause in the Arizona constitution was "intended to mean a judicially established guardianship . . . [and] has no application to the plaintiff or to the Federal status of Indians in Arizona as a class."[28] The court also noted that an extensive search of the proceedings of the Arizona Constitutional Convention failed to discover any evidence that the clause was intended to apply to Indians.[29] Justice Udall eloquently concluded that "to deny the right to vote, where one is legally entitled to do so, is to do violence to the principles of freedom and equality."[30] Finally, Indians in Arizona had the right to vote.

The same year that Indians in Arizona won the right to vote—1948—Indians in New Mexico also sued for a more favorable interpretation of imprecise constitutional language.[31] This case concerned the phrase "Indians not taxed," which appears in the United States Constitution (Article I, Section 2, and the Fourteenth Amendment) and in many state constitutions. By 1940 five states still prohibited "Indians not taxed" from voting.[32] The solicitor of the Department of Interior issued an opinion in 1938 concluding that a constitutional provision "which would exclude Indians not taxed from voting in effect excludes citizens of one race from voting on grounds which are not applied to citizens of other races. . . . I believe such laws are unconstitutional under the Fifteenth Amendment."[33] Eventually four of the states permitted Indians to vote, regardless of taxation, but New Mexico persisted in its efforts to disfranchise Indians on the basis of taxation. In 1948, Miguel Trujillo, an Indian from Isleta Pueblo, New Mexico, was denied the right to vote because he did not pay ad valorem state taxes on his property. Trujillo sued in federal court and a three-judge panel found in his favor. Judge Phillips's oral opinion is worth quoting:

The New Mexico Constitution . . . says that "Indians not taxed" may not vote, although they possess every other qualification. We are unable to escape the conclusion that, under the Fourteenth and Fifteenth Amendments, that constitutes a discrimination on the ground of race. Any other citizen, re-

111

gardless of race, in the State of New Mexico who has not paid one cent of tax of any kind or character, if he possesses the other qualifications, may vote. An Indian, and only an Indian, in order to meet the qualifications of a voter, must have paid a tax. How you can escape the conclusion that that makes a requirement with respect to an Indian as a qualification to exercise the elective franchise and does not make that requirement with respect to the member of any other race is beyond me. I just feel like the conclusion is inescapable."[34]

Political and Economic Justifications

Indians have also been denied the right to vote because of political and economic factors perceived to be related to the right to vote. Throughout the early development of Indian voting rights the government withheld voting privileges from Indians until they proved they were loyal to the Anglo government rather than to any tribal affiliation. The issue in *Elk* v. *Wilkins* in 1884 was whether the Indians maintained "direct and immediate allegiance" to the tribe or to the United States.[35] In *Swift* v. *Leach* in 1920 the counsel for the Indians argued that they deserved the right to vote because they did not "owe obedience to chiefs."[36]

Later, the issue of loyalty became a question of patriotism. During World War I the Congress extended citizenship to any Indian willing to fight in the war.[37] Indian participation in World War II enhanced the push for Indian suffrage in the late forties. Judge Phillips, in *Trujillo* v. *Garley*, noted that Indians had "responded to the need of the country in time of war in a wholehearted way . . . ."[38]

Another political factor that has affected Indian voting is their potential impact on policy. Opponents of Indian voting long argued that Indians should not be allowed to vote—at least at the state or local level—because they did not have to obey all state and local laws. In 1917 the Minnesota Supreme Court, in *Opsahl* v. *Johnson*, held that: "It cannot for a moment be considered . . . that those who do not come within the operation of the laws of the state, nevertheless shall have the power to make and impose laws on

112

others."[39] The Arizona Supreme Court reached a similar conclusion in *Porter* v. *Hall* in 1928: "It is almost unheard of in a democracy that those who make the laws need not obey them."[40] When *Porter* was overturned twenty years later, however, the court in *Harrison* v. *Laveen* argued that the "matter of determining what is 'good public policy' is for the executive and legislative departments and that courts must base their decisions on the law . . . ."[41]

The policy impact of Indian voting was also an issue in the 1956 case of *Allen* v. *Merrell.* The Utah Supreme Court justified the denial of Indian voting rights on the basis of their potential impact on policy:

> It is thus plain to be seen that in a country where the Indian population would amount to a substantial proportion of the citizenry or may even outnumber the other inhabitants, allowing them to vote might place substantial control of the county government and the expenditures of its funds in a group of citizens who, as a class, had an extremely limited interest in its function and very little responsibility in providing the financial support thereof.[42]

This issue evolved into an economic question concerning the possibility of Indians participating in revenue decisions that impose financial burdens on Anglos but not on Indians. This approach is often characterized by the cry of "representation without taxation" (Indians have at times feared that the right to vote would result in automatic state taxation of tribal property[43]). The courts have failed to uphold this argument; in 1975 the New Mexico Supreme Court ruled that Indians may vote on a school bond issue even though they are not taxed in order to repay the bond,[44] and the Arizona Supreme Court in 1973 held that an Indian may be elected to a county position even though he is immune from county and state taxation.[45] The present situation in regard to the political and economic implications of Indian voting was summed up in 1975 by Arizona's Attorney General (now governor) Bruce Babbitt:

113

What I think is safely established now is the principle that Indians can retain their sovereignty and their separateness politically from state governments, and at the same time, participate with full rights. In the state government it is essential to understand that because there are a lot of Anglos who do not accept that. In your slogans like "representation without taxation," "lack of equal protection," "special privileges for Indians," there is going to be more of them; the notion that somehow there is something fundamentally inconsistent about living on [an Indian] reservation . . . and at the same time saying the vote of every Indian on this reservation or any other one counts for just as much as anybody else's. . . . There is nothing fundamentally inconsistent about it. . . ."[46]

Cultural and Racial Discrimation

Federal Indian policy has long been characterized by two conflicting responses to the "Indian problem." One response demanded that Indians abandon their traditional culture, while the other refused to admit them to full participation in Anglo society. Both of these attitudes were evident in the struggle over Indian voting rights.

Abandonment of traditional Indian culture was for many years a prerequisite of Indian citizenship. Before it was amended the Minnesota constitution granted citizenship only to Indians who had "adopted the language, customs and habits of civilization."[47] The North Dakota constitution extended the right to vote only to "civilized persons of Indian descent who shall have severed their tribal relations . . . ."[48] The constitutions of South Dakota and Idaho contained similar language. This kind of cultural discrimination was not limited to state constitutions, however. The Supreme Court's decision in *Elk* v. *Wilkins* cites twelve treaties, four judicial decisions, four statutes, and eight attorney-general opinions that require "proof of fitness for civilization" before Indians can obtain citizenship and vote.[49]

Since the abandonment of Indian culture was required before Indians could become citizens, attorneys arguing for

Indian suffrage often attempted to convince the court that the Indians were assimilated. In *Swift* v. *Leach* attorneys for the Indians argued that the Indians "marry the same as white people; they have fixed abodes; they live as white people . . . they have severed their tribal relations and adopted the mode of civilization."[50]

The push for assimilation became even more evident during the termination period, and this is reflected in the controversy over Indian voting. The amicus curiae brief of the United States in the 1948 case of *Harrison* v. *Laveen* stated that the "Government's policy aims at the full integration of Indians into the political, social, and economic culture of the Nation,"[51] and therefore the right to vote was simply one part of that process of integration, leading ultimately to the "gradual removal of Federal supervision and control."[52] A similar attitude was expressed by the Utah Supreme Court in *Allen* v. *Merrell* in 1956. The court's opinion claimed that until federal supervision was terminated, Indians would be "neither acquainted with the processes of government, nor conversant with activities of the outside world generally."[53]

With the passage of time the requirement for total assimilation was gradually abandoned as a prerequisite for voting, but discrimination against Indian voters continues to this day. It is nothing new. As early as 1850 the First California Legislature limited suffrage to whites only.[54] Apparently there was a fear that "large land-owners might, on election day, lead troops of docile Indians to the polls."[55]

Since the passage of the Fourteenth and Fifteenth amendments it has been unconstitutional to deny the right to vote to any citizen on the basis of race. Most of the enabling acts for western states contain language similar to the Arizona act cited above which prohibits racial discrimination. Nevertheless, some subtle techniques have been used to actively discourage Indian participation. Many of these methods have also been used to great effect against other minorities such as blacks and Hispanics.

One of the most pervasive techniques for diluting the

minority vote is gerrymandering. In South Dakota three "unorganized" counties containing large numbers of Indians were administered in such a way that adjacent counties dominated by non-Indians controlled the Indian counties. This was ruled illegal in 1975.[56]

A somewhat different tactic was used in Arizona, where seats in the state house of representatives were apportioned according to voter turnout in gubernatorial elections. Since Indian reservations have traditionally experienced low levels of voter registration and turnout, this left them with inadequate representation in the statehouse.[57]

Prior to the passage of the 1965 Voting Rights Act, literacy tests were used to disfranchise Indians and other minorities. In Arizona, Indians were sometimes barred from voting because of this test.[58] The Navajo tribal chairman estimated that in the sixties half the adult population of his tribe were denied the vote on the basis of the literacy law.[59]

The 1965 Voting Rights Act outlawed literacy tests, which were inevitaby administered in a discriminatory manner. This forced opponents of Indian voting to adopt other methods. Registration on the Navajo Reservation was curtailed in 1976 because the county registrar's office, which is off-reservation, failed to supply a sufficient number of voter registration cards.[60] There were also charges of harassment during the registration drive.[61]

When the Voting Rights Act was renewed in 1975 a new section was added that required bilingual voting information and ballots. Indian voters have profited from this requirement. Despite extensive legislation, impediments to Indian voting are still being devised. Deloria and Lytle argue that: "Political establishments continue to devise new ways to perpetuate white political control in areas of heavy Indian population."[62]

Indians at the Polls

Despite this array of impediments to voting, Indians have been going to the polls in significant numbers for twenty-five years. There has been very little research on the impact or extent of Indian voting, however. There are two questions of interest: first, what are the registration and turnout levels for Indian voters, and second, do Indians vote along party lines or do they vote according to specific policies affecting Indians? First, the existing literature will be reviewed and then my findings from a sample of Arizona Indian voters will be presented.

Existing Literature

Helen Peterson examined a sample of Indian voters for the 1952 and 1956 elections. She found modest increases in registration and voting levels: "between 1952 and 1956 there was an average increase in voting from 31 to 37 percent for one Montana tribe, one South Dakota tribe and two Washington tribes."[63] She also cites evidence of Indians changing party affiliation in order to vote against specific policies affecting Indians.[64]

Jack Holmes completed a study of Navajo voters in New Mexico in 1967.[65] He examined the vote in twenty-three predominantly Navajo precincts for elections in 1960 and 1964. He found that support for Democratic nominees was strong but contingent upon their stand on Indian issues:

> In 1960, the twenty-three Indian precincts surveyed have posted a range of 29.7 to 79.8 percent in the Democratic share of their vote for president; in 1964 the range extended from 43.6 to 88.1 percent. If the precincts are lined up in an order determined by the increasing sizes of the Democratic percentage for president, the half in the middle set a range in 1960 of 44.0 to 58.0 percent. In 1964, the range of the middle half was from 63.2 percent to 72.9 percent—a notable shift, and one indicative of voters willing to use their votes for policy objectives.[66]

Although Holmes found evidence of issue voting, he did not discover a significant degree of ticket-splitting and concluded that "New Mexico's Indians are not yet highly sophisticated voters."[67]

117

Stephen Kunitz' and Jerrold Levy's study of Navajo voting in the 1968 national election discovered significant differences between samples of Navajos living on and off the reservation.[68] Off-reservation Navajos voted at a higher rate that their counterparts still living on the reservation. They also found that the off-reservation sample tended to vote Democratic while the on-reservation sample voted mostly Republican.[69] In a later study Levy concluded that Navajos are quick to participate when an election involves issues of importance to them.[70]

A recent study by Leonard Ritt examined the political attitudes and behavior of a national sample of self-identified American Indians who had been polled by the National Opinion Research Center between 1972 and 1978.[71] In this sample of primarily off-reservation Indians, forty-five identified themselves as Democrats, thirty-five as Independent, and sixteen as Republican. Ideologically, the Indian respondents tended to be moderates.[72] As in most samples of Indians, turnout was lower than the national average.[73]

There are a number of reasons why so few data exist on Indian voting. For one, many Indians live in remote areas of the country. There are obvious language and cultural barriers. These factors make survey research difficult. There is also considerable difficulty in separating Indians and non-Indians in aggregate data. In many voting studies Indians have simply been classified as "other." Nevertheless, limited information is available. The data presented below are based upon precinct election returns in Arizona.

Indian Voting in Arizona

The aggregate data presented in Table 1 offer a general view of Indian voting in Arizona. The data are for election outcomes for Indian precincts, defined as any precinct that lies completely within the boundaries of an Indian reservation. Thus the sample does not include all Indian reservation voters. Several precincts straddle reservation boundaries and therefore are excluded from the sample. For

Table 1. *Indian Voting in Arizona, By Tribe, Selected Precincts, 1952-1980*

| | 1980 | | | | 1976 | | | |
| | Pres | | Sen | | Pres | | Sen | |
Tribe	D	R	D	R	D	R	D	R
PAPAGO								
Party Total	406	165	466	168	237	93	235	80
Party %	71	29	74	26	72	28	75	25
Total Vote	634				330			
% Change	92				−2			
NAVAJO								
Party Total	6088	6757	11635	1540	11379	3143	12085	1622
Party %	47	53	88	12	78	22	88	12
Total Vote	13,175				14,522			
% Change	−9				62			
HUALAPAI								
Party Total	43	29	64	28	49	26	29	54
Party %	60	40	70	30	65	35	35	65
Total Vote	92				83			
% Change	11				36			
HOPI								
Party Total	150	190	152	233	148	169	103	216
Party %	44	56	40	60	47	53	32	68
Total Vote	385				319			
% Change	21				−34			
HAVASUPAI								
Party Total	7	12	1	19	20	19	10	27
Party %	37	63	5	95	51	49	27	73
Total Vote	20				39			
% Change	NA				NA			
COLORADO R.								
Party Total	149	332	224	274	236	311	236	321
Party %	31	69	45	55	43	57	42	58
Total Vote	498				557			
% Change	NA				NA			
APACHE								
Party Total	829	302	829	349	861	403	838	421
Party%	73	27	70	30	63	32	67	33
Total Vote	1178				1264			
% Change	−7				−17			

Tribe	1972				1968			
	Pres		Cong		Pres		Sen	
	D	R	D	R	D	R	D	R
PAPAGO								
Party Total	214	104	279	58	289	86	323	101
Party %	67	33	83	17	77	23	76	24
Total Vote		337				424		
% Change		−20				.01		
NAVAJO								
Party Total	5086	3721	6523	2428	1084	1612	1029	1638
Party %	58	42	73	27	40	60	39	61
Total Vote		8,951				2,696		
% Change		232				34		
HUALAPAI								
Party Total	26	29	17	44				
Party %	47	53	28	72				
Total Vote		61						
HOPI								
Party Total	254	205	314	173	97	176	89	173
Party %	55	45	56	36	36	64	34	66
Total Vote		487				273		
% Change		78				−24		
HAVASUPAI								
Party Total	23	32	na	na				
Party %	42	58						
Total Vote		55						
% Change		NA						
COLORADO R.								
Party Total	99	259	121	244				
Party %	28	72	33	67				
Total Vote		365						
% Change		NA						
APACHE								
Party Total	1024	480	1188	345	835	299	864	297
Party %	68	32	77	23	74	26	74	26
Total Vote		1533				1161		
% Change		32				−45		

Tribe	1964				1960			
	Pres		Sen		Pres		Cong	
	D	R	D	R	D	R	D	R
PAPAGO								
Party Total	328	93	296	115	112	100	135	57
Party %	78	22	72	28	53	47	50	30
Total Vote		421				212		
% Change		99				36		
NAVAJO								
Party Total	952	1057	788	1154	411	723	512	536
Party %	47	53	41	59	36	64	49	51
Total Vote		2009				1134		
% Change		77				29		
HOPI								
Party Total	121	237	103	243	40	94	41	82
Party %	34	66	30	70	30	70	33	67
Total Vote		358				134		
% Change		167				11		
APACHE								
Party Total	1780	336	1660	370	625	301	630	299
Party %	84	16	82	18	67	33	63	32
Total Vote		2116				NA		

Tribe	1956				1952			
	Pres		Sen		Pres		Sen	
	D	R	D	R	D	R	D	R
PAPAGO								
Party Total	76	80	134	20	91	91	118	60
Party %	49	51	87	−13	50	50	66	34
Total Vote		156				182		
% Change		−14						
NAVAJO								
Party Total	239	637	402	386	180	860	261	760
Party %	27	73	51	49	17	83	26	74
Total Vote		876				1040		
% Change		−16						
HOPI								
Party Total	36	85	49	69	73	120	82	108
Party %	30	70	42	58	38	62	43	57
Total Vote		121				193		
% Change		−37						
APACHE								
Party Total	224	246	343	113	245	323	277	244
Party %	48	52	75	25	43	57	53	47
Total Vote		470				568		
% Change				−17				

example, there are parts of four different reservations in Pinal County, but none of them contains an all-reservation precinct within Pinal County.

Table 1 includes general elections from 1952 to 1980 for the office of president and for the Senate race if there was one or the congressional seat when the Senate race did not correspond to a presidential election year (1960, 1972). The vote is divided by tribe. There are four figures given for each tribe; the "Party Total" is the cumulative vote for each party's candidate. This figure is the total for all the precincts that lie completely within that reservation. The second figure, "Party %," gives the percentage for each of the party total figures. The third figure, "Total Vote," records the total number of voters for the race (president or Senate/Congress) with the largest turnout. The final figure, "% change," indicates the percentage increase or decrease of the total vote from the previous election's total vote.

A number of limitations in this data should be explained. First, there is undoubtedly a small percentage of non-Indian vote in the sample since a limited number of Anglos vote on the reservations. The proportion of Anglo voters was undoubtedly higher in earlier years, but the marked increases in Indian turnout in recent years has reduced the proportion of Anglo vote to an insignificant percentage of the total vote.

Second, it must be understood that these figures do not represent all Indian voters in Arizona. Omitted are all Indians voting off the reservation, estimated at 19 percent of the state's total Indian population,[74] and the precincts of which only a portion lies within reservation boundaries.

Also, it should be emphasized that there is an undeterminable "hidden vote" that results in an undercount of total votes.[75] For example, if a person voted in only one of the races tabulated in Table 1, but another race with a higher absolute turnout was used as the total vote, then that person's vote would not show up in the total vote, but it would affect the party figures.

Although there have been innumerable changes in precinct boundaries over the past thirty years, the total area

122

encompassed by all of the reservation precincts has changed only marginally. The only time an actual increase in total precinct territory has occurred was when a precinct that straddled reservation boundaries was redrawn into an all-reservation precinct and a nonreservation precinct.[76] This is the only limitation to the data discussed thus far that would tend to slightly overestimate the percentage increase in the total vote. From a survey of precinct maps, over time the increase in territory of all-reservation precincts appears to be relatively small. With these caveats in mind, the data presented in Table 1 will be discussed tribe by tribe.

The three-million-acre Papago Reservation in southern Arizona is one of the largest in the nation. With an estimated population of 9,750, the Papagos have the numerical strength to influence local and regional elections.[77] Although the Papago vote is probably a fairly small proportion of all Papagos eligible to vote, there have been significant increases in registration and turnout in recent years. According to my sample the Papago vote is consistently Democratic, averaging 65 percent in presidential races and 73 percent in Senate/Congress races. The lone exception is the narrow margin for Eisenhower in 1956, although a large percentage of Papagos split their ticket that year and voted for the Democratic nominee for Senate. Since 1956, however, the Papago vote has strongly supported Democratic candidates. Congressman Morris Udall has done particularly well in Papago precincts, as evidenced by the 83 percent Democratic vote in the 1972 congressional race.[78]

The Navajo vote has undergone something of a metamorphosis over the years, changing from Republican to Democratic.[79] This trend was only recently reversed with a thin majority voting for Ronald Reagan in 1980, but the Navajos maintained a high degree of loyalty to Democratic nominees for Senate, primarily because of the Republican support for the very unpopular (among Navajos) Steiger Land Settlement Bill that partitioned the Navajo–Hopi Joint-Use Area.[80] This issue was so important to the Navajos that a very high percentage of them split their ticket in recent years in order to vote against the supporters of the Steiger bill. For example, in 1976, 88 percent voted for Democrat DeConcini, who ran against Sam Steiger, the author of the Joint-Use Land Settlement Bill. In 1980 the results of the vote in the Senate race were the same as in 1976; 88 percent voted for Democrat Bill Schultz, who ran against Republican Senator Barry Goldwater. This was despite a 53 percent vote for Republican presidential candidate Ronald Reagan.[81]

The Navajos have become an important political power in local and regional politics. In 1974 the tribe began a massive voter registration drive, coordinated by the Office of Navajo Political Affairs. According to the *Navajo Times*, total registration (including New Mexico and Utah precincts) increased from 11,500 in 1974 to 38,000 in 1976,[82] indicating that the registration drive was a success. In terms of the actual vote, there was a slight decrease in 1980 with an estimated 25,000 Navajos actually voting,[83] down from 28,704 voters in 1976.[84] This slight decrease is also reflected in my data, which only includes reservation precincts in Arizona. Despite the decrease, the Navajo Tribe will undoubtedly continue to play an important role in southwestern politics.

The Steiger Land Settlement Bill has had a profound impact on Hopi voting as well. Contrary to the position of the Navajos, the Hopi Tribe supports the Steiger bill. This support is reflected in their votes for Senate in 1976 and 1980; Steiger received 68 percent of the Hopi vote in 1976, and Senator Goldwater was supported by 60 percent of the Hopi voters in 1980. This support for Republicans is nothing new; Hopis have almost always voted for GOP candidates, giving them an average of 60 percent of their vote. The lone exception is 1972, when the Hopis voted for Democrats.

The Havasupai and Hualapai tribes from the northern part of the state are quite small and have only had their own reservation precincts since 1972. Although it is difficult to draw conclusions from such a small sample, it is evident that the Hualapai Tribe does not consistently support one major party to the exclusion of the other; there appears to be a shift away from Republicans and toward Democrats in recent elections. The very small sample from the Havasupai Reservation (which is in the Grand Canyon) indicates a fairly consistent pattern of Republican voting.

Voters from the Colorado River Reservation, another small reservation, have also supported Republican candidates. Since the establishment of a reservation precinct in 1972, they have voted for all the Republican candidates in the sample.

The vote for the Apache tribes combines the two contiguous reservations for Fort Apache and San Carlos. The "% change" figures for the Apaches indicate a somewhat erratic level of participation. This fluctuation may be due to changes in the territory covered by all-reservation precincts. Part of the difficulty in measuring the extent of the Apache vote is that the combined Apache reservations cover parts of five different counties. Since all voting data comes from official county election ledgers, it is extremely difficult to establish a total vote for the Apaches in Arizona. One fact is clearly obvious from the data: Apaches vote Democratic, averaging 65 percent for president and 70 percent for Senate/Congress.

To conclude this discussion of Table 1, it should be pointed out that though reservation Indians constitute only a small part of the total electorate, they have an important influence in local and state elections because of their geographic concentration and their apparent ability to issue-vote when a particular issue is perceived to have an impact on the reservation. The full extent of Indian political participation—the potential for increasing future Indian votes— cannot be determined without an examination of registration and turnout rates for Arizona Indians. Table 2 provides that information.

Thus far the concern has been with Indians living on reservations, but Table 2 includes both on- and off-reservation Indians living in select counties in Arizona. The data are not arranged by tribe and the names of the tribes should

Table 2. *Indian Registration and Voting by County, Arizona, 1976 Election*

Selected Counties	Total Eligible 18 yrs.	Total Reported Registered	Total Reported Voted	Turnout % of Eligible	Turnout % of Registered
Apache	16,783	8,491	7,282	43%	86%
Cochise	1,636	1,051	908	56%	86%
Coconino	7,900	5,206	4,322	55%	83%
Mohave	2,038	923	710	35%	77%
Navajo	15,408	8,068	6,525	42%	81%
Pima	11,250	6,295	4,481	40%	71%
Pinal	7,205	2,805	2,024	28%	72%
Yuma	3,812	1,622	1,171	31%	72%
TotalStatewide	107,088	51,442	40,882	38%	80%

Source: Bureau of the Census, Current Population Reports, Series P-23, No. 74, September, 1978. Standard error not shown on this graph.

not be confused with the names of the counties. For example, voters from Apache County are primarily Navajo. In some counties there is only one reservation, the Papago Reservation in Pima County, for example, but there is no way of determining the exact percentage of the Pima County total since there are a number of urban Indians in the county (in Tucson) from other tribes.[85] All of the counties in the table contain portions of reservations except Cochise County.

The first column of Table 2 contains the names of the counties. The second column represents all the Indians in that county that are eighteen years of age or older and therefore eligible to vote. The third column presents the total number of registered voters, and the fourth column gives the number of Indians that actually voted. The column titled "Turnout % of Eligible" indicates the percentage of legally eligible Indians that actually registered and voted. The last column, "Turnout % of Registered," is the percentage of registered voters who actually voted at the polls.

The "Total Statewide," the bottom line of the table, includes data from all Arizona counties and therefore is greater than the sum of the counties presented here.[86] Comparable figures for whites for the total statewide figures are 60 percent of the "Turnout % of Eligible" (compared to 38 percent for Indians). In other words, a smaller percentage of Indians register to vote, but those who go to the trouble of registering go to the polls and vote at a higher rate than whites.

The data in Table 2 are for Arizona only. They can be compared to a national sample by examining Table 3, which presents the same format as Table 2, but for a national sample. This set of data includes eastern Indians and probably a significant percentage of urban Indians. The figures tend to be high because the respondents are self-identified; hence, the sample includes "recognized" as well as non-recognized Indians. The results are remarkably similar to the Arizona sample, with "Turnout % of Eligible" being slightly higher for the total figure. Whether the two samples are similar in terms of partisanship is another question, but judging from Professor Ritt's study cited earlier, it appears

Table 3. *Indian Registration and Voting in Jurisdictions Covered by the 1975 Voting Rights Act Amendments*

State*	Total Eligible 18 years	Total Reported Registered	Total Reported Voted	Turnout % of Eligible	Turnout % of Registered
Alabama	89,347	59,846	45,697	51	76
California	19,942	10,134	9,614	48	95
Colorado	9,953	4,669	3,128	31	67
Florida	26,947	13,353	11,050	41	83
Hawaii	8,052	4,038	3,530	44	87
Louisiana	97,898	51,239	28,749	29	56
Maine	283	113	74	26	65
Mississippi	50,443	36,236	24,961	49	69
North Carolina	59,821	29,993	22,366	37	75
Oklahoma	5,546	3,745	2,901	52	77
South Carolina	35,130	16,352	13,989	40	86
South Dakota	6,395	3,363	2,153	34	64
Texas	388,518	224,740	190,270	49	85
Virginia	125,650	44,088	40,011	32	91
Total:	923,925	501,909	398,493	43	79

*These data include only the counties in these states that came under the jurisdiction of the 1975 amendments. Hence, they do not reflect the total number of potential Indian voters in the states listed.
  Source: Bureau of the Census, Current Population Reports, Series P-23, No. 74, September, 1978. Standard error not shown.

that both Arizona Indians and Indians in other states are not wed to any particular party.

Conclusion: The Impact of Indian Voting

Numerically, Indians are a small minority. Can their vote actually have an impact? The answer is yes; small minorities can decide elections if two conditions are met. First, the minority must bloc vote, and second, the race must be close. With respect to Indians, this has happened on a number of occasions. Helen Peterson cited four instances where the Indian vote may have been a deciding factor in the fifties, long before the recent increases in Indian voting.[87] Vine Deloria, Jr. identified eleven western states where the Indian vote could be decisive and cites five different races where the Indian vote has made the difference, including the elections of Senator McGovern (South Dakota), Senator Metcalf (Montana), Senator Church (Idaho), Senator Cannon (Nevada), and the governor of Minnesota.[88] Leonard Ritt writes that the Indian vote in 1974 "was deemed crucial to the [gubernatorial] victories of New Mexico's Jerry Apodaca and Arizona's Raul Castro."[89] Clearly the Indian vote can make a difference.

Another impact of Indian voting has been the election of Indians at the state and local level. In 1966 fifteen Indians were elected to state legislatures.[90] In 1972 the Navajos elected eight of their people to public office.[91] Today fourteen Navajos hold elective office, including positions in both houses of the New Mexico and Arizona state legislatures.[92] As Indian voting levels continue to rise, more Indians will undoubtedly be elected to office.

A great deal of research still needs to be done on Indian voting. Increased interest in the outcome and impact of Indian voting will probably accompany increased levels of participation. As Indians begin to take an interest in exercising more influence in politics, they will begin to keep track of their votes and demand more all-reservation precincts. As a result, more accurate tracking of Indian voting will be possible.

A great deal has been written about the political participation of other minority groups, especially blacks and Mexican-Americans. No other minority group voting data is comparable to the Indian experience, however, nor can the same generalizations be made about Indian voting. Indians are unique in many ways and one is the way they vote.

One of the more interesting theoretical questions posed by Indian voting concerns the relationship between community context (size, degree of urbanization, and so on), and levels of political participation. Verba and Nie found little correlation between community size and participation but did find a significant relationship between participation and what they call "boundedness," the extent to which a community is well-defined. But Verba and Nie were unable to locate any community that was very high on the "boundedness" variable; "of course, none of the communities in our study approaches being a completely autonomous community; all are embedded in American society . . . ."[93] Though Indian reservations are not perfectly autonomous, they are probably the best examples of that characteristic. If reservation political participation (not just voting, but the other "modes" of participation as well) could be compared to non-Indian participation near the reservation and to the participation of urban Indians, some interesting comparisons might occur that would help explain the impact of boundedness on participation.

There has been a significant increase in Indian political participation in recent years. Increased levels of voting is only one manifestation of the growing awareness on the part of American Indians that they have the potential to influence policy and elections. With their enormous landholdings, massive natural resources, and valuable water rights, the western tribes will undoubtedly play an increasingly important role in local, regional, and national politics.

NOTES

1. United States v. Kagama, 118 U.S. 375 (1886).
2. Monroe Price, *Law and the American Indian* (New York: Bobbs-Merrill Co., 1973), p. 219.

3. McKay v. Campbell, 16 Fed. Cas. 161 (1871) (No. 8840).
4. Elk v. Wilkins, 112 U.S. 94, 98 (1884).
5. 43 Stat. 253 (1924).
6. United States v. Kagama, 118 U.S. 375 (1886).
7. Opsahl v. Johnson, 138 Minn. 42, 163 N.W. 988 (1917).
8. Deere v. State, 22 F.2d 851 (N.D.N.Y.) (1927).
9. Porter v. Hall, 34 Ariz. 308, 321 (1928).
10. Trujillo v. Garley, (D.N.M. 1948).
11. Opinion of the Attorney General of Utah, March 23, 1956.
12. Opinion of the Attorney General of Utah, October 25, 1940.
13. Allen v. Merrell, 6 Utah 2d 32, 40 (1956).
14. Montoya v. Bolack, 70 N.M. 196 (1962).
15. 30 U.S. (5 Pet.) 1 (1831).
16. Swift v. Leach, 45 N.D. 437, 178 N.W. 437 (1920).
17. Arizona Constitution, Art. VIII, § 2.
18. 34 Ariz. 308 (1928).
19. Act of June 20, 1910, ch. 310, 36 Stat. 557, 568-79, § 20.
20. Porter v. Hall, 34 Ariz. 308, 324-25 (1928).
21. Ibid. at 332.
22. Ibid. (emphasis added).
23. Ibid.
24. See N. D. Houghton, "Wards of the United States—Arizona Applications," *University of Arizona Social Science Bulletin*, vol. 16 no. 3 (July 1, 1945): 19.
25. Helen L. Peterson, "American Indian Political Participation," *Annals, American Academy of Political and Social Science*, vol. 311 (May 1957): 123.
26. *Report of the President's Committee on Civil Rights* (U.S. Government Printing Office, Washington, D.C., 1947), p. 40.
27. 67 Ariz. 337 (1948).
28. Ibid. at 349.
29. Ibid. at 345.
30. Ibid. at 342.
31. Trujillo v. Garley, (D.N.M. 1948).
32. They were Idaho, Maine, Mississippi, New Mexico, and Washington. See *Voting in the United States*, published by The Council of State Governments, Chicago, Ill., August, 1940.
33. Opinion of the Solicitor of the Department of Interior, M. 29596, January 26, 1938, p. 8.
34. Trujillo v. Garley, 7, 8 (D.N.M. 1928).
35. Elk v. Wilkins, 112 U.S. 94, 102 (1884).
36. 45 N.D. 437, 178 N.W. 437 (1920).
37. Price, *Law and the American Indian*, p. 223.
38. – – –, 8 (D.N.M. 1928).
39. 138 Minn. 42, 163 N.W. 988, 990 (1917).
40. 34 Ariz. 308, 322 (1928).
41. Harrison v. Laveen, 67 Ariz. 337, 344 (1948).

42. 6 Utah 2d 32, 39 (1956).
43. Peterson, "American Indian Political Participation," p. 124.
44. Prince v. Board of Education, 88 N.M. 548, 543 P.2d 1176 (1975).
45. Shirley v. Superior Court, 109 Ariz. 510 (1973).
46. *Arizona's Indian Participation in the Political Process: Report on the 3rd Annual Indian Town Hall.* Sponsored by the Arizona Commission of Indian Affairs, Oct. 20-21, 1975, p. 15.
47. Minnesota Constitution, Art. 7, § 1.
48. North Dakota Constitution, § 121.
49. Elk v. Wilkins, 112 U.S. 94, 100 (1884).
50. 45 N.D. 437, 178 N.W. 437, 439 (1920).
51. Amicus curiae brief of the United States of America, Harrison v. Laveen, 67 Ariz. 337 (1948), p. 2.
52. Ibid. at p. 5.
53. 6 Utah 2d 32, 37-39 (1956).
54. Cal. Stat. 102 (1850).
55. Goodrich, *The Legal Status of the California Indian,* 14 *Calif. L. Rev.* 90-91 (1926).
56. Little Thunder v. South Dakota, 518 F.2d 1253 (8th Cir. 1975).
57. David A. Bingham, "Legislative Apportionment: The Arizona Experience." *Arizona Review of Business and Public Administration,* vol. 11, no. 10, (Oct. 1962), pp. 12-14.
58. Navajo Tribal Council, *The Navajo Times,* Nov. 5, 1964.
59. Stan Steiner, *The New Indians* (New York: Harper and Row, 1968).
60. *The Navajo Times,* Nov. 11, 1976.
61. *The Navajo Times,* Nov. 11, 1976.
62. Vine Deloria, Jr., and Clifford M. Lytle, *American Indians, American Justice* (Austin, Tex.: University of Texas Press, 1983).
63. Peterson, "American Indian Political Participation," p. 124.
64. Ibid., p. 125.
65. Jack E. Holmes, *Politics in New Mexico* (Albuquerque: University of New Mexico Press, 1967).
66. Ibid., p. 104.
67. Ibid.
68. Stephen J. Kunitz and Jerrold E. Levy, "Navajo Voting Patterns." *Plateau,* vol. 43, no. 1 (Summer, 1970): 1-8.
69. Ibid., pp. 2-3.
70. Jerrold E. Levy, "Changing Navajo Voting Patterns." Report for the Lake Powell Research Project, 1976.
71. Leonard G. Ritt, "Empirical Approaches to the Study of American Indian Political Behavior," delivered at the Annual Meeting of the Southwestern Political Science Association, Houston, Texas, April 2-5, 1980. This paper is an updated and expanded version of an article by Ritt in *Ethnicity,* vol. 6, no. 1 (Mar. 1979): 45-72. Ritt's work is to date the most comprehensive research on Indian political behavior.

72. Ibid., p. 14.

73. Ibid., p. 30.

74. From census data quoted in *Critical Issues for Indians-State Relations*, prepared by the Indian Planning Program, Arizona Office of Economic Planning and Development, Larry Landry, Executive Director (Jan. 1, 1981), p. 1.

75. There is also a "hidden vote" in the apparent extent of split-ticket voting created by the cancelling effect of voters who split their tickets in the opposite races. For example, if voter A voted for a Republican president and a Democratic senator, and Voter B voted for a Democratic president and a Republican senator, then it would appear as though neither voter had split their ticket.

76. The exception to this is the Havasupai Reservation, where both reservation precincts and reservation boundaries have changed in recent years. Because of these changes, and the low number of voters, it is not possible to establish a meaningful "% change" figure.

77. Indian Planning Program, *Critical Issues*, p. 2a.

78. Udall received 88 percent of the Papago vote in 1976, and 86 percent in 1980.

79. Figures for the Navajo Tribe are for Arizona precincts only. Large numbers of Navajo voters reside in the New Mexico and Utah portions of the reservation but are not included in this study.

80. See Levy, "Changing Navajo Voting Patterns."

81. Some precincts, particularly those in the Joint-Use Area, gave Schultz a 94 percent margin over Goldwater. *Navajo Times* (Nov. 13, 1980), p. 1.

82. *Navajo Times*, Nov. 11, 1976.

83. *Navajo Times*, Nov. 13, 1980.

84. *Navajo Times*, Nov. 11, 1976.

85. The Yaqui Reservation is in Pima County but was not created until 1978. For more information on urban Indians, see Joyotpaul Chaudhuri, *Urban Indians of Arizona*, Arizona Government Studies, No. 11 (Tucson, Ariz.: University of Arizona Press, 1974).

86. The Indians included in this table, as well as in Table 3, are self-identified.

87. Peterson, "American Indian Political Participation," pp. 124-26.

88. Quoted in Steiner, *The New Indians*, pp. 235-36.

89. Ritt, "Empirical Approaches to the Study of American Indian Political Behavior," p. 17.

90. Steiner, *The New Indians,* p. 234.

91. *The Navajo Times*, Nov. 16, 1972.

92. Telephone interview with Larry Foster, Director for Intergovernmental Relations, Navajo Tribe, September 5, 1984.

93. Sidney Verba and Norman H. Nie, *Participation in America* (New York: Harper and Row, 1972), p. 243.

6

The Crisis in Tribal Government

BY TOM HOLM

In recent years American Indian protests against their own tribal officials have seemingly become commonplace. Consequently, tribal operations have been crippled and in some instances completely brought to a standstill.[1] The reasons underlying the tribes' internal political strife are many and somewhat complex. Historic factionalism among some Indian people has surely contributed to the problem and controversies over reservation resource development and tribal funds have led to splits within several tribes. More important perhaps is the fact that many of the protests are actually made against the very political system under which the tribal governments operate.

In the United States, most Indian governments have written constitutions based on the American ideals of representative democracy. The powers and duties of elected tribal officers correspond to the functions of national, state, and local administrators, managers, and legislators. Under the constitutions tribal authority is vested in legislative, executive, and oftentimes, judicial branches of government. To many non-Indians steeped in European tradition this system, while not perfect, is at least equitable because it places political power in the hands of individuals who have received the approval of the majority of the electorate. To many Indian people, especially those who have knowledge of their traditional tribal value systems, democratic elections more often than not create artificial elites who then rule more or less in an arbitrary manner.

In many cases, tribal factionalism has been along "traditional" versus "modern" lines and is directly tied to differing concepts of authority. Authority in modern tribal governments is vested in certain positions within the tribal political system. The people elected to these positions then assume the power of the office. Authority, therefore, is related to the power of the office within the context of the tribal constitution.

According to many traditional value systems, however, authority is vested in individuals and not necessarily in particular tribal political positions. In most tribal societies authority is gained with status and does not imply arbitrary power. Status is accorded to individuals who have excelled in certain skills, practiced generosity, displayed great courage, have knowledge of ceremonial functions, possess spiritual powers, or who have strong analytical abilities or wisdom. Authority is given consistently to the person who has demonstrated over and over again that he or she has the spiritual and physical well-being of the rest of the tribe at heart.

Social consciousness was and is a primary factor in attaining a position of leadership among traditional-minded Indian people. The institution known as the "give-away" is demonstrative of this facet of Indian leadership. Persons in positions of leadership are expected to display generosity. Give-aways provide for a continual redistribution of wealth within the society. Leaders and those who aspire to leadership take great care to perpetuate this custom because it proves their social awareness and thus gives them status. In much the same way, warriors were admired for demonstrating bravery because it was assumed that since warfare was viewed in most tribal societies as being disruptive, they did so in defense of the group, the tribal identity, and the tribal ethos.

Status and authority were conferred by consensus. In addition, authority was seen generally in the intellectual sense of the word. Expertise was sought by society for answers to certain difficulties and those who had gained status within the society were presumed to have knowledge of the ways in which it operated. Leaders were recognized by society as a whole for the ways they dealt with problems.

This traditional concept of authority is very much alive today and has become, in some cases, a point of contention between recognized traditional leaders and elected constitutional officers. The takeover, occupation, and siege of Wounded Knee, South Dakota in 1973 was a good example of this traditional/nontraditional conflict. On February 27, a group of Indians, some of them members of the American Indian Movement, entered this small town on the Pine Ridge Sioux Reservation. During the takeover eleven hostages were detained only to be released forty-eight hours later. Over the next sixty-nine days, the Federal Bureau of Investigation laid siege to the village and numerous rounds of talks took place between occupation leaders, traditional chiefs and headmen, and United States government officials. It was also during this period of time that two Indian men were killed in exchanges of gunfire between Wounded Knee occupation forces and federal agents.[2]

The press coverage of the occupation and siege was intense and seemingly comprehensive. Reporters primarily focused on the American Indian Movement as an Indian version of militant minority organizations such as the Black Panthers. In the press the takeover of Wounded Knee appeared to be an attempt to focus American media attention on Indian poverty and government insensitivity to Indian problems. Wounded Knee was the site where federal troops buried in a mass grave the victims of a massacre perpetrated on a large band of Sioux in 1890. The village's symbolic value was not wasted on reporters.

Largely due to the press coverage and later white scholarship, the Wounded Knee crisis has not been widely regarded as a traditional/nontraditional confrontation. The American Indian Movement leaders were and are viewed as habitual dissidents striking out against authority in any form— Indian or white. The media and recent scholarly view of Wounded Knee holds it to have been a youthful protest in mimicry of inner-city rioting. Several people, in looking back at the event, have taken the view that the members of the occupying group were too young or had come from urban backgrounds and were therefore unable to know about traditional political thought.

The takeover, however, was not exactly an effort to gain media attention and, with it, more public involvement in Indian affairs. Some of the participants, in fact, expressed the honest hope that whites would stay out of the controversy. Simply put, many Indians on both sides of the question believed that whites could sympathize with or condemn the actions at Wounded Knee but never really understand the issues surrounding the crisis.

Despite the media coverage and later scholarly attempts to unravel the ideas that led to the takeover and siege, the crisis can be seen in traditional/nontraditional terms. At the center of the decision to occupy Wounded Knee was a controversy over Ogallala Sioux tribal leadership. The protesters at the village and a large portion of the Ogallala tribal membership were adamant opponents of tribal chairman Richard Wilson and the ways in which the Pine Ridge Council was conducting tribal affairs. Specifically, Wilson was accused of mismanagement, fraud, and several offenses ranging from refusing to publish the minutes of council meetings to denying certain Ogallalas the rights of free assembly, due process, and protection from unreasonable searches and seizures.[3]

Because of Wilson, the Wounded Knee protesters entered the village to declare their separation from the constitution under which the Ogallala tribal government operated. During the siege they openly stated that they were establishing a sovereign Sioux Nation under the treaty made with the federal government in 1868.[4] Tribal elders and traditional chiefs and headmen concurred with the idea that the 1868 treaty was made between two independent nations. It followed that if the Sioux Nation was sovereign, the people had the right to establish the type of government they wanted. Richard Wilson was not, according to this line of thought, a legitimate tribal chief or leader. He therefore could not have authority over the lives of the Ogallala people.

After the siege ended Senator James Abourezk of South Dakota conducted hearings regarding the incident as chairman of the Subcommittee on Indian Affairs of the Senate Committee on Interior and Insular Affairs. On the first day of the hearing, June 16, 1973, Wilson adamantly refuted AIM and traditional Ogallala charges leveled at himself and the tribal constitution. The tribal chairman argued before Abourezk that he objected to the interference in the tribe's affairs on the parts of both the federal government and the American Indian Movement because they were actively seeking to subvert tribal sovereignty. Wilson claimed that the takeover was a product of outside agitation and that the principle of self-determination for Indian tribes was being undermined.[5] The charges against him were false but even if they were true, they should be handled only by the duly constituted tribal government.

In his opening statement before Abourezk, Wilson stated that dissent on his reservation really came from a minority who were opponents of self-government and favored continued "fraternalism" with the Bureau of Indian Affairs. The Ogallalas had voted to accept a constitution in 1935 by a margin of 1,348 to 1,041 and had been governed under a democratic process since that time. "The minority will be heard," Wilson said, "but the majority shall rule."[6] It was obvious that Wilson did not want to recognize the treaty of 1868 because his government was a result of much later legislation.

The chairman had immediately cast his foes as being not only malcontents but against the ideal of tribal self-determination. He and the Ogallala council had already barred the members of AIM from using tribal property as of November 10, 1972, on the basis that the group threatened "the sovereign dignity of the Ogallala Sioux Tribe."[7] During the occupation of Wounded Knee Wilson garnered the support of the chief Indian lobby group in the United States, the National Congress of American Indians. In a memorandum to his organization's executive committee, NCAI director Charles E. Trimble wrote that the crisis was a "clear threat" to Indian political systems across the nation. Trimble moreover quoted one of Wilson's press releases that stated in effect that the federal government as well as AIM were ignoring the rightful authority on the Pine Ridge Reservation. Wilson also attacked the National Council of Churches' negotiation team for not including the tribal government in its activities. "We Indians," Wilson wrote, "must be reminded that unsolicited interference by the organized church in Indian affairs throughout history has always resulted in the loss of Indian lands, Indian rights and Indian lives." Indians, once again, were being told "how to run their lives."[8]

Trimble declared that NCAI would support Wilson and the constituted Ogallala tribal government. Although NCAI could not take a role in negotiating a settlement on the grounds that this activity would "further subvert tribal integrity," the organization planned to establish an advisory group at Pine Ridge in order to be "on call" to the Ogallala tribal government. NCAI further committed itself to assisting Wilson in regard to developing strategies, lobbying, and press relations.[9]

Trimble's and NCAI's support of Wilson was based solidly on upholding the ideal of tribal sovereignty. The federal government had controlled nearly every facet of Indian life between the years 1890 and 1934. Indian lands had been confiscated or dismembered; tribal governments had been dissolved; American Indian arts had been all but lost; and tribal religious ceremonies banned or destroyed. According to most observers of past American Indian policy, the Indian Reorganization Act of 1934 allowed at least a partial restoration of tribal integrity. It halted the allotment of tribal lands, permitted ceremonies to be held again, and generally attempted to preserve Indian arts. It thus promoted the maintenance of a tribal identity which was crucial to the continuity of American Indian values.

Tribal governments also began to be organized in anticipation of eventual self-rule. To the members of the National
Congress of American Indians the protection of this right
was all-important. Any subversion of it was perceived as a
return to the period prior to the Indian Reorganization
Act. The NCAI had already fought long and hard against
the termination policy of the 1950s because it was a blatant
effort to undermine self-determination for Indian tribes.
In principle, the preservation of home rule was to be protected at all costs—historic precedent demanded it.

To those who had captured Wounded Knee and to the
traditional Ogallala leaders, these arguments did not ring
completely true, nor did they seem to have real meaning.
Numerous complaints, issued primarily from traditional
Sioux people, had been lodged against tribal chairman Wilson since his assumption of office in early 1972. Particularly irritating and problematic to traditional chiefs and
headmen like Frank Fools Crow and Charles Red Cloud
had been Wilson's system of law and order at Pine Ridge.
Fools Crow, speaking before Abourezk's subcommittee,
told of telephone threats and the appearance of armed men
at his home.[10] Several Ogallalas testified that with federal
funds Wilson had established an auxiliary police force which
was being used to attack and silence his political opposition.
Red Cloud intimated to Abourezk that because of the roving
bands of armed agents, both the federal government's and
Wilson's, "people are really afraid to tell you these things."[11]
Because of apparent violations on the part of Wilson's
"goon squads," an "Ogallala Sioux Civil Rights Organization" had already been founded. This group in turn had
called on AIM for help.[12]

One of the stated purposes behind the occupation of
Wounded Knee was to produce a crisis in tribal government. It was intended to force a repudiation of Wilson's
methods and the 1935 Ogallala constitution. An earlier attempt to impeach Wilson under the constitution had been,
it was asserted, quelled by the use of the auxiliary police
force. Wounded Knee was an attempt to move away from

Wilson's government and reinstitute traditional Sioux values in the tribal political system.[13]

Traditional Sioux leaders were in agreement with this goal. After the siege on May 18, the traditional chiefs and headmen petitioned the federal government "to honor . . . the Indian people's desire to return to their traditional form of government." In essence, both the occupation forces at Wounded Knee and the traditional leaders wanted to retain the type of political system the Ogallalas had developed over the generations and which had never really been dissolved. They also wanted strict compliance with the Fort Laramie Treaty of 1868.[14]

In the main, these groups were protesting against Wilson's highly centralized system of government. Power, because of the "reorganization" constitution, had essentially fallen into the hands of a small group of people who ruled without benefit of widespread popularity. In fact, traditional leaders and AIM members asserted they ruled only by force of arms. In addition, traditional Sioux values did not equate "power" with "authority."

Authority obtained by force is alien to traditional Sioux thought. In traditional Ogallala society, leadership is placed on the shoulders of those men and women who have proven themselves worthy of it. Lakota men and women were taught from childhood that the only way to gain the respect of the group was to live up to certain social and individual standards. Of utmost importance for males were the virtues of bravery, honesty, generosity, and fortitude. Females were taught the same values, as well as industriousness, hospitality, and chastity.[15]

Like other tribal leaders, Sioux chiefs and headmen assumed positions of authority by consensus. In other words, they were leaders because the rest of society thought of them as such. Once in authority over a certain facet of Sioux life, the chief or headman had to demonstrate that he had the welfare of the tribe on his mind at all times. Otherwise he would lose status and authority simply because he no longer had a following. As Ogallala elder Matthew King put it, "The Chief is closely watched. If he makes a mistake he is out. There is no trial. He is out and that is all."[16]

Authority in traditional Sioux society was also less centralized. The Lakotas were organized politically in bands of small stable populations. The size of the group made it much more possible for leaders to understand and interpret public thought. When the bands met in large gatherings, such as for the Sun Dance, band headmen as well as widely recognized chiefs could confer in council and deal with human problems on a larger scale. Still, even in this larger gathering, group consensus opinion was always sought.

With the advent of the 1935 constitution, the United States government completely ignored the band structure and the authority of the recognized tribal elders. Consensus and the ability to work out problems in council gave way, at federal insistence, to majority rule. The government, the Bureau of Indian Affairs, and all other federal agencies focused on the very small group of elected officials and especially on the tribal chairman. So great was this focus that with government support these elected officials formed the National Tribal Chairmen's Association.

In a sense, United States concentration on an individual leader or a handful of elected tribal officials brought on the Wounded Knee crisis. Had the government recognized Sioux sovereignty since the 1868 treaty, there would have been no reason to institute the "reorganization" constitution of 1935. Wounded Knee, in the final analysis, was a challenge to government suppression of tribal self-determination.

Unfortunately for the traditional Ogallalas and the protesters at Wounded Knee, the United States was not about to recognize full Sioux sovereignty. In December, 1974 lawyers for the Wounded Knee protesters charged with criminal acts committed during the siege, moved that the allegations be dropped because the United States courts did not have jurisdiction over Sioux land. For thirteen days testimony was taken and arguments were presented concerning Sioux rights under the treaty of 1868. Judge Warren Urbom decided that his court was not the appropriate place for a decision of this magnitude. He ruled that jurisdiction was not a matter of treaties alone. Legislation, he maintained, also entered into the question. In effect he denied that the Sioux were sovereign because of congressional and bureaucratic modifications to the treaty of 1868.[17]

Urbom's decision did not end the sovereignty or the traditional/nontraditional questions. Federal judges had been especially leery of entering into intratribal conflicts. Instead of looking upon Wounded Knee as a genuine question of Indian sovereignty, Urbom chose to see the incident as a case of Sioux factionalism. He took a stand of noninterference but essentially gave the decision to the nontraditional element of the tribe.

In 1976, however, another federal judge reached quite a different opinion concerning government intervention in tribal politics. Eleven months before Urbom's decision in the Sioux matter took place, lawyers from the National Indian Youth Council and the Institute for the Development of Indian Law filed suit on behalf of Allen Harjo and three other traditional Creek leaders from Oklahoma against then Secretary of the Interior Rogers Morton and Creek Principal Chief Claude Cox. Later, the suit was revised to charge the new Secretary of the Interior under President Ford, Thomas S. Kleppe, instead of Morton. Cox was still included in the suit.

The issue in *Harjo* v. *Kleppe* was whether the Secretary of the Interior and Claude Cox had illegally refused to recognize the 1867 Creek constitution and the Creek National Council by disbursing tribal funds without the consent of the representatives of the Creek people. In other words, the federal government along with Cox had conspired to make the office of principal chief of the Creek Nation the sole embodiment of Creek government. Both the plaintiffs and the defendants requested summary judgment in the case.[18]

In a meticulously detailed historical argument Thomas E. Leubben, Jr. and Robert G. Vaughn presented the traditional Creek view of the ways in which Creek political

144

integrity had been stripped away. During the Civil War the Creeks had been forced into an alliance with the South. When the war was brought to an end the federal government imposed reconstruction on the Creek Nation under a new treaty and in spite of the fact that most traditional Creeks had remained loyal to the earlier treaties with the Union. Although the new treaty of 1866 forced the Creeks to cede large tracts of land to the United States and to grant access through their territory to the railroads, it recognized the power of the Creek National Council to make laws governing the body of land still remaining to them. The treaty further stipulated that the Creeks retained "the unrestricted right of self-government" and that no United States legislation could "interfere with or annul" their tribal organization, rights, customs, or laws.[19]

In the year following the ratification of the reconstruction treaty the Creeks adopted a new constitution in accordance with their right of continuous self-government. The Creek government was federalist in form with power strictly in the hands of a national council, the members of which were selected in a traditional manner from the leadership of the tribal towns. The members of the national council represented their own town constituencies. The constitution also provided for executive and judicial branches of government.[20]

In the thirty-six years between 1870 and 1906 the Creek Nation witnessed an unprecedented attack on its territorial and political sovereignty. Non-Indian intruders poured into the Indian Territory without permission and began to demand their rights as United States citizens. Hundreds of territorial bills were placed before Congress aimed specifically at the goal of making the Indian Territory a state in the Union and terminating all tribal entities. The tribal governments were able to hold off these attempts as well as the more concentrated effort to allot their lands under the General Allotment Act of 1886 because they held their lands in fee simple.[21]

In 1893, however, Congress formed a commission to force

the tribes of the Indian Territory into allotment, dissolving their governments and becoming part of a new state. Headed by the author of the Allotment Act, Henry L. Dawes, the commission was not well-received in the territory. The tribes refused to deal with Dawes, and Congress began to pass a series of laws designed to erode tribal sovereignty to the point that the tribes would have to come to agreement with the commission. In 1896, Congress directed that all Indian lands would be surveyed and that the commission would make a roll of all members of the tribes in anticipation of allotment. Congress also extended criminal and civil jurisdiction over the nations and in 1897 passed an act subjecting all tribal legislation to presidential veto. The tribes soon came to agreement with the commission under these various forms of duress.

In 1898, Congress passed the Curtis Act. This law contained most of the new agreements with the Dawes Commission and extended the provisions of the General Allotment Act over the Indian Territory.[22] In addition, it stipulated that the tribal governments would continue to exist only so long as it took to issue allotment deeds to tribal members and terminate any other tribal business. The final agreement with the Creeks was not ratified until 1901. In this pact it was provided that the tribal government would not continue "longer than March fourth, nineteen hundred and six."[23]

As long as the Creek government was to exist, however, it was to continue to operate under the constitution of 1867. The 1901 agreement mentioned this stipulation specifically and recognized the financial and legislative powers of the National Council. Under the 1897 Indian Appropriation Act all laws of the Creek Nation were still subject to presidential approval but recognition of the council was never withdrawn.[24]

The allotment process continued longer than had been expected and Congress was forced to extend the time period in which the tribal governments could continue to operate. In 1906, Congress began work on the Five Tribes

Act. Because there had been widespread dissent in comply-
ing with the allotment policy on the part of the traditional
Indians in the nations, it was feared that one of the tribes
would elect an executive officer who might very well decide
to refuse to sign allotment deeds. The Five Tribes Act would
provide that the president could remove from office any
executive who should refuse or neglect to perform the duty
of conveying, in the name of the tribe, allotments to tribal
members. Moreover, the president could appoint a new
principal chief or in the case of the Chickasaws, a governor,
should the position become vacant as a result of "removal,
disability or death."[25] The act did not deprive the tribes
of the right to elect officers nor did it dissolve the tribes'
legislative bodies. Because the time was fast approaching
for the termination of the Indian governments and the Five
Tribes Act was not yet complete, Congress secured a joint
resolution calling for the continuation of the tribal political
systems.[26] The Five Tribes Act was not passed until April
26, 1906.[27] Both acts stipulated that the tribal "governments" were to continue, thus implying that the national
council was to remain operative.

The Creek National Council in various forms and the office of principal chief have never been terminated. Continued problems with allotment and other business have prolonged the need for the Creek government to continue to
function. Succeeding secretaries of the Interior and com-
missioners of Indian Affairs, however, have undermined
the powers of the national council. As District Court Judge
William Bryant put it in his ruling in *Harjo* v. *Kleppe,*
the Department of the Interior ignored the provisions of
both the Curtis and the Five Tribes acts. It has regarded
the office of principal chief as its own fief. Under its advice
presidents appointed and reappointed executives who favored concentrating power into their own hands. For its
part, in the traditional Creek view, the office of principal
chief has become a creature of the Bureau of Indian Affairs.
Since the Five Tribes Act allowed the Creeks to retain
their government, presumably as organized under the con-

147

stitution of 1867, the Interior Department had no legal right to ignore the National Council. Bryant called the actions of the department "bureaucratic imperialism" and found for the traditional Creeks.[28]

Because the plaintiff argument was not put as a case of internal factionalism, Bryant had been forced to recognize United States culpability in undermining the Creek political system. Until his decision, most non-Indians had looked upon the collapse of traditional tribal government as an inevitable universal acceptance of representative democracy. In 1970, Congress passed an act that allowed the Creeks the right to select their own chief executives.[29] Claude Cox, the Creek principal chief and one of the defendants in *Harjo* v. *Kleppe,* had been popularly elected, yet he was not seen as having been delegated supreme authority.

The traditional Creeks were opposed to investing in a single person, even a democratically elected official, such great power. Before the advent of whites in North America the Creeks were a loose confederation of several tribes. They had a strong clan structure and a system of government that rested firmly on consensus values. Despite the fact that the Creek Nation was a confederacy, the principal Creek political unit was the tribal town. The towns handled all internal problems, most external difficulties, and maintained a high degree of autonomy. The Confederacy's council consisted of representatives from the towns and functioned only in extratribal affairs and only when the entire Creek Nation was threatened. Creek unity on a national level was primarily a function of ceremonial and clan ties.

When the whites came to Creek country the tribal towns began to rely more and more upon the Confederacy's council to meet the threat. By the 1830s the Creek central government had become a tightly knit unit with much greater authority than it had previously enjoyed. The tribal towns, however, maintained control over who was sent to the national council. At no time, even during removal from the Creek homelands in the East to Oklahoma, did the towns lose the right to appoint representatives to the council. The 1867 constitution merely reconfirmed the traditional political power base by stipulating that the delegates to the houses of Kings and Warriors would be elected by the towns they represented.[30]

Like the Sioux, the Creeks based leadership on consensus. Prominent men and women were awarded titles or special names. The title of "Beloved Woman" was indicative of this point. Women were very important in Creek society. Family lines were traced through the mother's side and the clan grandmothers were always consulted concerning every problem confronting the extended family. Certain women whose wisdom had been proven many times and who consistently lived up to the tribe's system of values were accorded great status and authority. Sometimes women who had demonstrated courage in battle were rewarded with a special place in the town's "Red" or war court. A "Beloved Woman" was just that—one who was looked up to and revered for her courage, virtue, and wisdom. Men gained status in war, for their knowledge of ceremony, and because they had excelled in one or more facets of Creek life. A leader in Creek society could not be a leader without continued, broad-based recognition of his or her abilities and status.[31]

When the United States government began to appoint people to the office of principal chief and look upon the position as the sole embodiment of Creek government, traditionally minded Creeks were thoroughly disillusioned. Creek ideas concerning the attainment of authority were totally ignored. In the eyes of traditional Creeks, their principal chief had become an agent of the federal government. Because the position derived its power from a source other than the Creek populace, the office of chief had lost its authority. In addition, the individual who had gained the office might not have first gained status within the perimeters of traditional Creek mores. He would thus be viewed as an illegitimate leader.

During the 1930s, when the United States began to allow

the reorganization of tribal political systems, a few Creek towns decided to form governing bodies of their own. The towns organized under the Oklahoma Indian Welfare Act of 1936, which had extended the provisions of the Indian Reorganization Act to the tribes of that state. The towns' willingness to incorporate independently of the central Creek government seemed to indicate a lack of strong ties to the office of principal chief as the personification of the Creek political system.

Significantly, two of the opposing parties involved in the *Harjo* v. *Kleppe* suit, Allen Harjo and Claude Cox, ran against one another for the office of principal chief. In 1970, Congress authorized the "popular selection" of the Five Tribes chief executives. The next year the Creeks elected Cox over Harjo by a margin of 2,674 to 1,846. Four years later the same two opponents ran again for the office. This time Cox received 1,840 votes to Harjo's 1,792, a difference of only forty-eight votes.[32] Harjo and the traditional Creeks were not at all satisfied with the results of the elections for several reasons. First, Harjo had promised a complete rein-statement of the national council while Cox proposed that a new constitution be submitted for approval by the secretary of the interior. Under the new constitution the members of the national council would be elected by districts rather than from the tribal towns. The new constitution had been finished before the decision in *Harjo* v. *Kleppe* had been reached.

Traditional Creeks believed that the 1867 constitution was more than sufficient for continued self-rule. Also, a new constitution would have taken electoral control out of the hands of the tribal towns. It was feared that the new electoral system would allow the principal chief, through the manipulation of the districts, to control the new legislature. In addition, a constitution that had to receive the approval of the Secretary of the Interior was hardly in keeping with traditional views of Creek sovereignty.

Another reason underlying traditional distrust of the principal chief was the very process under which Cox had gained

150

the office. The act of 1970, although it provided for elections, still required that the winner obtain the approval of the Interior Department. Also, Cox had won in 1975 on a simple majority vote. According to traditional views he had not received a strong enough mandate to assume the powers that had illegally been given to the principal chief.

Although Bryant's decision in *Harjo* v. *Kleppe* was favorable to the traditional Creeks, it did not produce a final resolution. With the idea of self-determination hovering over the ruling, the judge became unwilling to order a complete return to the constitution of 1867. Such an order would remove from Indian hands the right to determine their own political goals and would be no less "imperialist" an order than Interior Department interference. Instead, Bryant sought what he termed an "equitable" solution. The judge ordered that a commission be established composed of two persons selected by the traditional Creeks, two appointed by the defendants, and one person chosen by the four members already selected. With Bureau of Indian Affairs funding, the commission was charged with the task of educating the Creek populace concerning the case. It was also to ascertain the Creek opinion about the type of government the tribe as a whole really wanted.[33]

Problems beset the commission's work from the start. It became extremely difficult for the four chosen members to decide on a fifth party acceptable to both sides. This situation was not resolved until August, 1978 after Bryant ordered a thirty-day deadline on selecting a fifth member.[34]

Another problem involved finances. Gerald Wilkinson, the executive director of the National Indian Youth Council, stated that the Bureau of Indian Affairs failed to support the commission's educational program and had thus prevented a Creek tribal referendum on the constitution from taking place. The commission had ordered the printing of various materials relating to the Creek political impasse for mailing to Creek citizens. The referendum was to take place on January 27, 1979. The printed material was not completed in time for the deadline because insufficient funds had been released from the BIA to cover costs. The Bureau also failed to present the commission a list of Creek descendants in time for the planned mailing.[35]

In large part the difficulties over lists, membership, and mailing are minor points when compared to the commission's major task of unifying the Creeks politically. Compromise will be sought, to be sure, but the impasse seems bound to continue unless the tribe can actually reach a consensus opinion concerning their political structure. A referendum, although favorable from a non-Indian point of view, would impose another majority-rule situation on the tribe. Bryant's equitable solution to Creek political problems, when seen in this light, gave relief to no one.

In general, the *Harjo* case raised almost insolvable questions concerning Indian political sovereignty. Rightfully, Judge Bryant should have ordered the immediate convening of the Creek National Council. It was proved that the body had been illegally subverted. The Creeks had not given up the 1867 constitution despite Bureau actions. A return to the constituted political system, therefore, should not have been considered unfair or unjustified. The judge, however, was not convinced that he could order the "return" of a certain form of government. He feared being accused of exactly the same type of arbitrary colonialism that the secretary of the interior committed in undermining the Creeks' right to determine their own political system.

Bryant was particularly concerned over the fact that the 1867 constitution did not include suffrage for women.[36] Consequently, although he believed that the constitution had been wrongfully usurped, he did not think it formed the basis for an equitable system of government. In setting up the commission to decide on what form of government the Creeks should have, the judge necessarily imposed his own values on the tribe. Bryant believed that the tribe possessed the right of political self-determination, but only so long as it conformed to mainstream American ideals.

The *Harjo* suit and the Wounded Knee crisis brought traditional/nontraditional factionalism into focus. Both cases served to remind Indians and non-Indians alike that traditional tribal values still exist and that tribal sovereignty rests on the ability to recognize and deal with this fact. As was the case in both the *Harjo* suit and the Wounded Knee siege, traditionalists disliked the fact that power had been concentrated into the hands of a single person by the United States government. The crisis in tribal government, therefore, could very well be a product of political centralization in response to colonialism and consequent economic problems.

NOTES

1. See "Tribal Government . . . A Key Issue," *The Indian Historian,* 12 (Summer 1979): pp. 25-27.

2. New York *Times,* March 5, 8, 9, 26, 1973; Washington *Post,* March 1, 2, 4, 6-15, 29, 1973; 93rd Congress, 1st Session, U.S. Senate, *Occupation of Wounded Knee, Hearings Before the Subcommittee on Indian Affairs June 16-17, 1973* (Washington: 1974); Roxanne Dunbar Ortiz, *The Great Sioux Nation* (Berkeley, California: 1977).

3. U.S. Senate, *Wounded Knee Hearings,* pp. 251-52.

4. Washington *Post,* March 12, 1973.

5. U.S. Senate, *Wounded Knee Hearings,* p. 6.

6. Ibid., p. 4.

7. Resolution No. 72-55 of the Ogallala Sioux Tribal Council to Protect Property, Interests and Sovereign Dignity of the Ogallala Sioux Tribe. American Indian Studies Files, University of Arizona.

8. Charles E. Trimble to NCAI Executive Committee, March 14, 1973. American Indian Studies Files, University of Arizona.

9. Ibid.

10. U.S. Senate, *Wounded Knee Hearings,* p. 124.

11. Ibid., p. 125.

12. Ibid., p. 142.

13. Ibid., pp. 251-56.

14. Ibid., p. 311.

15. Bea Medicine, "Oral History," Roxanne Dunbar Ortiz, *The Great Sioux Nation,* p. 121.

16. Matthew King, "Rations Not Fit for Human Consumption," Roxanne Dunbar Ortiz, *The Great Sioux Nation,* p. 155.

17. Warren Urbom, "Excerpts from the Decision," Roxanne Dunbar Ortiz, *The Great Sioux Nation,* pp. 197-98.

18. 420 F. Supp. 1110 (1976).

19. Institute for the Development of Indian Law, *Treaties and Agreements of the Five Civilized Tribes* (Washington: n.d.), p. 242.

20. *Constitution and Laws of the Muskogee Nation,* American Indian Studies Files, University of Arizona.

21. See especially Angie Debo, *The Road to Disappearance* (Norman, Oklahoma: 1967); *And Still the Waters Run* (Princeton: 1973); Francis Paul Prucha, *American Indian Policy in Crisis* (Norman: 1976).

22. 30 Stat. 495.

23. 31 Stat. 62.

24. 30 Stat. 62.

25. 34 Stat. 137.

26. 420 F. Supp. 1110 (1976).

27. 34 Stat. 137.

28. 420 F. Supp. 1110 (1976).

29. 84 Stat. 1091.

30. *Constitution and Laws of the Muskogee Nation.*

31. For a look at Creek cultural history, see Debo, *Road to Disappearance.*

32. 420 F. Supp. 1110 (1976).

33. Gerald Wilkinson to Jack Leslie, Office of Senator Edward Kennedy, February 14, 1979. American Indian Studies Files, University of Arizona.

34. Ibid.

35. Ibid.

36. NIYC memorandum, n.d., American Indian Studies Files, University of Arizona.

7

Cultural Values and Economic Development on Reservations

BY DAVID L. VINJE

The 1960s witnessed a substantial effort by the Bureau of Indian Affairs in conjunction with the Economic Development Administration, Office of Economic Opportunity, and the Department of Labor to work with tribal authorities in promoting industrial development on U.S. Indian reservations. The basic strategy was that of attracting labor-intensive manufacturing activity to the reservations via an industrial promotion package. The package was designed to assist private firms in setting up plant and equipment and in obtaining a work force trained for the firm's particular needs.

The coordinated approach of government and tribe aided in the establishment of manufacturing activity on the reservations. In 1960 there were four reservation manufacturing plants in operation employing approximately 525 Indians. By 1970, the twenty-four most heavily populated reservations had approximately 3,465 Indians employed in durable and nondurable manufacturing, accounting for roughly 12 percent of reservation wage employment.[1]

However, it is questionable to label the 1960s approach a successful development strategy. For example, the Navajo Reservation was relatively successful in the establishment of manufacturing activity during this period. By the end of 1968, firms on the reservation employed approximately a thousand Navajos. But, for the same year, Aberle[2] estimates an increase in the reservation's labor supply of approximately three thousand individuals. Thus, in one year, 1968, three times as many Navajos were added to the labor force as had been absorbed by an eight-year effort in recruiting firms to the reservation. The recruitment of firms was expensive as well. Ruffing[3] estimates that in the case of their most important manufacturing employer, the Navajo Tribe earned a one percent rate of return on the fixed investment necessary to attract the firm to the reservation. And, since the completion of Ruffing's study, this particular firm has closed its plant and left the reservation.

Even when a manufacturing strategy generated industrial employment, the problem of poverty sometimes remained. Murray[4] cites a study done for the BIA which revealed that of 48 families employed during 1960–65 by a manufacturing firm operating on the Pine Ridge Reservation of South Dakota, 31 remained below a $3,000 poverty level of income. More generally, it can be demonstrated that the relationship between the involvement of a reservation in manufacturing activity and its level of per capita income is statistically insignificant. In a regression equation for the twenty-four most heavily populated reservations, manufacturing employment as an explanatory variable for reservation per capita income has an insignificant coefficient and an R^2 of 6.6 percent.[5]

The weakness of manufacturing as a development strategy for Indian reservations has been the subject of a number of studies.[6] A brief summary of the additional points raised by these studies is sufficient for the purpose of this paper. First, for other than a resource-based or footloose industry, the isolated location of many reservations constitutes a serious problem for the establishment of manufacturing activity, especially when combined with inadequate rail and highway systems. Second, many of the firms involved have been plagued by inexperienced management. In the case of some private firms, it appears that the willingness to establish a plant on the reservations is determined by the availability of federal assistance. Only when these firms are unable to make it on their own do they seem interested in the reservations. Third, the tribes do not have sufficient financial capital to establish operations that would have a better probability of success. The financial constraint pushes the tribe toward small-scale, under-financed, labor-intensive operations that can easily be jeopardized by a small change in technology or a small change in our import laws. An example of this constraint is found in the BIA's revolving loan fund in operation since 1934 as a source of development financing for the Indian tribes. In the fiscal year 1970, tribal requests to the revolving fund totaled $25.3 million while the cash available in the fund was $3.3 million.

Fourth, the cultural tradition of many Indians does not appear to lend itself to a manufacturing operation. The rights and responsibilities of the extended family system are still strong for many individuals. Since even reservation manufacturing jobs often require a residence relocation, manufacturing activity can be the basis for a disruption of family ties. The choice becomes especially difficult for the individual when it is recognized that the manufacturing job in most cases will: pay only the minimum wage, offer little opportunity for advancement, require quite rigid worker self-discipline, and oftentimes be of an indeterminant duration.[7] Vine Deloria, Jr. and Ruffing[8] maintain that a successful economic development strategy can exist only if it builds on the existing cultural traditions of a tribe. It would appear that a manufacturing strategy requires a substantial change in these traditions if it is to be successful.

Self-Determination

The 1970s witnessed a trend toward greater independence in decision making for tribal authorities. The federal government started to give more policy and administrative responsibility to the tribes, the emphasis being on "self-determination" for the Indian tribes.[9] Tribal officials did not interpret this trend as a movement toward termination by the federal government. Rather, they viewed the trend as a movement toward local control of existing federal programs as well as a greater voice for the Indians in the setting of Indian policy.

Given this trend, the paper's objective is to examine the

relationship between greater independence at a tribal or reservation level and the selection of an economic development strategy. If a reservation is no longer tied to a common federal strategy, what development path will it follow and how will the path chosen compare with the economic development strategy of the 1960s?

In an attempt to answer the questions just posed the remainder of the paper is devoted to an analysis of the development plans put forth by the tribal officials of three different reservations: the Navajo Reservation of New Mexico, Arizona, and Utah,[10] the Zuni Pueblo of New Mexico,[11] and the Standing Rock Sioux Reservation of North and South Dakota.[12] The reservations were selected to obtain a somewhat diverse sample in terms of reservation size, population, and resource base. In addition, each of the three reservations has a reputation for independence in drawing up its development plan; i.e., tribal officials had the major decision-making role. While examining all three plans, the paper will give a special emphasis to the Navajo plan since the Navajo Reservation is the nation's largest in both size and population.

Methodology

The three plans under study specify their primary objective to be closing or narrowing the gap that currently exists between living standards on the reservation and living standards for the rest of the United States. Given the objective, the development plans will be analyzed by categorizing activities and examining the percent of total plan expenditures devoted to each of the categories or components. The categories are listed in Figure 1.

The upper bracket consists of activities designed to increase living standards primarily through the creation of jobs. The lower bracket is composed of activities that should directly increase the living standards of the individuals and families involved. Education, located between the brackets, is delineated as a category which, more than others, has

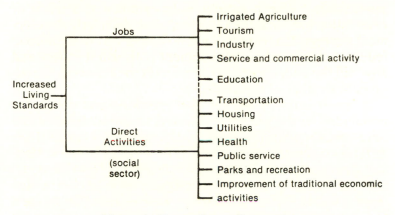

Figure 1. *Expenditure Categories*

elements of both brackets included in it. Also, as will be noted later, the reservations involved have varying responsibility for this particular activity.

The categories are established using a different methodology than found in some of the plans. The Navajo plan, for example, with its categories of Directly Productive Activity (DPA) versus Social Overhead Activity (SOA) uses the standard breakdown of developmental economics. The breakdown being used here is rationalized by a belief that the analysis should reflect the uniqueness of reservations as an example of rural or nonurban economic development. It is believed that the uniqueness of reservations is found in the cultural traditions of the Indians as a people.

In this interpretation, developmental projects that fall into the jobs bracket (DPA) are assumed to represent an approach or strategy to economic development that might be found in any regional economic plan. The stress is on the creation of jobs, often through the stimulation of new economic activities, as a means of raising income and thus the living standard of the individuals involved. In addition, like its off-reservation counterpart, this approach has the secondary objective of raising governmental real income.

159

Given tribal involvement in new economic activities, as either a partner or a taxing entity, it is assumed that successful projects within this category will aid tribal governments in their political and economic desire for increased self-sufficiency.

To the extent that cultural traditions are a factor, the jobs bracket of activities assumes traditions will give way to the new activities if a conflict exists. Dorner's study is an example of this approach, as can be seen in his statement that it is a delusion to believe that traditional values can be preserved while undergoing successful economic development.[13] This does not necessarily mean that traditional values are destroyed. Rather, it implies that the cultural traditions are relegated to a secondary position. They no longer constitute a way of life, but become similar in importance to the cultural traditions of other ethnic groups within the U.S.

It is recognized that the activities included in the direct bracket correspond to the social overhead activities discussed in developmental literature. Expenditures on utilities, roads, health, etc., should provide the groundwork for future economic activity, possibly in the next planning period. And, it is possible that an emphasis on this bracket today is merely a reflection of reservation planners sharing the belief held by many planners that SOA must precede investment in the DPA. However, it should be recognized that an emphasis on the direct activities bracket can also constitute a development strategy by which reservation officials may achieve the objective of increased living standards while minimizing the disruptions to the reservation's traditional way of life.

As alluded to previously, opinions vary as to the compatibility of traditional Indian values and successful economic development. Vine Deloria, Jr. and Ruffing maintain that successful development is possible only if it builds on existing cultural values. Dorner, as a spokesman for many, if not most, developmental economists, doubts the possibility of successful development unless traditional values are weakened. It is anticipated that the selected method of classifying activities will highlight the importance tribal leaders attach to the concept of allowing or encouraging traditional activity to continue.

The Plans

The Navajo Plan

The narrative section of the Navajo Ten Year Plan stresses jobs as an objective. The plan states that a primary factor in determining the investment required for the plan's operation is the desire to provide 46,000 Navajo jobs over the planning period. It is assumed that approximately 26,000 of these jobs will be in the public sector as a result of the tribe taking over more of the existing federal programs. The remaining 20,000 jobs are to be in the private sector.

Part of the plan's emphasis on jobs is a reflection of the Navajo tribal government's desire to increase the self-sufficiency level of the reservation. In particular, the plan talks of the need to increase the intrareservation multiplier effect of public and private investment activity. The plan emphasizes that primary jobs will more readily lead to secondary jobs in retailing and services if more of the individual's expenditures can be kept within the reservation's boundaries. By increasing the internal multiplier effect, it is also assumed that tribal government will benefit through increased revenue and decreased expenditures for welfare, etc. It is anticipated that private sector primary jobs will be found in the extractive, irrigated agriculture and manufacturing sectors. Coal gasification plants are currently being proposed as a new extractive-based industry capable of playing an important employer role. Large-scale manufacturing is not discussed as an important industry other than through the possible attraction of one or two "footloose" manufacturing firms to the reservation.

It is interesting, however, that the stress on jobs found in the narrative section does not evidence itself in the plan's

161

Table 1. *Development Plan Expenditure Allocations*

		Navajo	Zuni	Standing Rock Sioux
A.	Bracket Allocation (% of total exp.)			
	Jobs	9.68	17.02	24.34
	Education	30.16	7.07	40.50
	Direct (social sector)	60.16	75.92	35.16
B.	Category Allocation (% of Bracket total)			
	Jobs			
	Agriculture (irrigated)	56.70	0.0	2.74
	Tourism	9.28	70.70	17.59
	Industry	26.29	17.43	50.84
	Commercial and service activity	7.73	11.78	28.83
	Direct (social sector)			
	Transportation	30.27	37.65	19.47
	Housing	15.42	38.78	36.19
	Utilities	6.80	4.32	1.56
	Health	17.41	11.10	3.34
	Public Service	6.92	3.44	18.56
	Parks and Recreation	5.68	1.84	.47
	Traditional Ag and Grazing Activities	17.50	2.88	20.42
	Education (selected categories)			
	Head Start projects	5.21	25.41	0.0
	Adult education	4.30	4.46	.22
	Manpower projects	20.43	0.0	1.08
	K-12 programs	62.03	64.89	98.71

Source: The Navajo Tribe, *The Navajo Ten Year Plan,* Window Rock, Navajo Nation, 1972.

The Pueblo of Zuni, *Zuni Comprehensive Development Plan,* Zuni Pueblo, New Mexico, 1972.

Standing Rock Sioux Tribal Council, "Developmental Plan, Phase II," Ft. Yates, North Dakota, 1971.

expenditure breakdown (Table 1). Of the three reservations being examined, the Navajo plan devotes the smallest percentage of its total expenditure to the jobs category (9.68 percent versus 17.02 percent for the Zuni and 24.34 percent for the Standing Rock Sioux). An explanation is found in the Navajo's rich resource base. The tribe can and does anticipate that outside firms will be willing to invest private funds in extractive and processing activities. The plan anticipates that for every one dollar invested in directly productive activities by the tribe, two dollars will be forthcoming from private firms.

The plan also takes the development position that social sector activity will perform a dual function of reducing the gap in living standards while providing the basis for future expansion of the private sector. Given this view, expenditures in the social sector are compatible with an emphasis on jobs; i.e., improved transportation not only reduces the time and hardship involved in reaching needed services, but also supplies a basis for future industrial activity. And, transportation is the largest single category of expenditures in the Navajo direct or social sector bracket.

A somewhat different approach is found in the role assigned to traditional economic activity in the Navajo plan. Planned expenditures for the upgrading of traditional agricultural and grazing activities are quite high, ranking second only to transportation in the direct or social sector bracket. In addition, it is assumed that the upgrading activity will generate substantial employment, more than is to be generated by the large irrigated agricultural project. Yet, the plan does not view this sector as playing an important role in the future. Rather, it is assumed that absolute employment will soon level off, and, on a percentage basis, the population involved in this sector will decline as time passes.

The justification for a large expenditure on a sector that is expected to decline appears to be twofold. It is assumed that many of the older Navajos will be unable to move into the expanding wage sector. Thus, the plan hopes to achieve an adequate income for this group while allowing them to continue their present activities. In addition, political tension is thought to exist between tribal leaders and tradional groups at the grass-roots level.[14] It is possible that the tension is in part responsible for the magnitude of funds devoted to traditional activities. Regardless of which explanation has the greatest validity, the Navajo plan does not appear to view traditional activity as a building block for economic development. And, as will be seen, the Navajo plan's lack of emphasis on traditional activities is not that unique.

The Zuni Plan

The Zuni Pueblo is in a different position than either the Standing Rock Sioux or the Navajo in that its educational system is part of the Gallup-McKinley County School District. Thus, the Zuni Pueblo, while having the problem of its children being part of a wider non-Indian school system, does have the financial advantage of not being required to fund a complete school budget. As a result, the Zuni Pueblo is able to devote its planning effort to other areas.

In assessing employment opportunities, the plan discusses both the public and the private sectors. In terms of public jobs, the Zuni Pueblo has been a leader in contracting with the BIA to take over federal programs previously administered by the BIA. In the 1973 fiscal year, the pueblo, through individuals and as a public agency, contracted to administer $546,000 in program monies.[15] In addition to viewing contracting as a source of jobs, the pueblo sees it as an important element in tribal self-determination.

In the private sector, the pueblo is interested in further expanding job opportunities in the service and industrial sectors. The plan notes that currently 84 percent of individual income is spent off the reservation. It anticipates that increased on-reservation service facilities could counter this spending pattern. The plan also places a major stress on tourism as a private sector employer.

As is shown in Table 1, the Zuni plan calls for approximately 75 percent of its total expenditures to be spent on direct or social sector activity (versus 60 percent for the

Navajo and 35 percent for the Standing Rock Sioux). However, while the Zuni plan places a strong emphasis on direct activities, this is not the same as an emphasis on traditional economic activities. The Zuni plan devotes only 2.9 percent of its social sector budget to improvement of traditional economic activities.

The Zuni Reservation is small in size and has little in the way of natural resources. Currently only 4.1 percent of the Zuni labor force is employed in agricultural activities. (See Table 2.) The plan does not appear to view enhancement of traditional agricultural and grazing activity as a viable route to its goals. The plan's lack of interest in traditional activities appears to be based on more than just an economic assessment of the reservation's natural resources. The plan, in discussing a number of cultural restoration projects currently under way on the reservation, talks of the projects strictly in terms of their potential as tourist attractions. In discussing restoration of the pueblo itself, no mention is made as to whether a project of this nature might play a role in passing the pueblo's cultural traditions on to successive generations.

The Standing Rock Sioux Plan

The theme of the Standing Rock Sioux plan is the interrelationship between the physical sector and the social sector. The tribal leaders maintain that Sioux culture has always been based on a strong interrelationship between the people and the land.

In keeping with its theme, the plan calls for the establishment of Fort Yates as the reservation's growth center with five or six satellite centers being located in the more important of the remaining reservation communities. With this structure, tribal leaders hope to retain communication ties with the people at a grass-roots level in both an upward and a downward direction. In addition, it is believed that the structure will help the people retain a strong sense of their tribal identity and heritage.

Education is the largest single bracket of expenditures in

165

Table 2. *Reservation Data*

	Median for 24 Most Heavily Populated Reservations	Navajo Reservation	Zuni Pueblo	Standing Rock Sioux Reservation
1. Per capita income	$992.0	$776.0	$979.0	$1,002.0
2. Median family income	$4,300.0	$3,084.0	$5,291.0	$3,652.0
3. Median years of education, male and female 25 years and over	9.4 yrs	4.10 yrs	9.6 yrs	9.7 yrs
4. Housing with 1.51 persons per room or more	39.76%	64.69%	50.51%	34.61%
5. Housing with piped-in water	74.2%	36.5%	94.5%	50.4%
6. Percent of population under 18	53.53%	54.65%	56.31%	49.26%
7. Percent of all Indian reservation population		26.6%	2.2%	1.4%
8. Reservation size (thousands of acres)		12,540.0	407.0	849.0
9. Average male and female labor participation rate	41.20%	33.6%	30.5%	47.0%
10. Labor force employed (%)				
— manufacturing	12.15%	13.9%	18.2%	.0%
— government	46.9	55.6	47.1	66.0
— agriculture	11.13	4.62	4.12	14.58
— wholesale and retail trade	7.19	8.31	13.23	3.93

Source: U.S. Bureau of the Census, *Subject Report: American Indians,* U.S. Government Printing Office, 1973.

the Standing Rock Sioux plan.[16] The remaining development funds are split more equally than is the case for the
other two reservations with the jobs bracket receiving approximately 25 percent of all funds and 35 percent going
to the direct bracket.

The impression given by the plan is that the large allocation of funds to the jobs bracket results from the lack of
existing activity in this sector rather than from a disinterest
in the social sector. The reservation is not well endowed
with cultivatable land or with mineral resources. Thus, if
jobs are important, they will have to be found in nonagricultural activities. At the present time the reservation has
little in the way of nonagricultural activities such as industrial or service activities.

Within the direct bracket, housing is to receive the largest
allocation of funds followed by traditional agricultural and
grazing activities. While the traditional sector of the Standing Rock Sioux Reservation is to receive a higher percentage of social sector funds than is the case for the other two
reservations, this cannot be interpreted as a strong emphasis
on retaining a traditional way of life. The plan describes
the desired outcome from expenditures in this category in the
same terms as it describes the desired outcome from expenditures on other small business activities on the reservation.

The Standing Rock Sioux plan appears to reflect a strong
sense of cultural and community identity. However, the plan
also appears to view the economic sector as culturally neutral. They do not see existing traditions as a hindrance to
new economic activity, nor do they see new economic activity as a threat to cultural traditions.

Analysis of Plans

The three development plans examined do not reflect a
radical change from the 1960s. Rather, the change from the
1960s appears to be one of emphasis. Manufacturing is not
viewed as the key to economic development in the current
plans. In all three plans, it appears as just one possible

source of new economic activity. The one area of activity within the jobs sector that consistently is emphasized in the current plans is that of service activity. Each of the plans analyzed placed an emphasis on trying to establish viable shopping and service centers on the reservation.

The plans covered do not stand out as unique examples of rural or nonurban economic development. A development plan for a nonreservation, semirural area in north-central New Mexico, randomly pulled from the bookshelf, reveals a percentage breakdown quite compatible with the plans under discussion.[17] In the New Mexico plan, 16.3 percent of total expenditures is devoted to the jobs bracket, 79.3 percent to the social sector, and 4.4 percent to education.

As discussed earlier, Deloria, Jr. and Ruffing believe the economic development process has to be integrated with existing cultural traditions if the development process is to be successful. However, the plans under study appear to view new economic activity as culturally neutral. The plans express a strong interest in maintaining the cultural heritage of the tribes involved, and in encouraging new forms of economic activity. There is no attempt in the plans to portray new economic activity as a threat to cultural values, nor is there any indication that the success of the economic development process is viewed as being dependent upon a modification of these values.

Additional research is needed in this area. It is possible that the failure of the Deloria, Jr.-Ruffing–Dorner debate to materialize is a result of the plans reflecting the views of tribal officials as opposed to individuals at the grass roots level. It is also possible that the expenditure allocations revealed in the plans were skewed by the availability of federal funds. The plans may reflect some compromise between what is desired and for what in fact funds are available. Finally, it is possible that tribal officials believe that the adaptability component of the different tribal cultures is strong enough to encompass new forms of economic activity without a significant loss in traditional values.

However, Indian history, as well as the experience of

many third world countries, raises questions regarding the cultural neutrality of any economic development process. More specifically, Raffaele[18] believes that a relatively laissez faire approach to economic development is apt to be characterized by the breakdown of extended families as a creator of values, a diminution in the people's sense of responsibility, and a depersonalization of the individual. The result, according to Raffaele, is a nation, region, or community where the individual is easily manipulated and has, as a motivational characteristic, a high regard for expediency in his interpersonal relations.

In addition, given an objective of reducing the gap in living standards between groups both on and off the reservation, the post-World War II experience of many third world countries raises doubts as to the success of large-scale industrialization as an economic development strategy. In particular, the Navajo plan appears to fit the development strategy followed in the 1950s and 1960s by a number of third world countries. Given the rich resource base, the plan calls for large national and multinational companies to come onto the reservation for the purpose of establishing extractive-based industrial activity.

It is assumed that the combination of outside capital and tribal-owned mineral wealth will result in the creation of jobs for tribal members, as well as sufficient royalty income to assist the tribal government in establishing a more independent and self-sustaining reservation economy.[19] The tribal government is aware that the encouragement of coal gasification plants, electrical generating plants, etc., may be less than an ideal method of increasing economic activity. However, at this point few alternatives are thought to be available. Tribal officials have stated that if the reservation wants jobs and income, it has to build on the basis of what the tribe possesses that currently is in high demand, i.e., its coal, uranium, oil and natural gas resources.[20]

The economic development strategy called for in the Navajo plan is understandable. But, recent studies have indicated that a development strategy based on large-scale industrial activity, while generating substantial growth in GNP, may result in an increasing amount of unemployment and underemployment for the country or region involved.[21] The trickle-down theory does not appear to hold. In point of fact, it may work in reverse. The lower-income groups, instead of sharing in the benefits of growth, find that as a group their position may decline in both relative and absolute terms. According to Adelman,[22] even after the initial stage of development is passed, the income and employment effects being generated benefit the lower income groups only if the government takes strong policy actions to redirect the economy's path in such a way as to ensure that the benefits of growth are more equally shared.

Given sufficient royalty income, it is possible the tribal government will be able to redirect the income stream in such a way as to benefit tribal members beyond the initial employment effect. However, even with greater self-determination the process is not going to be that easy. In setting policy the tribal government has to negotiate with both the federal government and the corporations operating on the reservation. The experience with this policy negotiation process hasn't been that good. As recently as 1976, the federal government stepped in and overruled a contract between the tribe and a coal company since the tribe had agreed to accept a royalty income percentage that was less than federal law called for on Indian lands.[23]

Other points of concern have also been raised regarding the Navajo's development strategy. The adverse environmental effects apt to result from massive coal mining and coal burning on the reservation have been the subject of debate among reservation residents.[24] The critics view the acceptance of possible air pollution, water pollution, and the destruction of grazing lands as a gross violation of traditional values. In addition, there is a concern that a stress on energy production might well jeopardize other aspects of the development plan. While legal negotiations are still under way, at the present time the Navajo's allocation of water is not sufficient, in Lawson's view,[25] to support both

170

the energy projects and the large irrigated agricultural project called for in the plan.

Finally, the government has often been slow in delivering federal funds to the reservations for spending in the social and educational sectors. This factor combined with the uncertainty as to the economic effects of the Navajo strategy can result in some pessimism as to the ability of the tribe to achieve its goal as stated in the development plan. And, given the resource wealth of the Navajo Nation, this pessimism has to be increased substantially when addressing the probability of success for the other reservations under discussion.

Conclusion

The above-stated pessimism would seem to add weight to Deloria, Jr. and Ruffing's implicit criticism of the economic development strategy found in many reservation development plans. However, while neither unique nor radical, the reservation plans, to the extent the Navajo experience is transferable, do show a substantial change from earlier planning efforts. In the early 1950s, Congress authorized the Navajo–Hopi Long Range Rehabilitation Act.[26] Under that Act federal funds were authorized by category for expenditure on the Navajo Reservation. A comparison of the funds authorized under the 1951 Act with the current Navajo plan does show change occurring. The Act devoted a percentage of total expenditures to industry and transportation approximately double that called for in the current Navajo plan. The 1951 Act also devoted a percentage to health activities only one-half that found in the current plan. And, the percentage for housing in the current plan is ten times that found in the 1951 Act.

One of the advantages likely to result from the trend toward greater tribal independence is found in the diversity of the three plans. The ability of the tribal officials to individualize the plans to fit reservation needs, as they see them, shows up in the differing stress or emphasis the plans place on the various categories of activities. A second aspect of diversity in the plans is revealed in the institutional and administrative approach taken by the different reservations. The decentralized approach of the Standing Rock Sioux Reservation is quite different from the more centralized approach of the Navajo Reservation. As time progresses, it will be interesting to see if a plan's success can be correlated not only with the development strategy being followed, but also with the specific institutional or administrative approach being utilized.

Finally, it is possible that the split between Deloria and Ruffing's emphasis on integrating the development process with existing cultural values and the seeming emphasis of many tribal governments to follow development strategies that are interchangeable with non-Indian development plans may be bridged. Reno[27] has suggested that the key to successful Indian economic development rests with the technology utilized within sectors of the tribal economy. He maintains that economic success, as well as tribal unity and retention of cultural values, can best be achieved by an alternate form of technology.

He believes that an appropriate technology is one that stresses small-scale tribally operated economic activity of a labor-intensive nature. Following on the work of Hunter,[28] Schumacher,[29] and others, he maintains that with this approach tribal members will be less resistant to change and more willing to actively participate in increased economic activity on the reservation. With a more labor-intensive technology being utilized in firms under Indian control, the income distribution problems discussed earlier in conjunction with the recent experiences of third world countries might also be lessened. In Reno's view, the primary question is the mode and technology of production, and not whether traditional agriculture or resource extraction is stressed as the key sector in a development plan.

It is Reno's opinion that there is no *a priori* reason why the approach being advocated should be less productive than a more capital-intensive technology. However, while he believes immediate opportunities exist for an application of his approach, he also recognizes that substantial research and development work is required before a decentralized, small-scale, labor-intensive technology is apt to be as productive as the technology utilized by the major industrial companies. As a solution, Reno advocated the establishment of an office of appropriate technology within the Navajo tribal government as a vehicle for carrying on the necessary research and development work.[30] In the context of this paper such an office would appear to be a first step in bridging the gap between Deloria and Ruffing's approach to economic development and that of many tribal officials.

NOTES

1. U.S. Bureau of the Census, *Subject Report: American Indians* (Washington, D.C.: U.S. Government Printing Office, 1973).

2. D. Aberle, "A Plan for Navajo Economic Development," in *Toward Economic Development for Native American Communities* (Washington, D.C.: U.S. Government Printing Office, 1969).

3. L. Ruffing, "Economic Development and Navajo Social Structure" (mimeographed article, 1974).

4. J. Murray, *Industrial Development on Indian Reservations in the Upper Midwest* (Saint Paul, Minnesota: Upper Midwest Research and Development Council, 1969).

5. D. Vinje, "An Exploratory Study of Inter-Reservation Variations in Per Capita Income and Labor Participation," *Growth and Change,* vol. 8 (July, 1977), p. 38.

6. U.S. Bureau of Indian Affairs, Missouri River Basin Investigation Project, *The Fort Berthold Reservation Area* (Billings, Montana: Missouri River Basin Investigation Project, Report No. 196, 1971); Vine Deloria, Jr., "The Lummi Indian Community: The Fisherman of the Pacific Northwest" (mimeographed article, 1974); S. Fuller, "Indian Problems in Acquiring Development Capital," New Mexico State University, Agricultural Experiment Station, Special Report No. 11 (December, 1971): J. Murray and A. Sorkin, *American Indian and Federal Aid* (Washington, D.C., Brookings Institution, 1971); H. Striner, "Toward a Fundamental Program for the Training, Employment and Economic Equality of the American Indian," in *Federal Programs for the Development of Human Resources* (Washington, D.C.: U.S. Government Printing Office,

1968); B. Taylor and D. O'Connor, *Indian Manpower Resources in the Southwest* (Tempe, Arizona, University of Arizona Press, 1969); U.S. Commission on Civil Rights, *The Southwest Indian Report* (Washington, D.C., U.S. Government Printing Office, 1973).

7. D. Vinje, "Private Firms and U.S. Indian Reservations: An Hypothesis," *Liberal Arts Review,* vol. 1 (Winter 1975), pp. 18-28.

8. L. Ruffing, "Navajo Economic Development Subject to Cultural Constraints," *Economic Development and Cultural Change,* vol. 24 (April 1976), pp. 611-21.

9. J. Taylor, *The States and Their Indian Citizens* (Washington, D.C., BIA, U.S. Government Printing Office, 1972).

10. The Navajo Tribe, *The Navajo Ten Year Plan* (Window Rock, Navajo Nation, 1972).

11. The Pueblo of Zuni, *Zuni Comprehensive Development Plan* (Zuni Pueblo, New Mexico, 1972).

12. Standing Rock Sioux Tribal Council, "Developmental Plan, Phase II" (Fort Yates, North Dakota, 1971).

13. P. Dorner, "The Economic Position of the American Indians: Their Resources and Potential for Development" (unpublished doctoral dissertation, Harvard University, 1959).

14. L. Ruffing, "Economic Development and Navajo Social Structure."

15. U.S. Bureau of Indian Affairs, Albuquerque Area Office, "Contracts" (Albuquerque, New Mexico, 1973).

16. While the development plan is essentially a ten-year plan, the actual project allocations specified in the plan are for only the first two years of its operation.

17. North Central New Mexico Economic Development District, *Overall Economic Development Program, Phase II* (Santa Fe, New Mexico: College of Santa Fe, 1969).

18. Joseph Raffaele, *The Economic Development of Nations* (New York, New York: Random House, 1971), chapter 8.

19. The Navajo Tribal Government, "The Navajo Times" (March 18, 1976), p. A-3.

20. "The Navajo Times" (April 29, 1976), p. A-2.

21. F. Stewart and P. Streeter, "New Strategies for Development: Poverty, Income Distribution and Growth," *Oxford Economic Papers,* vol. 28 (November 1976), pp. 381-405.

22. Irma Adelman, "Development Economics—A Reassessment of Goals," *American Economic Review,* vol. 65 (May 1975), pp. 302-309.

23. *The Navajo Times* (August 18, 1977), p. A-19.

24. *The Navajo Times* (March 24, 1977), p. A-1.

25. Michael Lawson, "The Navajo Indian Irrigation Project: Retrospect and Prospects," paper presented at Western Social Science Association Annual Meetings (Denver, Colorado, April, 1977).

26. R. Young, *The Navajo Yearbook: 1951-1961* (Window Rock, Arizona, Bureau of Indian Affairs, Navajo Area Office, 1961).

27. Philip Reno, "Navajo Resources and Economic Development" (mimeographed article, 1976), chapter 3.

28. Guy Hunter, "The Transfer of Institutions from Developed to Developing Countries," *African Affairs,* vol. 67 (January 1968), pp. 3-10.

29. E. Schumacher, *Small is Beautiful: Economics as if People Mattered* (London, England: Bland and Briggs, Ltd., 1973).

30. C. Kolstad, D. Grimmer, P. Reno, and J. Tutt, *Appropriate Technology and Navajo Economic Development* (Los Alamos, New Mexico: Los Alamos Scientific Laboratory of the University of California, 1976).

8

Bureau of Indian Affairs Influence on Indian Self-determination

BY ROBERT A. NELSON AND JOSEPH F. SHELEY

The issue of self-determination is at the heart of any analysis of American Indian relations with white America. Given the complexities of contemporary societal interrelationships, self-determination is not an "either-or" proposition. Rather, it is a matter of degree: the degree to which Indians can keep intact their cultural heritage and social structures, the degree to which they can provide their own subsistence, and the degree to which they can legally govern themselves. During the late 1960s and early 1970s, the question of Indian self-determination became particularly visible to the public through Indian seizures of public institutions such as Alcatraz Island and occasional violent confrontations with government agents such as occurred at Wounded Knee. As with the black riots of the 1960s, Indian demonstrations brought some *apparently* positive government relief in the form of official recognition of the need for Indian self-sovereignty.

In this paper, however, we argue that Indian self-determination remains in relatively the same position it held prior to the 1960s primarily because the government's chief Indian agent, the Bureau of Indian Affairs (BIA) of the U.S. Department of the Interior, has thwarted efforts to diminish its control over Indians. We seek to illustrate this point by focusing on a major source of Indian-BIA tension: criminal justice planning. We shall describe the BIA administration of reservation crime control programs with special atten-

177

tion given to the strategies and tactics utilized to exert control over tribes despite federal mandates to reduce control. Finally, we offer a general approach to criminal justice planning on reservations which affords considerably greater self-determination to Indians without denying the inevitability of BIA influence.

Tribal-Federal Relations

For the roughly two hundred years of their relationship, the federal government has dictated the life situation of Indians. Indians are wards of the state, governed by the state. Yet, while clearly always the dominant partner in the relationship, the federal government has vacillated regarding both the method and goal of its domination. Indian tribes sometimes have been recognized as governments through treaties with the United States.[1] They also have been viewed as "immigrants" as the government has implemented plans to assimilate them into "mainstream society." They have been viewed often as a "natural attraction" to be preserved from twentieth-century corruption. And, most recently, they have seen the government promise them self-determination, i.e., the eventual power to assimilate and to preserve their heritage to the degree they, the Indians, desire.

Whatever its current position toward Indians, the government has not relinquished control over them. The government acts as the trustee of lands, resources, and rights granted Indians under the provisions of various treaties and the U.S. Constitution. In executing this trust, the government has given responsibility to the BIA to expend appropriations for the "general support and civilization of Indians" under the Snyder Act of 1921.[2]

In its role of protector and governor of Indians, the BIA has also come to bear the brunt of Indian dissatisfaction with the tribal-federal government relationship:

> The Indian is never alone. The life he leads is not his to control. This is not permitted. Every aspect of his being is

178

affected and defined by his relationship to the Federal Government—and primarily to one agency of the Federal Government: the Bureau of Indian Affairs.

. . . Even when exercised illegally, the total power of the Bureau is virtually unchallengeable and unreviewable. Where the normal citizen has three avenues of redress political, judicial, administrative—the Indian has none.

. . . Through the pervasiveness of the Bureau's role, the exercise of power and administration of programs by the BIA have come to ensure that every effort by the Indian to achieve self-realization is frustrated and penalized; that the Indian is kept in a state of permanent dependency as his price of survival; and that alienation from his people and past is rewarded and encouraged for the Indian.[3]

Dilution of Formal BIA Power

Through 1970, the BIA's mission was to provide for and to civilize the Indian. However, in 1970, President Richard Nixon laid the foundation for a federal policy of Indian self-determination. Responding to public concern about the plight of the Indian, Nixon stated that "the time has come to break decisively with the past and to create the conditions for a new era in which the Indian future is determined by Indian acts and Indian decisions."[4]

The response of the Congress to Nixon's message took the form of the passage of Public Law 93-638, the Indian Self-Determination and Educational Assistance Act of 1975. Through this law Congress recognized

> . . . the obligation of the United States to respond to the strong expressions of the Indian people for self-determination by assuming maximum Indian participation in the direction of . . . Federal services to the needs and desires of those communities. [Further, Congress declares its] . . . commitment to the maintenance of the Federal Government's unique and continuing relationship with and responsibility to the Indian people through the establishment of a meaningful transition from Federal domination of programs for and services to Indians

179

to effective and meaningful participation by the Indian people in the planning, conduct, and administration of those programs and services.[5]

As the federal government's primary agent of Indian affairs, the BIA was automatically affected by the 1975 federal policy change. Its formal role of "governor" of Indians was reduced, at best (in BIA eyes), to "diplomat" or, perhaps, "advisor" or, even, to "servant." Indeed, Public Law 93-638 mandated the BIA to enter "upon the request of any Indian tribe into a contract or contracts with any tribal organization of any such tribe to plan, conduct and administer [tribal government programs and functions]."[6] Not only was the formal goal of the BIA altered but the agency was given specific directions to alter administrative processes.

BIA Reactions

Organizations as Interest Groups

To best understand the BIA response to the government's mandate for change, it is necessary to view the agency as an interest group in a conflict situation. Service organizations rarely are content to stand ready to be called by the population they serve. Once created, a service organization becomes an interest group. Like that of any interest group, its primary goal is self-preservation, and, beyond this, enhancement of its present position. As Eizenstadt notes, "from the very beginning a bureaucratic organization is put in what may be called a power situation, in which it has to cast its influence and to generate processes of power on its own behalf and in which it is under pressure from different centers of power in the society that would control it."[7] To survive and to gain strength, the organization must constantly adjust its goals, structure, and interests. These adjustments are most often reactive, but also are often anticipatory.

Examples of such interest group self-preservation and

self-service abound. Having conquered polio, for example, the March of Dimes avoided extinction by extending its sphere of interest to other childhood diseases.[8] The Pentagon spends millions simply to convince the Congress and the public of threats to U.S. military security rather than waiting, as the ideal-type service organization might, for the Congress to perceive a problem and call for military services. Similarly, Becker has described the role of the Treasury Department's Bureau of Narcotics in the passage of the Marijuana Tax Act.[9] In an effort to stamp out use of the drug, the Bureau enlisted the support of powerful interest organizations and the press to sway public opinion regarding marijuana and to convince Congress to enact prohibitive legislation. The Bureau acted, in Becker's terms, as both rule creator and rule enforcer and, in so doing, extended both its influence and its mandate.

Strategies and Tactics

Studies of occupations and professions as interest groups provide a useful framework for analysis of the BIA response to the dilution of its official power. Manning,[10] in his study of police, and Friedson,[11] in his research on the medical profession, both suggest that occupational organizations gain and hold power through use of strategies and tactics aimed at projecting the appearance that a necessary service is being performed well by the only group that can do the job. *Strategies* refer to the general plans by which appearances are projected (e.g., a declaration of war on crime by the police), and *tactics* to the specific means by which strategies are carried out (e.g., placing police on every downtown corner).[12] For the most part, strategies of occupational organizations take the form of projection of the professional appearance, and the tactics utilized to implement the strategies generally emphasize bureaucratic efficiency and scientific technology.

History provides at least one clear example of BIA tactics designed to perpetuate control over Indians. The Indian

Reorganization Act of 1934, also known as the Howard-Wheeler Act, provided for the restoration of the status and authority of tribal governing bodies. While the act did not directly threaten BIA control of Indians, it did carry the potential for Indian-BIA tension over legal authority in certain disputes among tribal members which could ultimately lead to greater erosion of BIA control. The 1934 act called for the restoration of traditional power through adoption by referendum vote of a constitution. Yet, most tribes operated without constitutional governments and lacked the necessary skills to develop constitutions. This inexperience, together with a lack of legal assistance, opened the door to a BIA strategy of projecting an image of professional expertise. The specific tactic to implement this strategy was the BIA's preparation of a "model" constitution. It was this model which was adopted almost verbatim by all tribes organizing under the Indian Reorganization Act. Hence, the BIA was able to retain and increase its power through a new line of legitimation of its services as unique and necessary.[13]

The BIA and Public Law 93-638

The above examples facilitate understanding of the BIA's response to the dilution of its formal power by Public Law 93-638 in 1975. While mandated to support Indian self-determination, the BIA still maintained a number of responsibilities as a trustee of Indian affairs. The trustee role afforded the BIA the opportunity to make its presence felt in Indian affairs and, though less formally, to maintain roughly the same degree of sovereignty over Indians as it held prior to the passage of Public Law 93-638. More to the point, the BIA has retained its powerful position through increased bureaucratization, a tactic relatively unnecessary prior to Public Law 93-638. During the past seven years, the BIA has maintained and increased its dominance over Indians through 1) a planning orientation suited more to its bureaucratic needs than to tribal needs, and 2) the conversion of tribes themselves to a bureaucratic planning orientation. As the bureaucratic "ideology" has been increasingly legitimated, traditional tribal approaches to problems and their solution have been similarly delegitimated. Traditional tribal social structure has therefore suffered. In the following section of this paper, we focus on a major illustration of increasing BIA bureaucratization.

An Illustration: Criminal Justice Planning on the Reservation

Responding to what it and many tribes perceived as a major crime and delinquency problem on Indian reservations, the BIA—through its Division of Law Enforcement Services (DLES)—devised its Reservation Law Enforcement Improvement Plan. DLES, responsible for direct and indirect law enforcement services on reservations, introduced its plan in 1977 as an aid to the attainment of Indian self-determination, stating as its aim the provision of "planning resources and assistance to your reservation to help you, your planning committees, your council, and the community identify your law enforcement problems and needs."[14]

The Reservation Law Enforcement Improvement Plan entailed the compilation and reporting of information required in two planning documents described as "Guidebooks." *Guidebook I* required reservation planners to "analyze conditions of the past five years, particularly crime incidence, and to estimate what they think would happen in the future."[15] *Guidebook II* required planners to project solutions, based on data obtained through *Guidebook I* instructions, "in the form of specific programs five years into the future."[16] Together, the Guidebooks "will comprise the law enforcement plan for the reservation for several years to come. The plan should serve as a blueprint for directing future funding requests, source allocations and policy decisions."[17]

Despite formal statements to the contrary, the DLES plan functions both to maintain and to fortify federal dominance of Indians. It does so indirectly through flaws in the management and administration of the plan.

Design Limitations

The DLES plan suffers from a number of problems common to many criminal justice system plans. First, little leeway is granted the tribe in defining its problems. The "significant" crimes to be addressed are pre-identified and predefined and reflect the simple adoption of the FBI's *Uniform Crime Reports* definition and priority system.[18] Second, assessment of the reservation crime problem relies on official enforcement statistics. There is abundant evidence that such statistics carry reliability and validity problems in the nonreservation setting.[19] Their usefulness in the reservation setting is yet more questionable.[20] Most observers feel that Indians traditionally do not report victimizations to outside law enforcement agencies and that Indian criminal justice policy has been spotty and records-keeping minimal (the very reason for the DLES plan in the first place). Finally, the plan calls for DLES to act as the primary agency in setting and implementing enforcement policy on the reservation. Thus, tribes are faced with plans based on DLES-generated statistics, which probably do not reflect community crime problems, and must live with DLES policies which may reflect DLES bureaucratic needs more than community needs.

Management and Administration Tactics

While the basic design of the Reservation Law Enforcement Improvement Plan represents indirect suppression of tribal self-determination, certain tactics employed by DLES in implementing the plan suggest more direct suppression. First, tribes were faced with time controls. They were given little opportunity to consider or to voice opinions concerning the efficacy of the plan. Time to complete the planning process was negligible. DLES allowed tribes in the Phoenix area only two months to complete *Guidebook II* requirements, for example. Some tribes entered into contracts with the BIA to complete their Guidebooks and thus were faced with contractual obligations to complete the documents by a specified date. Recent oversight reports filed by the U.S. General Accounting Office indicate that the BIA commonly imposes severe and disadvantageous time constraints on tribes.[21]

Second, DLES placed heavy financial restrictions on tribes' efforts to complete the Guidebooks. Tribes thus were forced to limit the scope of the data they could collect to determine the nature and extent of their crime problems. So limited, they were channeled further into relying on DLES definitions of crime and DLES-generated official crime data. The same economic limitations constrained production of imaginative solutions to perceived crime problems.

Third, tribes were denied information necessary for sound program planning. Exhibiting a trait for which the BIA has recently drawn criticism, DLES provided tribes with inadequate crime data.[22] Crime statistics were so poor that some tribes appeared to have no crime problem though they were nonetheless required to develop crime control plans.[23] Tribes received little information regarding available resources for planning and funding. Instead they received volumes of relatively useless information about "policing," such as catalogs of police equipment. Most problematic, tribes were not given indicators regarding the potential adoption of their plans by DLES. Though the plans were to be individually tailored for tribes through cooperation with DLES, the BIA was under no obligation to follow the dictates of the plan, in some ways making the entire planning process a mere formality.

In sum, it is important to relate the nature of the dilemma encountered by reservation planners. They were faced with the highly complex task of identifying and addressing crime control needs based upon methodologically questionable data with tremendous time constraints, few resources of their own choosing, and little assurance that their efforts would influence policy. It must be remembered, as well, that the entire process was to be accomplished by untrained, part-time "committees." The result was a forced reliance on the BIA for technical assistance and movement back into the mainstream of the BIA system.

Bureaucratic Ethos

The management and administrative tactics described above are neither new to the BIA-Indian relationship nor do they represent the more severe negative influence on tribal sovereignty. Tactics are situation-specific, and lack of strong resistance to those presently described may be viewed by some tribes as preferable to an escalation of BIA-Indian tensions. More constant and more culturally disabling to Indian culture are the BIA's bureaucratic structure and consciousness. It can well be argued that the BIA has forced Indians to seek out reservation problems through bureaucratic means and to attempt solutions through bureaucratic structure. As this occurs, tribes change from less to more predictable and more manageable by the BIA system. As Turk suggests, greater reliance on legalism "promotes adherence to the ground rules of conventional politics" and reinforces the status quo.[24]

Structurally, bureaucracy has four distinctive features: a highly specialized division of labor, a hierarchical authority structure, written rules, and impersonal relations between bureaucracy and workers and between workers. None of these features coincides with traditional Indian governing and problem-solving cultural patterns. BIA labor segmentation and segmented interaction with tribes counters traditional Indian holistic world views by removing problems from the cultural environment in which they are implicated. While Indians traditionally utilize consensus decision-making processes within tribal and kinship groups,[25] the BIA uses and encourages hierarchical authority arrangements by which "top-down" decision making occurs. A reliance on abstract written rules is predicated on the assumption that behavior can be effectively controlled by them. Contrasted with this is the traditional tribal mode of governance based upon concepts of communal property, consensus norms, and oral history. Informal social controls rather than formal legal systems predominate. Finally, bureaucratic impersonal detachment engenders equal treatment of all persons within the bureaucracy in accordance with written rules which codify abstract "rights." Contrasted with this, again, is the communalism of traditional tribal culture in which relationships are governed by the ties of family and tribe, and rights are considered only within the context of social interaction.

Bureaucratic consciousness is more subtle and more significant in the BIA exercise of control over Indians. Such consciousness represents a cognitive style, a manner of organizing and manipulating knowledge. It "presupposes general and autonomous organizability. In principle everything is organizable in bureaucratic terms. Because of its abstract formality, bureaucracy is applicable in principle to just about any human phenomenon . . . Organization can be set up autonomously, that is, as following no logic but its own."[26]

Organizing reality according to the dictates of bureaucratic consciousness involves categorizing human experience according to a system of formalized, abstract rules. All experience is quantifiably organizable. For example, a "crime problem" is bureaucratically knowable in terms of statistics and charts. Human behavior is more effectively governed by adherence to a body of abstract rules and rights. Crime control therefore is to be accomplished by making abstract rules more explicit and by increasing sanctions for deviance.

Traditional Indian cultures adhere to "logic of interaction contexts" rather than to more formalistic, abstract logic which characterizes bureaucracy. Human actions are governed in accordance with social norms which provide "limits" for behavior. These limits are not formally, bureaucratically fixed but instead emanate from the immediate experience of social interaction.[27] While bureaucratic consciousness is future-oriented and emphasizes the individual within a competitive setting, traditional Indian culture highlights the present, the group, and cooperation. The very concept of "planning"—the ability to predict and influence behavior—is a bureaucratic construct which contrasts with the traditional, dialectic Indian approach to social phenomena.

It becomes clear, then, that control of one group by another hinges not only on the responses of the group aspiring to dominate situations which threaten its position but, more importantly, on the extent to which the would-be power can instill its world view on the less powerful.

Through the design and management of the "Planning for the Improvement of Indian Criminal Justice Services on Reservations" program, the controls inherent in bureaucratic structures, and the limitations imposed by bureaucratic consciousness, the Bureau of Indian Affairs has acted to the detriment of tribal self-determination. Little evidence exists that the "plans" developed as the result of the planning program represent the crime control problems and needs of Indian communities. It is suggested that such plans more appropriately address the needs of the BIA. Further, the present planning program functions to legitimate bureaucratic structure and consciousness and, conversely, delegitimate traditional tribal social institutions. In the present situation, crime—a social problem—is to be remedied according to formalistic, rational mechanisms (laws, sanctions, enforcement). Traditional forms of social control cannot be accommodated by bureaucratic consciousness (i.e., cannot be monitored or evaluated) and, therefore, are granted no authority. As a result, traditional tribal social structure is further eroded to the point that self-determination becomes an academic issue.

The Potential For Compromise

While we have focused on BIA actions throughout this paper, it is less our intention to take sides in this traditional dispute than to outline its dynamics. Indeed, it is our opinion that neither side will succeed in gaining its way with the other. The BIA will always meet opposition from its "clients." Indians will not be rid of the BIA and will not be able to halt inevitable cultural changes. It seems wise, then, to seek some middle ground which affords Indians greater control over the speed and manner in which their culture changes without threatening the BIA's self-perceived needs. To illustrate this possibility, we offer the following general criminal justice planning proposal for reservations.

Tribal Involvement

The basic goal of a criminal justice program for a reservation must be involvement of the tribe both in the definition of the crime problem and in the implementation of the plan. As we have seen in previous pages, this goal has been kept barely in sight. Beyond this, the criminal justice plan must recognize both formal and informal deterrents to crime. That is, the traditional formal social control response to crime, i.e., law enforcement,[28] must be complemented by programs designed to take advantage of informal forms of social control already extant within tribes. Precisely which types of informal social control will be emphasized depend upon tribal culture, definition of the crime problem, and the degree to which tribes wish to involve themselves in crime prevention. We note also that there is currently considerable emphasis in the field of criminology on crime deterrence through informal social control.[29] Most such criminological theories center on the relative strengths of individuals' attachments to conventional persons, commitments to conventional goals and lines of activity, and belief in the validity of societal norms.[30] Given the traditional strength of Indian cultures and the still largely homogeneous nature of tribes, this theoretical orientation seems especially suited to the problem at hand.

Crime Data

The reservation criminal justice plan begins by seeking better information for planning than is now feasible through traditional reliance on law enforcement agencies. We suggest a household victimization survey of tribal members. Entire populations of smaller tribes and random samples of larger tribes can be interviewed. The technology for victimization studies is currently highly refined and easily adaptable to the reservation setting.[31] While having problems of its own,[32] a crime-counting method which actively seeks information from members about crimes committed against them is considered superior to a passive system which waits for members to report crimes.

In addition to the victimization survey, we suggest a self-reported criminality and delinquency survey of tribal youth, probably between the ages of twelve and twenty years. Again the technology for such surveys is well developed and easily adaptable to reservation settings.[33] Given proper administration procedures and respondent anonymity, self-report studies produce surprisingly reliable results.[34] These results will aid in identifying the types and amounts of crime committed by youth, as well as providing information about which types of youth commit which types of crime.

Finally, we suggest a survey of tribal members concerning their attitudes and fears about crime on the reservation, ideas about crime control priorities, and notions about tolerable levels for various types of crime. This survey can be conducted separately or in conjunction with the victimization survey.

In sum, the above suggestions would produce extremely high-quality data on which to base policy. Tribes would know much about their "crime problem" and their members' ideas about that problem. The potential for BIA participation in and satisfaction with this data-gathering process is great. Funding should come through the BIA. The BIA can contract for the researchers needed to conduct the surveys. Probably most important, the process is bureaucratic in nature, providing data which represent the crime problem and which are gathered systematically. These data will form the basis for criminal justice planning and constitute baseline data for future evaluation of programs arising from the plan.

Planning

Once data have been collected, criminal justice planning can proceed. In line with the desire for greater tribal involvement in this process, we suggest the organization of a tribal crime control committee. The committee should consist of about eight members and should represent the tribal council, the tribal laity, and the BIA. Committee members should be oriented toward the underlying themes of this proposal and should probably draw at least nominal salaries for their work. Reporting directly to the tribal council (which deals with the BIA), the committee's tasks are analysis of researcher reports on tribal crime data and the major tribal concerns and translation of the research information into planning priorities.

We note here that all aspects of its crime problem need not be addressed simultaneously on a reservation. This is as unrealistic a goal as it is in the larger Anglo society. Indeed, a realistic number of types of crimes to gain attention should be arrived at and adhered to and should be based on information on tribal members' concerns.

Whether and to what extent crime control plans include both formal and informal social control mechanisms will depend on the priorities established by crime control committees. Clearly, some forms of crime (e.g., rape) will call for a concerted law enforcement effort. Others may rely on informal control mechanisms. For example, theft and vandalism—major problems on most reservations—may best be combatted through strengthening ties between youth and conventional persons whose respect might be lost through criminal behavior, or by the strengthening of the socialization process which impresses youngsters with normative values. In line again with previous efforts to involve tribal members in the crime control process, receptivity surveys might be conducted to determine the extent to which programs are acceptable to the members.

Implementation

Perhaps more than at any other phase of the criminal justice planning process, the BIA must be involved in coordination of efforts to implement programs. Programs will not run themselves. Funding must be found and technical expertise brought in. As stated above, this is precisely the role chosen by the BIA in its DLES *Guidebooks.*

Evaluation

Too often, program evaluation represents an afterthought. That is, after a program has run for a time, someone suggests evaluating it. In many cases, this proves impossible because the data necessary for true evaluation are irretrievable or nonexistent. We suggest that evaluation strategies be included in the planning stages so that all persons involved in the program will know what evaluation will entail.[35] We cannot overemphasize the need for participation in the evaluation by the crime control committee. To divorce the committee from evaluation is to discourage tribal participation in the crime control process.

We feel that an approach to criminal justice planning like that suggested above will at once offer tribes some semblance of self-determination and the BIA some semblance of self-preservation. Nothing in our general plan counters the letter or the spirit of the DLES *Guidebooks.* Our plan is open-ended, allowing for modifications and changes of direction as new data are analyzed. The plan not only allows but actually requires tribal participation. While it is bureaucratic in nature, it does not represent the imposition of outside bureaucracy on tribes.

Conclusion

This paper has detailed a conflict between reservation Indians and the Bureau of Indian Affairs. The BIA has been characterized as an interest group whose foremost goal is preservation of its dominant position regarding Indian tribes. The powerful status of the BIA has been threatened in recent years through legislation which provides tribes with greater participatory power in matters of tribal interest and mandates that the BIA work to facilitate Indian participation in their own affairs. The BIA response to its mandate has taken the forms of a program-planning orientation which forces tribes to refer most decisions to the BIA and the perpetuation of a bureaucratic ethos among tribes which serves to compartmentalize tribal problems to the point that tribal members desire no active role in their solution. The delegation of solution tasks to the bureaucracy of the BIA both perpetuates BIA dominance and works against preservation of traditional Indian culture and social structure. These general points are well illustrated in a description of BIA criminal justice planning on the reservation.

Through the example of a recommended general plan for reservation crime control, we have argued that, given certain facts of life regarding BIA-Indian relations, the conflicting positions of both parties may be made considerably more compatible. Critics will surely respond that we have fallen into the social problems–social planning "trap" which preaches solutions through research and technology. To some extent, this is correct. Yet, we have no illusions that crime on the reservation or BIA-Indian tensions will be solved fully by our plan. Rather, we feel that, given the facts that the BIA will remain a powerful agency and that Indian culture will indeed change, our criminal justice plan (and similar plans for other reservation problems) offers some satisfaction to both parties. Within a traditional BIA orientation, Indians are given maximal input into reservation planning. They can, in fact, define their own social problems and monitor their proposed solutions.

On the face of it, we do not see the plan as "selling out" to the BIA or as abandonment of resistance to BIA violence to traditional Indian culture. We feel that some cultural erosion will inevitably occur and that our plan gives tribes a degree of determination of the speed, direction, and impact of the erosion. In our view, the BIA will not suffer by this arrangement. However, it is clear that if the agency perceives a loss through such plans, the plans can be easily undermined in the same manner as have previous plans. We realize, as well, that if enthusiasm for such plans cannot be stirred among tribal members, perhaps it is too late to expect any gains in the area of self-determination.

NOTES

1. C.F. Wilkinson and J.M. Volkman, "Judicial Review of Indian Treaty Abrogation: 'As Long as Water Flows or Grass Grows Upon the Earth'—How Long a Time Is That?" *California Law Review* 63 (1975): 601-61.

2. Snyder Act of 1921, 42 Stat. 208, 25 USC 13, Nov. 2, 1921.

3. E. Cahn, (ed.) *Our Brother's Keeper: The Indian in White America* (New York: New American Library, 1969) 5, 10, 13.

4. R. Nixon, Message from the President of the United States Transmitting Recommendations for Indian Policy. H.R. Doc. No. 363, 91st Cong., 2d Sess. 1 (1970).

5. Pub. L. 93-638, 93rd Congress, S. 1017, January 4 1975 (25 U.S.C. 450): 1.

6. Pub. L. 93-638, 4.

7. S.N. Eizenstadt, "Bureaucracy, Bureaucratization, and Debureaucratization." *Administrative Science Quarterly* 4 (1960): 306.

8. H.S. Becker, *The Outsiders* (New York: Free Press, 1963) 153.

9. Becker, *The Outsiders:* 135-46.

10. P.K. Manning, "The Police: Mandate, Strategies, and Appearances." Pp. 149-193 in J.D. Douglas, (ed.). *Crime and Justice in American Society.* (Indianapolis: Bobbs-Merril, 1971).

11. E. Friedson, *The Profession of Medicine.* New York: Dodd, Mead, 1973.

12. Manning, *The Police,* 16.

13. American Indian Lawyer Training Program, *Indian Self-Determination and the Tribal Courts.* 1977:23.

14. E.F. Suarez, Sr., Chief, Division of Law Enforcement Services, Bureau of Indian Affairs. Memorandum introducing the Reservation Law Enforcement Improvement Plan documents of tribes, 1977.

15. Bureau of Indian Affairs, Division of Law Enforcement Services, *Planning for the Improvement of Indian Criminal Justice Services on Reservations, Guidebook I,* (Washington, D.C.: U.S. Government Printing Office, 1977): I-1.

16. Bureau of Indian Affairs, Division of Law Enforcement Services, *Planning for the Improvement of Indian Criminal Justice Services on Reservations, Guidebook II* (Washington, D.C.: U.S. Government Printing Office, 1977) I-1.

17. Bureau of Indian Affairs, *Guidebook II:* i.

18. Of chief concern are what are known as FBI Index Offenses:

homicide, rape, robbery, aggravated assault, burglary, larceny, and motor vehicle theft.

19. For a summary of problems with official crime statistics, see J.F. Sheley, *Understanding Crime* (Belmont, Calif.: Wadsworth, 1979) 28-30.

20. For estimates of Indian criminal behavior, see N.S. Hayner, "Variability in the Criminal Behavior of American Indians." *American Journal of Sociology* 47 (1942): 602-13; "Juvenile Delinquency Among the Indians." *Interim Report of the Subcommittee to Investigate Juvenile Delinquency to Committee on the Judiciary,* 84th Congress 1st Sess., Washington, D.C., 1955; M.S. Minnis, "The Relationship of the Social Structure of an Indian Community to Adult and Juvenile Delinquency." *Social Forces* 41 (1963) 395-403; O. Stewart, "Questions Regarding American Indian Criminality," *Human Organization* 23 (1964): 61-66; H. Von Hentig, "The Delinquency of the American Indian, " *The Journal of Criminal Law* 36 (1945): 75-84.

21. Report of the Comptroller General of the United States, *Tribal Participation in the Bureau of Indian Affairs Budget System Should be Increased.* General Accounting Office, February 15, 1978 (CED-7F-62): 11.

22. Report of the Comptroller General of the United States, *The Indian Self-Determination Act—Many Obstacles Remain.* General Accounting Office, March 1, 1978 (HRD-78-59).

23. R.A. Nelson, K.K. Keiser, and G.J. Evans, *Supplemental Report to Guidebook II: Planning for the Improvement of Indian Criminal Justice Service on Reservations.* Washoe Tribe of Nevada and California, 1978: 1, 16-17.

24. A.T. Turk, "Law as a Weapon in Social Conflict." *Social Problems* 23 (Fall 1976): 281.

25. *Report of the American Indian Policy Review Commission Task Force No. 4 on Federal, State, and Tribal Jurisdiction* 254 (July 1976).

26. P. Berger, B. Berger, and H. Kellner, *The Homeless Mind* (New York: Vintage Books, 1974) 80.

27. For a detailed discussion on this point, see E.T. Hall, *Beyond Culture* (New York: Anchor Books, 1976).

28. Law enforcement on the reservation can involve tribal members to a far greater extent than is now the case. For a discussion of such involvement within tribes in Canada, see F.M. Starr, "Indians and the Criminal Justice System." *Canadian Journal of Criminology* 20 (July 1978): 317-23.

29. For a summary of this trend, see L.T. Empey, *American Delinquency: Its Meaning and Construction* (Homewood, Ill.: Dorsey, 1978) 228-39.

30. T. Hirschi, *Causes of Delinquency.* (Berkeley: University of California Press, 1969).

31. See, for example, U.S. Department of Justice, *Criminal Victimi-*

zation in the United States—1976. Washington, D.C. U.S. Government Printing Office, 1978.

32. J.P. Levine, "The Potential for Crime Over-reporting in Criminal Victimization Surveys." *Criminology* 14 (November 1976): 307-30.

33. See R.H. Hardt and G.E. Bodine, *Development of Self-Report Instruments in Delinquency Research.* (Syracuse: Youth Development Center, Syracuse University, 1965).

34. Sheley, *Understanding Crime,* 31.

35. See L.T. Empey, A Model for the Evaluation of Programs in Juvenile Justice (Washington, D.C., U.S. Government Printing Office, 1977).

9

The Supreme Court and Indian Water Rights

BY MARY WALLACE

For more than seventy-five years, since the holding in 1908 in *Winters* v. *United States*[1] the Supreme Court and the federal courts have consistently expanded the scope of the *Winters* doctrine, which implicitly reserved Indian water rights. Recent Supreme Court decisions indicate that the Court is now reassessing the concept of federal reserved rights, especially where federal-state conflicts are involved. The emphasis has shifted from the protection and expansion of federal reserved rights to concern over "[the] impact upon those who have obtained water rights under state law and to Congress' general policy of deference to state water law."[2]

This new sensitivity to state water law and the rights held under it has influenced some recent Supreme Court decisions. Beginning in the early 1970s, in a series of cases involving the state of Colorado, the Court repeatedly referred to a congressional policy of deference to state water law and especially to the McCarran Amendment, as the basis for its decisions to allow state courts to adjudicate federal reserved water rights. Beginning a "new era in the adjudication of water rights for Indian tribes," in these cases the court discounted long-standing traditions in Indian law and policy.[3] In 1983, again citing congressional intent and also for the sake of "efficiency," in *Arizona* vs. *San Carlos Apache Tribe*,[4] the Court held that state courts are the preferred forum in which to adjudicate Indian water rights, and it indicated that the McCarran Amendment also waived the sovereign immunity of the Indian tribes.

After first reviewing the Supreme Court's previous interpretations of the McCarran Amendment, it will be submitted herein that the Court erred in its holding in the *San Carlos* case. When viewed in the context of previous Court holdings in cases involving the adjudication of Indian rights and Indian tribal sovereignty, it is clear that the *San Carlos* case breaks a long tradition of leaving the tribes free from state jurisdiction. In addition, when the legislative history of the McCarran Amendment is analyzed, no support for the Court's position can be found. On the contrary, a number of other acts passed by Congress demonstrate a congressional policy of leaving the tribes free from state jurisdiction. Finally, Congress could not have intended to include reserved rights under the scope of the McCarran Amendment. When the Act was passed in 1952, federal reserved rights had not yet been extended to non-Indian reservations; most of the water rights held by the United States had been acquired under state law. It was not until *Federal Power Commission* v. *Oregon,* [5] in 1955, and *Arizona* v. *California,*[6] in 1963, when the Court extended the *Winters* doctrine to non-Indian federal reservations, that federal reserved rights became of such magnitude as to cause disputes with the states.

State and Federal Water Rights

From the arrival of the first settlers in the West there has been conflict over water. As Corker states: "Ever since Western water rights were first established in the mining camps of the Sierra Nevadas, it has frequently been nip and tuck whether the difference of opinion would be solved by briefs or bullets."[7] To resolve these conflicts over water use and to direct water to its "best" use, western states have allocated water under the doctrine of prior appropriation, which allows the first user of a water source to divert the water from its natural course and put it to a beneficial use. Every western state has established either an administrative or a judicial proceeding to manage conflicts arising under this system. One common method of settling disputes is a general stream adjudication in which all the water rights held on a stream are adjudicated.

As a proprietary interest of the United States, federal reserved rights and federal water rights acquired under state law are outside the scope of state jurisdiction. Until passage of the McCarran Amendment, the major obstacle to adjudication of these rights by the state courts was the sovereign immunity of the United States. Simply stated, the doctrine of sovereign immunity protects the government from suit unless it consents to be sued.[8] Only Congress can waive the immunity of the United States,[9] and the Court has ruled that statutes waiving immunity must be strictly construed.[10]

In the early 1950s, a number of disputes requiring general stream adjudication arose, including one in Senator McCarran's district in Nevada.[11] The United States could not be drawn into any of these suits without its consent, and the states either had to wait for the government to initiate the suit, or proceed with the adjudications and hope the federal government did not contest the result. Then, in 1952 the McCarran Amendment allowed a limited waiver of sovereign immunity in the area of water rights litigation. In part, the amendment provides:

(a) Consent is hereby given to join the United States as a defendant in any suit (1) for the adjudication of rights to the use of water of a river system or other source, or (2) for the administration of such rights, where it appears that the United States is a necessary party to such suit. The United States, when a party to any such suit, shall (1) be deemed to have waived any right to plead that the State laws are inapplicable or that the United States is not amenable thereto by reason of its sovereignty, and (2) shall be subject to the judgments, orders, and decrees of the court having jurisdiction, and may obtain review thereof, in the same manner, and to the same extent as a private individual under like circumstances . . . .[12]

Thus, the McCarran Amendment allowed state courts to adjudicate federal water rights acquired under state law. There is, however, no mention of reserved rights or Indian water rights in the amendment.

The Supreme Court has greatly expanded the scope of the amendment, and in its latest interpretation, in *San Carlos,* the Court held that Congress intended to include Indian water rights under the scope of the amendment. In this interpretation, the Court holds that "it [the amendment] commands the federal court to defer to state court water rights proceedings, even when Indian water rights are involved."[13] More specifically, the Court also holds that the waiver of sovereign immunity by the United States includes the tribes and that "water rights suits brought by Indians and seeking adjudication only of Indian rights" are also within the scope of the McCarran Amendment.[14]

Supreme Court Interpretations of the McCarran Amendment

Supporters and critics alike concede that the McCarran Amendment is a "poorly drafted law, full of ambiguities and conflicts."[15] These ambiguities have enabled the states to use the amendment to try to bring all federal water rights, including reserved rights, into the state courts. After the Court's decision in *Arizona* v. *California,* one that greatly expanded the scope of the *Winters* doctrine, the western states had a new incentive to use the amendment to their advantage. The federal government and the Indian tribes became the owners, at least on paper, of much of the water in the West. By the 1970s, with water overallocated in many basins, the unknown, but potentially large, water-right claims of the federal government and the Indian tribes began to cast a cloud over economic growth in the West. In an attempt to force the quantification of these water rights, the states, especially Colorado, began to test the limits of the McCarran Amendment.

The line of cases preceding the *San Carlos* case answered administrative questions and defined the scope of the amendment. Although in *In re Green River Drainage Area*[16] the Court ruled that the statute itself did not confer federal question jurisdiction, it was not until a series of cases in the late 1950s and early 1960s that the amendment began to be clarified. The early cases centered around one point: What kind of proceedings were included under a provision in the amendment that requires it to be an adjudication of a "river system or other source."[17] In *California v. Rank,* the Court said in part:

> There can be little doubt as to the type of suit Congress had in mind. It was not a private dispute between certain water users as to their conflicting rights to the use of waters of a stream system, rather it was the quasi-public proceeding which in the law of western waters is known as a "general adjudication" of a stream system; one in which the rights of all claimants in a system, as between themselves, are ascertained and officially stated.[18]

By holding that suits brought under the McCarran Amendment must be general and comprehensive in nature, the appeals court ruled out suits that were intended to adjudicate the water rights of the United States alone. In *Dugan v. Rank,*[19] this position was affirmed; federal claims may not be the primary focus of adjudication.

It was not until the 1970s that the question of what kind of federal water rights were included under the waiver contained in the McCarran Amendment was answered by the Court. These cases, originating in Colorado, form the basis for the Court's decision in the *San Carlos* case. They represent the beginning of a radical departure from the congressional policy underlying the amendment. Using its interpretation of the amendment as the basis for its decisions, the Court ruled that the state courts had jurisdiction over federal and Indian water rights.

In *United States v. District Court for Water Division No. 5*[20] and its companion case, *United States v. District Court for Eagle County,*[21] the Court broadened the scope of the amendment in two ways. First, in *Eagle County,* in interpreting which water rights of the federal government were included under the act, the Court held: "We deal with an all-inclusive statute concerning 'the adjudication of rights to the use of water of a river system' which in §666(a)(1) has no exceptions and which, as we read it, includes appropriative rights, riparian rights and *reserved rights*."[22] Rejecting the principle of *ejusdem generis* (of the same kind), and stressing a legislative intent of drafting an "all-inclusive" statute, the Court held that the *or otherwise* found in the phrase "where it appears that the United States is the owner of or is in the process of acquiring water rights by appropriation under state law, by purchase, by exchange, or otherwise,"[23] included the reserved water rights of the United States. The Court reaffirmed that any court decision is reviewable by the Supreme Court, but the Court must agree to hear the case and it is unlikely to review issues of fact.

In the joined cases of *Eagle County and Water Division No. 5,* the Court discarded "the extremely technical" argument of the United States that the Colorado proceedings did not meet the requirements of a general adjudication as expressed in *Dugan* v. *Rank,* and held that the Colorado supplemental proceedings did involve the "whole community of claims."[24] The Court said that adjudications by monthly proceedings were "inclusive in the totality."[25] These decisions have been interpreted by some commentators as allowing state administrative proceedings, such as the Wyoming system, to qualify under the McCarran Amendment.[26] This issue is, however, unresolved.

In two other Colorado cases decided in 1976, *United States* v. *Akin*[27] and *Colorado River Water Conservation District* v. *United States,*[28] the Court again expanded the scope of the McCarran Amendment. In these cases, relying on the legislative history of the amendment and on dicta in *Eagle County,* the Court "concluded that the state court has jurisdiction over Indian water rights under the Amendment."[29] Moreover, "bearing in mind the ubiquitous nature of Indian water rights in the Southwest," it is clear "that a construction of the Amendment excluding those rights from its coverage would enervate the Amendment's objective."[30] The Court concluded that concurrent jurisdiction existed in regard to both Indian and non-Indian water claims but gave preference to state court proceedings. The basis for this decision was not constitutional grounds nor even the amendment itself, but as Justice Brennan wrote, on a consideration of "wise judicial administration giving regard to conservation of judicial resources and comprehensive disposition of litigation."[31] In effect, the Court reversed the previous policy of allowing Indian property rights to be adjudicated only in federal courts, and did it primarily on grounds of judicial efficiency.

The San Carlos Decision

Arizona v. *San Carlos Apache Tribe*[32] and *Montana* v. *Northern Cheyenne Tribe,*[33] decided concurrently in June, 1983, are sequels to the Colorado cases. For these cases, the Court relied on the framework drawn in the Colorado cases. In fact, both the Federal District Court and the Supreme Court relied on the *Colorado River* case as the basis for their rulings. The issue, as enunciated by the Ninth Circuit Court of Appeals, was whether the "disclaimers" in the constitutions of Arizona and Montana removed Indian water rights from state court adjudication. In addition, in *San Carlos* the issue of the sovereign immunity of the Indian tribes and whether it too was waived by the McCarran Amendment was addressed. Questions of wise judicial administration were left unresolved and remanded to the lower court.

In the majority opinion, delivered by Justice Brennan, the Court said that "whatever limitation the Enabling Acts or federal policy may have originally placed on state court jurisdiction over Indian water rights, those limitations were removed by the McCarran Amendment."[34] Relying on the congressional intent behind the McCarran Amendment, the Court concluded that any other interpretation would frustrate the purpose of the amendment, which was that state courts should adjudicate all water rights.

In deciding whether the sovereign immunity of the tribes was waived by the statute, the Court first had to decide whether the tribes, bringing federal suits in their own behalf, rather than by the United States, and seeking adjudication only of their own water rights, were included under the amendment. The Indian respondents and the United States presented five arguments why this question should be answered in the negative. Among the arguments were that as reserved rights the adjudications could be decided in federal courts and later included into any comprehensive state decree; that Indian rights have traditionally been left free of state interference; and that Indian sovereignty was not waived by the McCarran Amendment.[35] The Court rejected these arguments and concluded:

> More important, all of these arguments founder on one crucial fact: If the state proceedings have jurisdiction over the Indian water rights at issue here, as appears to be the case, then concurrent federal proceedings are likely to be duplicative and wasteful, generating "additional litigation through permitting inconsistent dispositions of property."[36]

Thus, refusing to "be guided by general propositions,"[37] and relying heavily on the "policy underlying the McCarran Amendment,"[38] the Court chose to emphasize judicial efficiency and held that Indian water rights, even when suits are brought by the tribes themselves, are included under the McCarran Amendment, and that the preferred forum for adjudication is the state courts. These holdings are contrary to other Supreme Court decisions in the area of tribal sovereignty and state jurisdiction.

Tribal Sovereignty and State Jurisdiction

The Supreme Court has long recognized and defined the "peculiar relation" between the Indian tribes and the federal government.[39] In fact, it is the early interpretations of the

Constitution by Chief Justice John Marshall that form the basis of much of modern Indian law. In addition, many of the early controversies presented to the Court revolved around disputes between the federal government and the states as to which should exercise jurisdiction over the tribes. Thus, there is a formidable body of law dealing primarily with federal-state relations vis-á-vis the Indian tribes. In reviewing Indian policy throughout the last two centuries, one commentator concludes that the tribes are in a "unique position as a congressionally acknowledged and judicially confirmed third unit of government, within the nation but not included in the federal system."[40]

This is a body of law that the majority of the Court chose to ignore in the *San Carlos* decision. The Court ignored a long-standing tradition of leaving tribal property rights free from state jurisdiction. When the states have been allowed to exercise jurisdiction in Indian country, it has been by specific act of Congress. Moreover, traditionally any ambiguities have been resolved in the favor of the Indians. The Court's decision in *San Carlos* contradicts all of these policies.

The early opinions penned by Chief Justice Marshall cannot be underestimated, for not only did they provide an analytical framework for many decisions issued by the later Court, but "it is important that the Constitution was initially applied to Indian affairs by Justices in the formative years who were statesman at the time of its adoption."[41] Foremost among these early cases is *Worcester* v. *Georgia.*[42] Relying on the supremacy clause, the commerce clause, and other key provisions in the Constitution, Marshall held: "The treaties and laws of the United States contemplate the Indian territory as completely separated from that of the states; and provide that all intercourse with them shall be carried on exclusively by the government of the Union."[43] This tradition of leaving the Indian tribes free from state control, in the absence of specific congressional authorization, governed Court decisions throughout most of the twentieth century.

Although some writers will argue that "from the beginning Worcester was rejected" by the Court,[44] it is clear that the Court has long recognized the potentially hostile treatment the tribes may receive from the states. For example, in *United States* v. *Kagama,* the Court declared: "They owe no allegiance to the states, and receive from them no protection. Because of the local ill feelings, the people of the states where they are found are often their deadliest enemies."[45] Sixty years later in 1945, Justice Black concurred "The policy of leaving the Indians free from state jurisdiction and control is deeply rooted in the Nation's history."[46] The Court has also held in *Williams* v. *Lee,*[47] in 1959, and in *McClanahan* v. *Arizona Tax Commission,*[48] in 1973, that when Congress does allow state jurisdiction, it will do so expressly. Although these two cases can also be criticized as contradictory, and the Court can be accused of failing to "replace *Worcester* with any clear analytical test,"[49] some pertinent points can be drawn from them.

Without doubt, the Court has moved away from the standard enunciated in *Worcester* that Indian reservations are distinct nations within which boundaries state laws cannot intrude, to a much less rigorous standard. Some writers have argued that the Court has used different tests, such as the "infringement test" or the "preemption test," but for the purposes of this paper it is more useful to simply look at the kind of exceptions the Court has allowed. For example, in *Williams* v. *Lee,* the Court said: "Essentially, absent governing Acts of Congress, the question has always been whether the state action infringed on the right of the reservation Indians to make their own laws and be ruled by them."[50] In *Mescalero Apache Tribe* v. *Jones,* the Court held that "even on reservations, state law may be applied unless such application would interfere with reservation self-government or *would impair a right granted or reserved by federal law.* "[51] Finally, in *McClanahan* v. *Arizona Tax Commission,* although the Court ruled that tribal sovereignty will serve as a "backdrop against which the applicable treaties and federal statutes must be read" when con-

sidering whether the states have jurisdiction, it also emphasized that "Doubtful expressions are to be resolved in favor" of the Indians.[52]

As this brief review indicates, the Court has allowed some
state jurisdiction over Indian affairs but has emphasized
that it must not infringe upon the tribes' rights to govern
themselves nor upon rights reserved or granted by federal
law. In addition, the Court has indicated it will look to
federal statutes when considering grants of jurisdiction to
the states, and it reaffirmed that it must be a specific grant
from Congress and that unclear areas will be resolved in
favor of the Indians.

In *San Carlos* the majority violated all of these holdings. There was no express delegation of jurisdiction to the
states and the ambiguity was resolved in favor of the states.
Indian water rights are a right granted or reserved by federal law and a persuasive argument can be made that state
adjudication of Indian water rights substantially interferes
with the tribes' ability to govern themselves. The regulation
and control of water resources is at the core of tribal sovereignty. Instead of following these principles, the Court
created its own version of the legislative intent behind the
McCarran Amendment.

Indian Property Rights, Water Rights, and Federal Court Jurisdiction

Given that a valuable proprietary interest of the United
States is involved in the adjudication of federal reserved
rights, it is useful to review some other considerations the
Court has noted. Although in *Eagle County* the Court ruled
that the assertion of federal proprietary rights by the United
States alone did not require adjudication in federal court,
it can be argued that it is more significant when the United
States initiates the suit in federal court.[53] The Court recognized in *Akin* that "the priority of the court which first
acquires jurisdiction over the subject matter is entitled to
recognition, and where the plaintiff has selected the forum

and filed first, his right to try his case in that court is not to be lightly dismissed."[54] (The Court reversed and remanded the *San Carlos* case, though.) Moreover, one writer argues that because the United States voluntarily joined water proceedings in Colorado Water Divisions 4, 5, and 6, and initiated proceedings in federal court for Water Division 7, the home of the Ute Indian Reservation, this represents a substantial federal interest and should have remained in the federal courts.[55] The Court did not address this issue in *Akin.*

There are a number of compelling reasons why Indian reserved rights should be adjudicated in the federal courts. First, the adjudication of Indian water rights involves questions that arise under the Constitution and under statutes and treaties of the United States. Through Section 331 of Title 28 of the United States Code, Congress has conferred jurisdiction of these matters on federal courts.[56] Second, most will agree that many questions still remain under the *Winters* doctrine and the Supreme Court itself is reassessing *Winters.* These questions should be resolved in federal courts, not in state courts that have hesitated to recognize federal reserved rights. Finally, Congress specifically denied state court jurisdiction of Indian property under sections 1160 and 1162 of Title 28 of the United States Code.

Many critics of the Court question how it could ignore obvious directives from Congress and allow state court jurisdiction over Indian water rights. Earlier it was shown that the Court relied heavily on the Colorado cases, especially the *Colorado River* case, for its decision in *San Carlos.* In doing so, the Court in effect considers Indian reserved rights as primarily *federal* reserved rights, as the property of the federal government. In this assumption lies one of the Court's errors.

Others will argue that Indian water rights are of a special character.[57] Harold Ranquist states: "The United States is not the 'owner' of rights reserved for the benefit of the Indians in the same way that it is the 'owner' of water rights reserved for use on federal parks or forests held for the benefit of the general public."[58] He also adds that the tribes' right to use the water is held in trust, but that this is "equitably owned and exercised by individual Indians and Indian tribes in connection with this possession of reserved lands."[59]

Justice Stevens, in his dissent in *San Carlos,* also argues that: "Although in some respects Indian tribes' water claims are similar to other reserved federal water rights, different treatment is justified."[60] He then cites the various statutes passed by Congress and hostile state courts as justification. Citing *Moses H. Cone Memorial Hospital* v. *Mercury Construction Corp.*[61] a case decided four months earlier, he also argues that the Court has emphasized the "phantom command of the McCarran Amendment" over substantial federal questions.[62] In part, the dissent reads:

> We emphasize that our task in cases such as this is not to find some substantial reason for the *exercise* of federal jurisdiction by the district court; rather the task is to ascertain whether there exist "exceptional circumstances, the clearest of justifications" that can suffice under *Colorado River* to justify the *surrender* of that jurisdiction. Although in some rare circumstance, the presence of state-law issues may weigh in favor of that surrender . . . the presence of federal law issues must always be a major consideration against surrender.[63]

In *San Carlos,* the Court substituted the "phantom command of the McCarran Amendment" that state courts should adjudicate Indian water rights for longstanding principles of law. As will be shown, nothing in the legislative history of the amendment supports this conclusion. Because of the Court's unflagging reliance on congressional intent, it is essential to review the history of the amendment.

Legislative History of the McCarran Amendment

Given the ambiguous language of the McCarran Amendment the Court had no choice but to review the legislative history. One writer argues that in Indian law, "Where a statute on its face is ambiguous, no resort to its legislative history should be necessary."[64] The Court did not agree. This point aside, there is another good reason the Court should not have interpreted the amendment so broadly: The amendment was passed as a rider on an appropriations bill.[65] Therefore, there was no preamble that defined the intent of Congress as to the amendment. It is doubtful that Congress would give away a major proprietary interest of the United States in such a fashion. In most important pieces of legislation that deal with a major policy change, a preamble is included that specifically defines the intent of Congress. The McCarran Amendment is a clear example of judicial legislation. The Court reviewed a legislative history that is inconclusive at best and created a new federal policy.

After a careful reading of the legislative history behind the McCarran Amendment, one wonders where the Court finds support for its position that "the policy underlying the McCarran Amendment" is to allow state courts to adjudicate Indian water rights. Indeed, there is very little legislative history to examine. There is no discussion or even reference to Indian water rights or reserved rights except by inference. What legislative history there is shows that the McCarran Amendment was meant to be interpreted narrowly, not broadly, as the Court has done. One writer argues that the amendment may have been designed to correct a problem in Senator McCarran's home state of Nevada.[66] The attorney general of Nevada wrote a letter to Senator McCarran apprising him of a dispute involving an adjudication decree on the Quinn River in Nevada. The federal government had successfully contested in the Federal District Court that it had not consented to be sued and was immune from any suits. The Court agreed and the suit was dropped, leaving the dispute unresolved.[67]

The key to the Court's holding that reserved rights and Indian water rights are included under the amendment is its interpretation of the phrase "where it appears that the United States is the owner of or is in the process of acquiring water rights by appropriation under state law, by purchase, by exchange, or otherwise."[68] The Court concluded that reserved rights were intended to be covered under the phrase "or otherwise." Rejecting the principle of *ejusdem generis* that would have required the court to conclude that the " 'or otherwise' provision does not encompass the adjudication of water rights having a source in the powers over navigation and over reserved lands,"[69] the Court concluded that: "We deal with an all-inclusive statute concerning the adjudication of rights to the use of water of a river system which in § 666(a)(1) had no exceptions and which as we read it includes appropriative rights, riparian rights and reserved rights."[70]

Nothing in the legislative history supports this decision by the Court to include reserved rights in the waiver of sovereign immunity. There is only one reference in the Senate Report to the type of suit envisioned. It states: "Congress has not removed the bar of immunity even in its own courts in suits wherein water rights *acquired under State law* are drawn in question. The bill ... was introduced for the very purpose of correcting this situation and the evils growing out of such an immunity."[71] From this reading, it is clear that only rights acquired under state law would be covered by the statute. There is no mention of reserved rights.

One other reference to reserved rights can be found in a letter from the Acting Assistant Secretary of the Interior to Senator McCarran that was included in the Senate Report. In this letter, the secretary lists the interests of the United States, including reserved rights and Indian reserved rights, and suggests that the bill be clarified to include only those rights acquired under state law.[72] There was no discussion of the secretary's concerns in the report. The letter can be construed in at least two ways. One, the letter served as notice to Congress that the statute could be construed to include reserved rights and Indian water rights. Thus, by not acting to limit the waiver, Congress intended that these rights be included.[73] Two, Congress thought the bill already expressed the narrow waiver proposed by the secretary and there was no need to change the language.[74] Whatever the interpretation, it is clear that there was certainly no express delegation from Congress conferring jurisdiction of Indian water rights to the states. In fact, in response to questioning on the Senate floor, the McCarran Amendment excluded Indian water rights from a proposed cataloging of federal water rights, a provision that was later dropped from the bill.[75]

Other Acts of Congress

Since there is so little reference to Indian water rights in the legislative history of the amendment, other statutes passed by Congress that do deal specifically with Indian rights, especially Indian property rights, must be examined. Two statutes, one passed in 1953, only thirteen months after the McCarran Amendment was passed, and another passed in 1966 help determine congressional policy in regard to state jurisdiction over Indian tribes.

In 1953, Congress enacted Public Law 83-280.[76] Proposed during the "termination era," Public Law 280 was one of a number of acts that were intended to end the federal responsibility over the Indians. Although there is some dispute over whether Public Law 280 itself is a termination act or one designed to improve law and order on the reservation,[77] it is clear that the intent of Congress during this period was to terminate federal involvement in Indian affairs. In five states Public Law 280 transferred civil and criminal jurisdiction over reservation Indians and extended the law to all other states willing to assume jurisdiction. The act was later amended to require the consent of the tribes' before jurisdiction could be assumed. Of importance to this paper is the savings clause, a section that limits state jurisdiction. This provision states in part:

> Nothing in this section shall authorize the alienation, encumbrance, or taxation of any real or personal property, *including water rights,* belonging to any Indian or any Indian tribe, band, or community that is held in trust by the United States or is subject to a restriction against alienation imposed by the United States; or shall authorize regulation of the use of such property in a manner inconsistent with any Federal

treaty, agreement, or statute, or with any regulation made pursuant thereto; *or shall confer jurisdiction upon the state to adjudicate, in probate proceedings or otherwise, the ownership or right to possession of such property or any interest therein.*"[78]

Given the termination sentiment in Congress, the specific language in this section is especially significant. During hearings on Public Law 280, when asked by Congressman D'Ewart of Montana whether the bill protected Indian treaty rights and "the tribal estates," the chief counsel for the Bureau of Indian Affairs replied yes and referred D'Ewart specifically to the savings clause.[79] Unlike the McCarran Amendment, no speculation is required; there is no other way to read Public Law 280 except to say that it denies state jurisdiction over Indian water rights. At a time when many in Congress wished to throw the Indians to the wolves, this clause is evidence of a congressional intent to keep Indian water rights in the federal courts.

Another statute passed by Congress in 1966 also is a clear expression of congressional intent. It states: "The district courts shall have original jurisdiction of all civil actions, brought by an Indian tribe or band with a governing body duly recognized by the Secretary of the Interior, wherein the matter arises under the Constitution, laws, or treaties of the United States."[80] Designed to remove the $10,000 jurisdictional amount limitation, this statute demonstrates a clear congressional intent to provide Indian tribes with a federal forum, a promise that the San Carlos Tribe acted upon. As Justice Stevens notes in his dissent, the Senate Report accompanying this statute stated:

There is a great hesitancy on the part of the tribes to use State courts. This reluctance is founded partially on the traditional fear that tribes have had of the states in which their reservations are situated. Additionally, the Federal courts have more expertise in deciding questions involving treaties with the Federal government, as well as interpreting the relevant body of Federal law that has developed over the years.[81]

Recognizing the potential conflicts between federal claims and Indian claims, a situation often found in water rights, the report stated: "The proposed legislation will remedy these defects by making it possible for the Indian tribes to seek redress using their own resources and attorneys."[82] Thus, Congress assured the tribes that not only would they have a federal forum in which to air their grievances, they could also use their own attorneys. This is exactly what the San Carlos Apache Indians did in 1979, they filed suit in the Federal District Court for the District of Arizona requesting federal determination of their water rights. Section 1362 of Title 28 of the U.S. Code, especially when considered in light of Public Law 280, clearly demonstrates a congressional intent to allow Indian water rights to be adjudicated in federal court. In fact, it represents a *promise* that they have access to a federal forum, a promise that the majority of the Court chose to ignore in the *San Carlos* case.

State Courts and Indian Water Rights

There are a number of practical arguments that support the adjudication of Indian water rights in federal courts only. For example, citing the *Colorado River* case, the majority in *San Carlos* said: "Mere subjection of Indian rights to legal challenge in state court . . . would no more imperil these rights than would a suit brought by the Government in district court for their declaration. . . . Indian interests may be satisfactorily protected under regimes of state law."[83] Given the past treatment of Indians in state courts, this statement is naive.

If an address to the Rocky Mountain Mineral Law Institute's Annual Convocation, Robert Pelcyger reviewed a number of cases that had reached the Supreme Court after decisions had been rendered at the state court level. Pelcyger stated that during its last three terms, the Court has "reversed or vacated seven decisions of state courts that were adverse to Indian property or sovereign interests in which a state, or one of its agencies, sought affirmance."[84]

He also reviewed three other terms of the Court in which a number of Indian cases were decided and found that the official positions of the states were rejected in nine cases.[85] These cases include *Williams* v. *Lee,*[86] *Arizona* v. *California,*[87] and *Menominee Tribe* v. *United States.*[88] He also added that the last time a decision was reached favorable to the Indians at the state court level and subsequently reversed in the Supreme Court was in 1949 in *Oklahoma Tax Commission* v. *Texas County.*[89]

Practical considerations, as opposed to legal precedent, were important factors influencing the Court's decision in *San Carlos.* As noted earlier, the Court said, "concurrent federal proceedings are likely to be duplicative and wasteful generating 'additional litigation through permitting inconsistent dispositions of property'."[90] The Court noted "the comprehensive nature of the state proceedings" and enunciated a desire to avoid "piecemeal litigation" and provide "convenience to the parties."[91]

As Justice Stevens points out in his dissent, this may be an erroneous concept of the adjudication process. He argues:

> Since Indian reserved claims are wholly dissimilar to state-law water claims, and since their amount does not depend on the total volume of water available in the water source or on the quantity of competing claims, it will be necessary to conduct separate proceedings to determine these claims even if the adjudication takes place in state court. Subsequently, the state court will incorporate these claims—like claims under state law or federal Government claims that have been formally adjudicated in the past—into a single inclusive, binding decree for each water source.[92]

He also argues that if state courts do err, "the entire comprehensive state water rights decree may require massive re-adjustment."[93] Given Pelcyger's review, this scenario appears likely.

In its majority opinion, the Court rejects this argument as presented by the United States and the Apaches because "they assume a cooperative attitude on the part of the

215

state courts, state legislatures, and state parties which is neither legally required nor realistically always to be expected."[94] It is ironic that the Court acknowledges the lack of cooperation at the state level in this context, but not in the broader context of a proper forum initially. As Justice Stevens states: "If state courts cannot be expected to adhere to orderly processes of decision making because of their hostility to the Indians, the statutory right accorded to the Indian tribes is even more important."[95]

On a final note, the Supreme Court has repeatedly recognized that water, especially in the West, is one of a state's most important resources. In many cases, state judges are elected and remain very conscious of the viewpoints of those instrumental in the judge's elections. These interests are often contradictory to the interests of the Indian tribes. As one tribal attorney says:

> It's like going to your banker to act as judge to find out whether you owe the bank a note. I mean, after all they're dealing with state assets and they're preserving state assets and they have State law and the Indians don't fall within that jurisdiction. . . . I'm not saying judges aren't fair. A lot of them are, but they are somewhat, whether they like it or not, biased, and they do have a certain amount of political pressure and other pressures to bear upon them. I just don't think the Indians can get a fair trial in state courts dealing with major state issues. The state's a party on one side and the Indians are a party on the other side and the state is the judge.[96]

Conclusion

The Court committed a number of errors in its decision in the *San Carlos* case. Only by ignoring long-standing principles of Indian law and by ignoring or misinterpreting congressional intent could the Court rule that state courts are the preferred forum for the adjudication of Indian water rights. Nothing in the legislative history supports this conclusion, and two other laws—Public Law 280 and Section

1362 of Title 28 of the United States Code—directly contradict this holding. The Court took two words, *or otherwise,* and a fictionalized legislative intent and held that reserved rights and Indian water rights were included under the waiver of sovereign immunity found in the McCarran Amendment.

Coming at a time when many Indian tribes are debating between litigating or negotiating their water rights, this case will undoubtedly force some tribes to try to influence the legislative branch. It is a fact that many tribes are unwilling to litigate their water rights in the state courts. As a result, the *Winters* doctrine takes on a new meaning. Instead of being an unenforceable court doctrine, it becomes a source of power for Indian tribes. Because the assertion of *Winters* rights by Indian tribes can act as a cloud over economic growth in the West, the filing of a well-researched lawsuit can be a powerful resource before the case reaches the courtroom; it can bring the non-Indian water users to the bargaining table.[97] Attempting to influence Congress requires different resources than are required for the courtroom and Indian tribes are at a disadvantage because they lack the traditional political resources. Thus the tribes will have to develop a new strategy to retain their rights to water.

NOTES

1. 207 U.S. 564 (1908) (water rights reserved by implication when the reservations were created). See Shrago, *Emerging Indian Water Rights: An Analysis of Recent Judicial and Legislative Developments,* 26 ROCKY MOUNTAIN MIN. L. Inst. 1107 (1980).

2. United States v. New Mexico, 438 U.S. 696, 718 (1978).

3. 66 Stat. 560, ch. 651, § 208a-c, codified at 43 U.S.C. § 666 (1970) [hereinafter cited as McCarran Amendment]; Elizabeth McCallister, "The McCarren Amendment and Indian Tribes' Reserved Water Rights," in 4 *American Indian Law Review* (1936) 303.

4. Arizona v. San Carlos Apache Tribe, 103 S. Ct. 3201 (1983), revd. and remanded.

5. 349 U.S. 435 (1955).

6. 373 U.S. 546 (1963).

7. Corker, *Water Rights and Federalism—The Western Water Rights Settlement Bill of 1957,* 45 CALIF. L. REV. 604 (1957).

8. R. CLARKE, WATER AND WATER RIGHTS. 6 vols. (Indiana: The Allen Smith Co., 1967), vol. 2 at p. 87.

9. Dalehite v. United States, 346 U.S. 15 (1935).

10. McMahon v. United States, 342 U.S. 25, 27 (1951).

11. Comment, *Adjudication of Water Rights Claimed by the United States—Application of Common-Law Remedies and the McCarran Amendment of 1952,* 48 CALIF. L. REV. 94 (1960).

12. McCarran Amendment, *supra* note 3.

13. Arizona v. San Carlos Apache Tribe, 103 S. Ct. 3201, 3217 (1983) (Stevens, J., dissenting).

14. *Id.* at 3215.

15. CLARKE, *supra* note 8, at 97.

16. 147 F. Supp. 127 (D. Utah 1956).

17. McCarran Amendment, *supra* note 3.

18. California v. Rank, 293 F.2d 340, 347 (9th Cir. 1961).

19. 372 U.S. 609 (1963).

20. 401 U.S. 527 (1971).

21. 401 U.S. 520 (1971).

22. *Id.* at 524 (emphasis added).

23. McCarran Amendment, *supra* note 3.

24. United States v. District Court for Eagle County, 401 U.S. 520, 525-26 (1971); United States v. District Court for Water Div. No. 5, 401 U.S. 527 (1971).

25. United States v. District Court for Water Div. No. 5, 401 U.S. 527 (1971).

26. See Frank Trelease, "Federal-State Relation in Water Law," prepared for the National Water Commission, Legal Study No. 5: Comment, *Determination of Federal Water Rights Pursuant to the McCarran Amendment: General Adjudications in Wyoming,* 12 LAND & WATER L. REV. 457 (1977).

27. 504 F.2d 115 (10th Cir. 1974).

28. 424 U.S. 800 (1976).

29. *Id.* at 809.

30. *Id.* at 811.

31. *Id.* at 817 (Brennan, J.), *citing* Kerotest Mfg. Co. v. C-O-Two Fire Equip. Co., 342 U.S. 180, 183 (1952).

32. Arizona v. San Carlos Apache Tribe, 103 S. Ct. 3201 (1983).

33. Decided with *San Carlos* case, 103 S. Ct. 3201 (1983).

34. Arizona v. San Carlos Apache Tribe, 103 S. Ct. 3201, 3212 (1983).

35. *Id.* at 3213.

36. *Id.* at 3214, *citing* Colorado River Water Conservation Dist. v. United States, 424 U.S. 800, 819 (1976).

37. *Id.* at 3216.

38. *Id.* at 3215, *citing* Colorado River Water Conservation Dist. v. United States, 424 U.S. at 820 (1976).

39. Cherokee Nation v. Georgia, 30 U.S. (5 Pet.) 1, 17 (1831).

40. Comment, *The Indian Battle for Self-Determination,* 58 CALIF. L. REV. 445, 487 (1970).

41. Veeder, *Indian Prior and Paramount Rights Versus State Rights,* 51 N.D. L. REV. 107, 112 (1974).

42. 31 U.S. (6 Pet.) 515 (1832).

43. *Id.* at 556.

44. Martone, *American Indian Tribal Self-Government in the Federal System: An Inherent Right or Congressional License,* 51 Notre Dame Lawyer 600 (April, 1976).

45. 118 U.S. 383 (1886).

46. Rice v. Olson, 324 U.S. 786 (1945).

47. 358 U.S. 217 (1959).

48. 411 U.S. 164 (1973).

49. Clinton, *State Power Over Indian Reservation: A Critical Comment on Burger Court Doctrine,* 26 S.D. L. REV. 434, 439 (1981).

50. 358 U.S. 217, 219 (1959).

51. Mescalero Apache Tribe v. Jones, 411 U.S. 148 (1973) (emphasis added).

52. McClanahan v. Arizona Tax Comm'n, 411 U.S. 164, 174 (1973), *citing* Carpenter v. Shaw, 280 U.S. 363 (1930).

53. Comment, *Adjudication of Indian and Federal Water Rights in the Federal Courts,* 46 COLO. L. REV. 555 (1975).

54. United States v. Akin, 504 F.2d 115, 121 (10th Cir. 1974).

55. Comment, *supra* note 53, at 572.

56. 28 U.S.C. § 331 (1970).

57. Veeder, *supra* note 41, at 198.

58. Ranquist, *The Winters Doctrine and How it Grew: Federal Reservation of Rights to the Use of Water,* 1975 BRIGHAM YOUNG U. L. REV. 639, 698.

59. *Id.* at 698.

60. Arizona v. San Carlos Apache Tribe, 103 S. Ct. 3201, 3218 (1983).

61. 103 S. Ct. 927 (1983).

62. Arizona v. San Carlos Apache Tribe, 103 S. Ct. 3201, 3221 (1983).

63. *Id* at 3220, *citing Mercury Construction Co.*

64. Ranquist, *supra* note 58, at 707.

65. McCarran Amendment, *supra* note 3.

66. Comment, *supra* note 11.

67. *Id.* at 104.

68. McCarran Amendment, *supra* note 3.

69. Comment, *supra* note 11, at 94.

70. United States v. District Court for Eagle County, 401 U.S. 520 (1971).

71. S. REP. No. 755, 82d Cong., 1st Sess. 5-6 (1951) (emphasis added).

72. *Id.* at 8.

73. Comment, *supra* note 53, at 577.

74. Comment, *supra* note 11, at 112.

75. 97 CONG. REC. 12948 (1951).

76. Act. of Aug. 15, 1953, 67 Stat. 588, 25 U.S.C. § 1360b.

77. Comment, *State Jurisdiction Over Indian Land Use: An Interpretation of the "Encumbrance" Savings Clause of Public Law 280,* 9 LAND & WATER L. REV. 421, 427 (1974).

78. Pub. L. 83-280, 67 Stat. 588, 25 U.S.C. § 1360b (emphasis added).

79. See Goldberg, *Public Law 280: The Limits of State Jurisdiction Over Reservation Indians,* 22 U.C.L.A. L. REV. 535 (1975).

80. 28 U.S.C. § 1362 (1970).

81. S. REP. No. 1507, 89th Cong., 2d Sess. 2 (1966).

82. *Id.*

83. Arizona v. San Carlos Apache Tribe, 103 S. Ct. 3201, 3205 (1983), *citing* Colorado River Water Conservation Dist. v. United States, 424 U.S. 800, 819 (1976).

84. Pelcyger, *Indian Water Rights: Some Emerging Frontiers,* 21 ROCKY MOUNTAIN MIN. L. INST. 743, 745 (1975).

85. *Id.* at 746.

86. 358 U.S. 217 (1954).

87. 373 U.S. 546 (1963).

88. 391 U.S. 404 (1968).

89. 336 U.S. 342 (1949).

90. Arizona v. San Carlos Apache Tribe, 103 S. Ct. 3201, 3214 (1983), *citing* Colorado River Water Conservation Dist. v. United States, 424 U.S. 800, 819 (1976).

91. *Id.* at 3215.

92. *Id.* at 3217-18.

93. *Id.* at 3220.

94. *Id.* at 3214.

95. *Id.* at 3220.

96. William Strickland, Papago Tribal Attorney, at Arizona Groundwater Comm'n Meeting, January 5, 1978, at pp. 10-11.

97. Mary Wallace, "Papago Participation in the Formulation of the Southern Arizona Water Rights Settlement Act" (Master's thesis, University of Arizona, 1984).

10

Indians and the First Amendment

BY JOHN PETOSKEY

Since the late 1970s a new issue in First Amendment law has confronted the federal judiciary. American Indians are increasingly making claims to the protection of the First Amendment for their religious practices in opposition to the decisions of federal land managers.

Although the First Amendment prevents governmental interference with the free exercise of religion, this protection has been substantially denied by the United States government in regard to Indian religions based on specific sites. This denial is based not so much on any improper application of Supreme Court First Amendment principles and analysis, although it is that; rather, the denial is rooted in a religious ethnocentrism that permeates the legal relationship between the United States and Indian societies whereby the courts are judging Indian religious claims by standards developed for Judeo-Christian religions.

The relationship between Indian societies and the United States has been one of continuing conflict. Since the Indian tribes unquestionably lost the physical conflict, at no small cost to the United States, the present fight continues in other realms of tribal beliefs. A principal issue confronting the federal courts in this continuing conflict has been the application of First Amendment free exercise analysis to the Indians' collective right of access for religious practices to lands under federal jurisdiction when those lands are subject to competing land-use policies.

Because of the wide variety of Indian tribal societies, traditions, and religious perceptions, it is almost impossible to arrive at a level of generalization about Indian societies comparable to the level of generalization possible when describing non-Indian societies. The non-Indian religious tradition in the United States is largely Judeo-Christian, and certainly in the development of American constitutional law the standard of reference for legal issues involving religion has been Judeo-Christian. To hear a court quote from the Koran, the Bagavagita, or the Tao is not a common experience for the law student or the practicing attorney yet, to hear the same court refer to the Bible or to Jewish tradition is part of the rhetoric of American law. It was, of course, problems of religious interpretation that motivated the Founding Fathers to include the First Amendment's well-known language on religion: "Congress shall make no law respecting an establishment of religion, or prohibiting the free exercise thereof. . . ."

The provision was written to govern the sometimes tumultuous relationships between Judeo-Christian religions and secular governments. The religious clauses, Free Exercise and Establishment, are in a dynamic relationship that is constantly developing to meet the changing needs of a pluralistic society. In general, both clauses are a bar to governmental action when that action either threatens the free exercise of religion or entangles the government in the establishment of a religion.

An establishment clause analysis generally includes the following elements: The particular governmental action must be of secular purpose with a principal effect that neither advances nor inhibits religion nor causes excessive government entanglement with religion. The free exercise clause prohibits governmental burdens, direct or indirect, on the practice of religion. There is an absolute right to believe; however, the regulation of practices or conduct is permissible when the government can show a compelling state interest in the regulation that burdens the free exercise practice of religion.

First Amendment issues addressed by courts have generally been within the mainstream of Judeo-Christian religions, and the principal cases that have established the standards for a valid free exercise claim have been derived from religions within that tradition. As a consequence, the courts have had to rely on traditions not apposite to the asserted free exercise claims by Indians when determining whether a valid free exercise claim has been presented.

For purposes of Indian claims of access to federal public lands for the practice of religion, the important cases are the free exercise standards of *Wisconsin* v. *Yoder*[1] and *Sherbert* v. *Verner*[2] since the principal Indian decisions relied on these cases in deciding whether to protect Indian free exercise interests.

Yoder is the Court's bench mark for claims of free exercise impairment. A group of Amish citizens sought exemptions from prosecution under Wisconsin statutes that required school attendance for their children until age sixteen. Because of the Amish belief that integration into the religious community is only accomplished by vocational training on the farm and in the home, they refused to send their children beyond the eighth grade. The Supreme Court exempted the Amish from prosecution under the statute on the basis that mandatory high school attendance interfered with the Amish's ability to practice their religion. In addition, the state failed to show a compelling interest in requiring the two years of additional education.

Under *Yoder*'s analysis, a free exercise claim must first prove that the government has burdened important religious interests. Once this is established, the burden of proof shifts to the government to show "[that] there is a state interest of sufficient magnitude to override the interests claiming protection."[3] The balancing test set out in *Yoder* weighs the severity of religious impairment against the importance of the state's policies.

Sherbert was decided ten years before *Yoder* and is crucial to a free exercise analysis. *Sherbert* held that states may not impose indirect burdens on religious practices unless a compelling state interest justifies the state activity. In *Sherbert* a Seventh-day Adventist challenged the statute that denied her employment benefits because she refused to accept available work. Plaintiff's observance of a Saturday Sabbath caused her to be fired from a job and prevented her from accepting another job. Plaintiff claimed that withholding of statutory benefits was unconstitutional because it forced her to choose between the precepts of her religion and the benefits of the unemployment program. Although the Court did not address whether the state had a sufficient and compelling interest, the Court agreed that plaintiff's unavailability for Saturday work was motivated by her religious conviction. The remedy proffered by the Court was either to confer the direct benefit to the plainiff or to abandon completely the unemployment benefits program. *Sherbert* establishes the proposition that the First Amendment requires the government to refrain from acting unless it affirmatively protects religious practices.

The holding that direct and indirect religious burdens will be balanced against the governmental interest is the proper test to apply to Indian access claims. Although both *Yoder* and *Sherbert* conceded the government may burden religious practices to serve an important governmental interest, the decisions required the courts to scrutinize government programs before permitting such religious impairment. In proving the importance of its interest, the government must do more than assert a general need to effectuate important policy. It must make a particularized showing that the accommodation of the religious practice would specifically harm the state's interest.

Sherbert and *Yoder* also required the government to prove that in order to implement its policy that would burden religion, a no less restrictive or intrusive means is available to implement the policy. *Sherbert* stated that in order to justify the burden of plaintiff's religion, the state would have to be required "to demonstrate that no alternative forms or regulations would combat abuses without infringing First Amendment rights."[4] *Yoder* incorporated this standard when addressing the state's interest in educating Amish children.

Recent Federal Cases of Indian Access Claims

Traditional Indian religious sites are still located within this country. For historical and political reasons, virtually all of those sites are located on land controlled by the federal government. Thus, the federal government's insensitivity to Indian religious beliefs has an especially high First Amendment cost because there is no alternative place of worship for many Indian religious practices.

A number of recent lower federal court decisions may have hastened the demise of Indian religions. For example, the Cherokee in *Sequoyah* v. *TVA*,[5] the Navajo in *Badoni* v. *Higginson*,[6] the Cheyenne and Lakota in *Fools Crow* v. *Gullet*,[7] the Inupiat in *Inupiat Community* v. *United States*,[8] and the Navajo and Hopi in *Wilson* v. *Block*,[9] all lost in their efforts to protect religious sites under federal ownership. The only decision finding that the actions of the federal public land manager were proscribed by the free exercise clause is *Northwest Indian Cemetery Protective Association* v. *Peterson*.[10]

The rationales for the above decisions have not been consistent. Although other courts have favorably and intelligibly addressed the First Amendment rights of individual Indians for specific practices,[11] the issue of collective Indian rights to religious expression have been almost consistently denied when the expression of the right has conflicted with other federal policies.

Sequoyah, Badoni, Fools Crow, Inupiat, and *Wilson* all have a common factual base. In all cases, Indians were asserting a collective right of access for specific religious practices on land under the control of various federal agencies. The Indians predicated their claims of access on the free exercise clause of the First Amendment. The federal land manager made an adverse decision that directly or indirectly burdened the specific practice of the alleged collective right to practice religious ceremonies on federal land.

In *Sequoyah* the Tennessee Valley Authority flooded sacred Cherokee sites, in *Badoni* the Glen Canyon Dam flooded Rainbow Bridge and made it possible to have a floating marina bar for tourists in the vicinity of Rainbow Bridge National Monument, thereby destroying the atmosphere necessary for conducting Navajo ceremonies. In *Fools Crow* the state of South Dakota made a tourist attraction out of Bear Butte, thereby destroying the pristine quality of the site that was necessary for Lakota and Cheyenne ceremonies. In *Inupiat* the development of off-shore oil in the Arctic has impaired the conducting of ceremonies. In *Wilson* the development of a ski resort has inhibited ceremonies performed by Navajo and Hopi religious practitioners. A detailed analysis of the cases will point out some problems with the courts' interpretations of the free exercise claim asserted by Indians.

In *Sequoyah*, Cherokees brought suit to enjoin the completion of a dam on the grounds that if completed the dam would flood "sacred homelands" and destroy sites of cultural and medicinal importance. The court of appeals upheld the district court's grant of summary judgment on the basis that the Cherokee failed to demonstrate the centrality of land to be flooded to the practice of their religion. In *Fools Crow*, Lakota and Cheyennes alleged that the construction of roads and parking lots disturbed the natural features of Bear Butte, a site of tremendous religious significance to Indians, located in the Black Hills. The Indian plaintiffs also asserted that the state had failed to control tourist behavior that interfered with plaintiffs' religious practices on Bear Butte and that the state's attempted regulation of Indian campers visiting Bear Butte for religious purposes similarly interfered with the religious practices of Indians. The district court's grant of defendant's motion for summary judgment was grounded on a finding that the construction did not burden plaintiffs' religious practices but instead actually facilitated them by improving Indian access to Bear Butte. The court also made a finding that occasional "misbehavior" by tourists did not impair the religious practice of Indian vision seekers.

In *Badoni* the court directly addressed the kind of governmental burden that would be sufficient to override a free exercise claim. The court found that the Lake Powell Reservoir was "a crucial part of a multistate water storage and power generation project" and that no less restricted means of serving that interest existed. In addition, the court also found that the state had a strong interest in assuring public access to a natural wonder. Of particular interest is that the court intimated that the American Indian Religious Freedom Act[12] may be unconstitutional. Language in the *Badoni* decision suggests that if the act had been before the court on a constitutionality claim, the court would have found the act unconstitutional.[13] If this had indeed been the situation, it would have been the first time in the history of federal legislation that an act passed by Congress, under its plenary power over the Indians, to be found unconstitutional.

In *Inupiat*, the federal district court did not address the claim by the Inupiats of religious impairment because there was an insufficient factual base in the record. The Inupiats had made general allegations that off-shore oil development inhibited their ceremonial use of ice floes and that the continual development would stop certain religious practices. Since the Inupiat did not submit specific evidence in the record, however, the court found that there was no burden.

In *Wilson*, Indian plaintiffs of the Navajo and Hopi tribes sought to enjoin the development of a ski facility known as the Arizona Snow Bowl in the San Francisco Peaks located in the Coconino National Forest. Defendants in this case were private parties who had received a land-use permit from the Forest Service to develop a ski resort on 777 acres of land. The Indian plaintiffs alleged that the development of a ski resort would impair specific religious practices performed in the Snow Bowl area and that medicinal herbs found only in that area would also be destroyed. The Indian tribes also claimed that deities inhabited the peaks and that development would harm the deities. In finding that the Indians had not submitted a free exercise claim, the court held that in order to show a free exercise claim the Indians would have to prove that the religious practices would absolutely be prevented rather than impaired or indirectly burdened. The court stated that the initial burden of proof is upon the plaintiffs to demonstrate that the governmental action burdens their practices of religion and that one element of the burden of proof for plaintiffs would be a showing that no alternative site is available for the practice.

As practitioners of Indian religions continue to seek protection for their beliefs and practices, the inconsistent legal analysis that is being applied to Indian religious claims is becoming more apparent. In two cases, *Fools Crow* and *Wilson*, plaintiffs had sought discretionary review by the U.S. Supreme Court for the 1983 term. Unfortunately, review was not granted and therefore the future course of collective access claims by Indians is still largely uncertain. Substantial basis had existed for the granting of review. The following principal points had been raised in the briefs of attorneys representing the tribes upon which review was urged. Because the issues were not addressed in a definitive manner by the U.S. Supreme Court, the presently pending cases, such as *Northwest*, or, future cases, will probably address similar issues.

The Decisions in the Lower Courts are in Conflict

The Sixth, the Eighth, and the Tenth circuits are in conflict. The Sixth Circuit Court of Appeals focused its attention upon the nature of the religious beliefs and practices which would be affected by the federal action. *Sequoyah* held that to warrant protection, "worship at the particular geographic location" must be "inseparable from a way of life," "the cornerstone of religious observance," or "play a central role in religious ceremonies."[14] There is no basis for a secular court to assume the responsibility of making such theological determinations.

228

The Tenth Circuit in *Badoni* held that a compelling governmental interest maintaining the capacity of Lake Powell for interstate water needs outweighed the religious interest and that any governmental accommodation of Indian religious practices at Rainbow Bridge would be a violation of the establishment clause.

In *Fools Crow* the Eighth Circuit affirmed the decision of the district court, which held that the development of Bear Butte was not in violation of the free exercise clause because recreation was a compelling state interest that outweighed the burden on the practice of Indian religion and that governmental accommodation of Indian religious practices would violate the establishment clause.

The District of Columbia appellate court in *Wilson* held that in order to trigger the free exercise analysis the religious practices of Indians would have to be absolutely *prevented* and that since it was still possible for Indian religious practitioners to perform the ceremonies despite the presence of skiers, the protections of the free exercise clause were therefore not available to the Indians.

The first two federal district courts considering collective access claims to federal public land took a different approach. They focused on the government's property interest, concluding that the free exercise clause could never supersede the government's rights as landowner.[15] In both instances the court of appeal rejected this analysis on the basis that "[t]he government must manage its property in a manner that does not offend the Constitution."[16] The *Wilson* court has resurrected that argument by distinguishing the only relevant non-Indian decision on the basis of land ownership. In *Pillar of Fire* v. *Denver Urban Renewal Authority,*[17] the court held that members of a church threatened with destruction as part of an urban renewal project were entitled to a hearing at which their interests could be weighed against those of the Urban Renewal Authority. "[R]eligious faith and tradition," said the court, "can invest certain structures and land sites with significance which deserves First Amendment protection."[18] The court of appeals in *Wilson* held that its opinion did not conflict with *Pillar of Fire* because "a governmental taking of privately-owned religious property . . . involves different considerations than does a claimed First Amendment right to restrict the government's use of its own land."[19]

Court of Appeal Rulings in Fools Crow *and* Wilson *Are Inconsistent with First Amendment Principles*

The holding in *Wilson* was unless government *prevents* religious practices, it does not burden religious practice. Attorneys for the Navajos argue that the court of appeals failed to apply the proper free exercise analysis to Hopi and Navajo claims and that the actions of the Forest Service burden their free exercise of religion. In *Bob Jones University* v. *United States* the Supreme Court restated the free exercise analysis in the following manner:

> This Court has long held the Free Exercise Clause of the First Amendment an absolute prohibition against governmental regulation of religious beliefs, *Wisconsin* v. *Yoder, Sherbert* v. *Verner, Cantwell* v. *Connecticut,* . . . [Citations omitted]. As interpreted by this Court, moreover, the Free Exercise Clause provides substantial protection for lawful conduct grounded in religious belief, see *Wisconsin* v. *Yoder, supra, Thomas* v. *Review Board of the Indiana Emp. Security Div.,* [Citation omitted.] However, "[n]ot all burdens on religion are unconstitutional. . . . The state may justify a limitation on religious liberty by showing that it is essential to accomplish an overriding governmental interest." *United States* v. *Lee* [Citation omitted]. See, e.g., *McDaniel* v. *Paty, Wisconsin* v. *Yoder, supra, Gillette* v. *United States* [Citations omitted].[20]

The *Wilson* decision required Indian religious adherents to show that the practice of their religions would be absolutely prevented not burdened by the development of the recreational use before that court would even apply the First Amendment balancing test. *Wilson* also held that the

Indians must show that the proposed government action *"penalized* Plaintiffs for their beliefs."[21]

The attorneys for the Navajo and Hopi argue that the lower courts did not properly apply the First Amendment analysis. The tests applied in the lower courts imposed a greater burden of proof on adherents of Indian religions to show that their free exercise is burdened than is imposed on any other religion making a similar claim.

Decisions Permit National Park Service and State Parks to Continue to Discriminate Against Traditional Indian Religions

The attorneys for the Navajo and the Hopi are arguing that the Federal Government discriminates among religions in a manner that encourages Judeo-Christian faiths to have religious facilities or activities on federal lands, but which prohibits adherents of minority traditional Indian religions from practicing their religions on those same lands. The National Park Service has put aside over a hundred separate locations for Christian worship,[22] yet the Forest Service claims in the *Wilson* case that the need for more ski resorts in Arizona makes it impossible to accommodate the Navajo and Hopi need for their religious sites. Whether characterized as a violation of the equal protection principles incorporated in the due process clause of the Fifth Amendment,[23] or as a violation of the First Amendment, this federal action constitutes invidious discrimination on the basis of religion, race, and culture.

There is no doubt that the First and Fifth Amendments protect Indians as a class.[24] The United States has never argued that the beliefs of the practitioners are other than sincerely held religious beliefs, and neither the United States nor the *Wilson* court suggested that the Navajo or Hopi traditional religious practices are "so bizarre, or so non-religious in motivation, as not be entitled to protection under the Free Exercise Clause."[25] Thus, these religious beliefs *are* entitled to the full measure of protection afforded to Judeo-Christian religions.

The attorneys for the Navajo and Hopis also argue that the federal government effectively prohibits Indian religious practices and beliefs on federal lands and promotes the practices and beliefs of more established religions. Any government program that has the effect of discrimination among religious faiths "must be invalidated unless it is justified by a compelling governmental interest,[26] and unless it is closely fitted to further that interest."[27] No party has even suggested that the operation of a ski resort could meet this test.

The Navajo attorneys argue that the federal government should not be permitted to discriminate among religious faiths on federal public lands. To urge and facilitate the development of Judeo-Christian religions on national public lands, while at the same time destroying Indian religions on the same lands, constitutes invidious racial, religious, and cultural discrimination by the federal government. The government can not show a compelling governmental interest to justify this discrimination.

A Holding in Favor of Petitioners Would Not Create a Veto Power Over Federal Land Use by Religious Adherents

The history of federal Indian policy in the United States has been characterized by dramatic shifts in perspective. At one time the official policy of the United States was to assimilate Indians into the mainstream of society. A central part of this policy was the suppression of Indian religions. It is well documented that in the nineteenth century the United States government allocated various Indian tribes to specific religious sects to indoctrinate the tribes into the mainstream of non-Indian society. In accordance with this federal policy, anything associated with Indian religions was ruthlessly suppressed.

Early federal land managers received their policy guidance from the general temper of the times and, as a matter of course, prohibited Indian access to sacred sites. A new era of Indian administration was instituted by Commissioner of Indian Affairs John Collier in the 1930s and, despite the ups and downs of the last fifty years of federal Indian policy, no one would seriously contend that the policies of religious suppression should be reinstituted. In accordance with the renewed policy of supporting Indian cultures, the American Indian Religious Freedom Act was passed in 1978 to remedy and to alleviate past practices that suppressed Indian religions.

The act became effective August 11, 1978. Section 1 reads:

> [H]enceforth it shall be the policy of the United States to protect and preserve for American Indians their inherent right of freedom to believe, express, and exercise the traditional religions of the American Indian, Eskimo, Aleut, and Native Hawaiians, including but not limited to access to sites, use and possession of sacred objects, and the freedom to worship through ceremonies and traditional rites.

The legislative history of the Act is clear in finding that religion is an intrinsic part of Indian culture.

Under the authority of Section 2 of the act a Task Force prepared a report documenting areas of conflict and procedural changes necessary to effectuate the policies of the act. The American Indian Religious Freedom Act Report identified problems of Indian religious access in twenty states that affected more than forty tribes. The kinds of access problems that were to be presented to federal agencies and to federal courts are certainly manageable, and it is unlikely that a new host of access problems will arise in the future.

Implied in the *Sequoyah, Badoni, Fools Crow,* and *Inupiat* holdings is that Indian religious adherents would have a veto power to all federal land use. The courts may believe the implied argument that a dying religion of a tiny minority seeking a permanent, open-ended religious easement on all federal property would effectively control federal use and enjoyment of public lands, but this fear is largely unwarranted. Although Indian cultures and religions have been diminished, they certainly are not dying and they are adapting to changing circumstances. After centuries of official federal policy designed to destroy their cultures and religions, Indian societies are renewing their efforts to sustain themselves. The task force identified all potential religious access claims and no further claims are likely to arise.

All of the Indian plaintiffs in the above cases alleged violations of the American Indian Religious Freedom Act by federal officials as part of their claim for relief. Unfortunately, the act does not confer a private right of action. The direction of the act is simply agency review of existing policies. In that sense, the act is a paper tiger and the *Wilson* court so held. The court quoted language from the legislative history in which Congressman Udall stated that the act has no teeth and that it was simply a resolution stating the intent of Congress. Although this may be true, the point of the act is a shift in federal policy. This shift is one from destroying Indian cultures to sustaining them, and to the extent that the act supports sustaining Indian cultures, the courts should take it into consideration when addressing First Amendment claims of Indians. The reports pursuant to the act clearly established that a "parade of horribles" is not going to come forth as a result of allowing Indians access to federal land areas.

Finally, the briefs of the Navajo, Hopi, Lakota, and Cheyenne petitioners seeking review are addressing the question of the only case that upheld Indian free exercise claims. *Northwest Indian Cemetery Protective Association* v. *Peterson*,[28] held that the development of a logging road in northern California was impermissible because it burdened the free exercise of religion by three small tribes in the area. The court distinguished all prior decisions in the following manner. The court found *Sequoyah* not applicable because the plaintiffs in *Northwest Indian Cemetery* asserted that the area was central to their practice of religion. The court found *Wilson* inappropriate for the same reason. *Fools Crow* was distinguished on the basis that the Indians in that case

234

only asserted an inconvenience to their worship at Bear Butte. After finding that the religious area in *Northwest Indian Cemetery* was central and indispensable to the Indians' religious practices, the court then went on to determine which state interest was being urged as compelling to override the free exercise claim. The state interest interest included economic and recreational development. The court held that these interests were not sufficient to override the free exercise claims of the three tribes involved.

The tribes in *Northwest Indian Cemetery* were essentially claiming the same type of free exercise claim as the Navajo, Hopi, Inupiat, Cheyenne, and Lakota were claiming. The fundamental basis that all of these tribes are claiming is a *pristine environment* as a prerequisite to the successful practicing of their religion. Their argument is that resource development destroys the pristine environment and thereby directly and indirectly burdens the free exercise of Indian religions. *Northwest Indian Cemetery* was the only case that upheld the right of Indians to practice religion in a pristine natural environment.

The defendants in this case suggested that a reasonable accommodation could be made with the Indians' religious interest by establishing a protective radius of one-half mile around sites where Indians conducted ceremonies. The court rejected this proposed accommodation by saying that a pristine environment was a fundamental prerequisite for the successful free exercise of Indian religious interests. The court also held that accommodation of Indian religious interests was not in violation of the establishment clause and that the lack of excessive governmental entanglement precluded a finding of any establishment clause violation.

Conclusion

The Indian religions are entitled to the same protection under the First Amendment as any other religion or belief. The distinctions that must be drawn, however, is that in determining the scope of rights to which Indian religions are entitled, standards must be developed that are relevant to the nature of those beliefs and not based on the different beliefs, needs, and concerns of totally different religions. Judeo-Christian religions have been the primary standard of reference for the development of tests under the free exercise clause of the First Amendment. These tests have been developed in relation to economic interests. For example, *Sherbert* turned on the question of whether the person was to receive unemployment benefits. *Yoder* turned on the kind of economic integration into a community.

A fundamental misconception exists when an economic analysis is applied to Indian religious aspirations. The collective Indian access claims discussed all required a pristine environment. In our resource-starved times any pristine environment is becoming more difficult to find. Resource development, whether for recreational interests or for interstate water needs, is in opposition to Indian religious interests in an undisturbed environment in which to conduct the proper ceremonial activity. If the courts will recognize that tests evolved from Judeo-Christian religions are not applicable to Indian religions, then manageable standards can be developed to fully accord free exercise rights to Indian religions.

The courts appear to fear an implied veto power, through Indian religious site easements, on all federal actions that may conflict with religious claims asserted by Indians. This implied veto power is not likely to be asserted in the future simply because not that many religious access claims exist. The American Indian Religious Freedom Act Report listed approximately twenty states and forty tribes that are affected by access issues. Not all the access issues require a pristine environment. Certain tribes can make reasoned accommodations with other land uses. Yet, because of the nature of most Indian religions, which generally is a seeking for a personal revelation or vision, a suitable environment for such activities is almost mandatory. This is not to say that denial of Indian claims is going to cause all Indian religions to fade from their societies, it is only to say that

236

reasonable accommodations should be made for free exercise claims by Indian tribes and that the courts should not use standards developed by cases that address economic interests. Rather the courts should look at the prerequisite of practice the need of a pristine environment that characterizes Indian religious practices.

NOTES

1. 406 U.S. 205 (1972).
2. 374 U.S. 389 (1963).
3. Wisconsin v. Yoder, 406 U.S. 205, 214 (1972).
4. Sherbert v. Verner, 374 U.S. 389, 407 (1963).
5. 620 F.2d 1159 (6th Cir.), *cert. denied*, 449 U.S. 953 (1980).
6. 638 F.2d 172 (10th Cir. 1980), *cert. denied*, 452 U.S. 954 (1981).
7. 541 F.Supp. 785 (D.S.D. 1982).
8. 548 F.Supp. 182 (D. Alaska 1982).
9. 708 F.2d 735 (D.C. Cir. 1983).
10. 565 F.Supp. 586 (N.D. Cal. 1983).
11. People v. Woody, 61 Cal. 2d. 716, 394 P.2d 813, 40 Cal. Rptr. 69 (1964) (the ceremonial use of peyote); Frank v. Alaska, 604 P.2d 1068 (Alaska 1979) (the ceremonial use of moose meat); Teterud v. Burnes, 522 F.2d 357 (8th Cir. 1975) (ceremonial use of long hair); Peyote Way Church of God v. Smith, 556 F. Supp. 632 (N.D. Tex. 1983) (upholding the Indian exemption for criminal prosecution for the possession of peyote).
12. Pub. L. No. 95-341, 92 Stat. 469, codified at 42 U.S.C. §1996.
13. Badoni v. Higginson, 638 F.2d 172, 180 (10th Cir. 1980), *cert. denied*, 452 U.S. 954 (1981).
14. Sequoyah v. TVA, 620 F.2d 1159, 1164 (6th Cir.), *cert. denied*, 449 U.S. 953 (1980).
15. Sequoyah v. TVA, 480 F. Supp. 608 (E.D. Tenn. 1979); Badoni v. Higginson, 455 F.Supp. 641 (D. Utah 1977).
16. Badoni v. Higgison, 638 F.2d 172, 176 (10th Cir. 1980), *citing* Sequoyah v. TVA, 620 F.2d 1159, 1164 (6th Cir.), *cert. denied*, 449 U.S. 953 (1980).
17. 181 Colo. 411, 509 P.2d 1250 (1973).
18. *Id.* at 419, 509 P.2d.
19. Wilson v. Block, 708 F.2d 735, 742, n.3 (D.C. Cir. 1983).
20. Bob Jones Univ. v. United States, 103 S.Ct. 2017, 2034-35 (1983).
21. Wilson v. Block, 708 F.2d 735, 744 (D.C. Cir. 1983).
22. Among these locations are such famous churches as the Christ (Old North) Church, Boston, Massachusetts; Gloria Dei (Old Swedes)

Church in Philadelphia, Pennsylvania. The National Park Service also maintains and operates churches at scores of national parks. Some of the more notable examples are the shrine of the Ages Chapel, Grand Canyon National Parks and the Yellowstone National Park Chapel.

23. *See* Bolling v. Sharpe, 347 U.S. 497 (1954).

24. *See* Morton v. Mancari, 417 U.S. 535 (1974).

25. Thomas v. Review Bd. of Indiana Employment Security Div., 450 U.S. 707, 715 (1981).

26. *Cf.* Widmar v. Vincent, 454 U.S. 263, 267-70 (1980).

27. Larson v. Valente, 456 U.S. 228, 247 (1982), *citing* Murdock v. Pennsylvania, 319 U.S. 105, 116-17 (1943).

28. 565 F.Supp. 586 (N.D. Cal. 1983).

11

The Evolution of Federal Indian Policy Making

VINE DELORIA, JR.

The federal-Indian relationship, as Chief Justice John Marshall commented, is like no other in the world. Indian tribes are denominated "domestic dependent nations," but their practical relationship with the United States "resembles that of a ward to his guardian."[1] Indian tribes appear to have the same political status as the independent states of San Marino, Monaco, and Liechtenstein, yet they have little real self-government and seem to be forever mired in a state of political and economic pupilage. One benefit of this pupilage is that Indians receive a wide and sometimes bewildering variety of social services that the smaller European states—and other American racial and ethnic minorities—do not receive from their relationship with larger governments. The Indian tribal status is therefore of dubious blessing, conferring some benefits but exacting a tremendous price in self-esteem and independence. Making sense of this confused state has taxed the best minds in American jurisprudence and left them perplexed. Inevitably many scholars turn to the field of policy formulation with the hope of discovering a conceptual framework in which the status of Indians makes sense and justifies the twists and turns of American history.

Underlying the study of Indian policy is the assumption that the fundamental doctrines of federal Indian law are consistent with each other. This belief originated in the early days of contact when European nations attempted to justify their invasion of the Western Hemisphere by adhering to the tenets of the doctrine of discovery. Promulgated in its basic form in 1493 by Pope Alexander IV in two bulls, *Inter Caetera,* which granted Spain all lands not under a Christian prince, and *Inter Caetera II,* which set a demarcation line at one hundred leagues west of the Azores and the Cape Verde Islands, beyond which all future discoveries of land not held by a Christian prince on Christmas, 1492, would belong to Spain. Prolonged theological debate by Spanish theologians, who sought to place a moral basis under Spanish exploitation of the New World, and acceptance of Catholic doctrine by other European nations eager to lay claim to western lands produced a consensus that conceived the natives of the New World as childish creatures in need of the civilizing benefits of Christianity and European commerce.

The United States laid claim to Great Britain's rights and responsibilities in protecting American Indians following the Revolution and, although hardly a discoverer in the traditional sense, the United States adopted the doctrine of discovery as its basic theoretical framework within which its political relationship with Indians was understood. One of John Marshall's earliest decisions, *Johnson* v. *McIntosh,*[2] used the American claim to the doctrine of discovery rights to void previous land patents issued while the Illinois area was under French rule. The principle was established in American domestic law that the Indians owned the equitable title to their lands subject only to the superior title exercised by the discoverer, or his successor, in this instance the successfully independent United States. Relying on the *Johnson* v. *McIntosh* theory and the commerce clause of the Constitution, the executive branch negotiated treaties with Indian tribes as a function of its responsibility under international law. Indian treaties were kept with other American treaties by the State Department. The Department of War dealt with Indians on the frontier and feted visiting Indian dignitaries in a manner officials of foreign countries might expect. The purveyor of supplies, a staff member of the Treasury Department, kept the Indian accounts, and some of the earliest treaties pledged mutual aid in case of hostilities or required passports of American citizens wishing to visit the Indian lands. The post-Revolution political context visualized Indians as semi-independent nations; the Supreme Court provided the theoretical framework in which this interpretation made sense.

Had Indians been able to maintain themselves apart from whites, had they continued their traditional customs and practices without adopting the ways of the whites, the executive branch of the federal government might have continued to deal with them as quasi-independent nations. Before the Revolution had been brought to a successful close, however, there was substantial evidence that Indians living on the frontiers of the colonies had made significant changes in their way of living, preparing themselves for even closer accommodation to the ways of the whites. The Five Civilized Tribes of the Deep South and the Miamis of the Wabash and Illinois country already had a strong mixed-blood leadership that desired the best of the two diverse worlds. The Iroquois had flirted with Catholicism and were in the process of transforming their longhouse villages into settlements resembling the English and French outposts. Most of all, the desperate need of the Indians for manufactured trade goods, such as iron kettles, steel hatchets, gunpowder, and firearms, in exchange for furs and land cessions made it evident that Congress would have to devote considerably more energy to protecting Indians from themselves than in restricting the activities of American citizens who were intruding on the Indian lands in the western country.

Early congressional activity in Indian policy began with a series of appropriation acts for the civilization of the Indians in the last decade of the eighteenth century.[3] There also was an increasing demand for preemption laws to give good title to settlers squatting on Indian lands. This was the beginning of a conflict of interest between congressional concern for internal domestic development of the

241

United States and the trust relationship with the Indians that Marshall would create and articulate in his *Cherokee* decisions. Congress reached back to colonial times and brought forward the old demarcation line announced in the Proclamation of 1763 and modernized it, drawing now a series of mythological lines between "Indian country" and the established settlements of the American frontier. Indian country had to be largely fictional because of the migratory ways of the Indians and the predatory habits of the whites. Its chief virtue was its relationship to older doctrines, which gave Indian country the aura of rationality and respectability.

The removal policy of 1830 represented the first instance in which a political platform became realized on the national agenda. Andrew Jackson had campaigned vigorously for western votes and represented expansionism and manifest destiny, which certainly meant difficult times for Indians if brought to fruition. The margins of victory for the removal bill in the House and Senate and the extensive debates on the morality of removal testify to the feeling in the Congress that Indian policy had momentous consequences for the future that could not be casually swept aside in the expediency of the moment. William Ellsworth of Connecticut, in the House debate, reminded Congress that:

> We must be just and faithful to our treaties. There is no occasion for collision. We shall not stand justified before the world in taking any step which shall lead to oppression. The eyes of the world, as well as of this nation, are upon us. I conjure this House not to stain the page of our history with national shame, cruelty, and perfidy.[4]

The final House vote for passage, 103 to 97, suggests that had Jackson not worked hard to obtain passage, the removal policy would not have become the dominant federal Indian policy of the nineteenth century.

More important, from the perspective of the present posture of federal policy, was the passage of the two acts of June 30, 1834, that updated the trade and intercourse provisions and gave institutional structure to the Department of Indian Affairs.[5] In the House Committee report dealing with Indian trade, the reality of the frontier situation was addressed.

> The Indians do not meet the traders on equal terms, and no doubt have much reason to complain of fraud and imposition. . . . Power is now given to refuse licenses to persons of bad character, and for a more general reason, "that it would be improper to permit such persons to reside in the Indian Country," and to revoke licenses for the same reasons.[6]

Recognizing that a new precedent was being established, the report continued:

> The committee are aware that this is granting extensive power to the agents, and which may be liable to abuse; yet, *when it is recollected that the distance from the Government at which the traders reside,* will prevent a previous consultation with the head of the department, . . . the rights of the traders will be found as well secured as is compatible with the security of the Indians.[7]

Here the Congress was attempting to realize two distinct and contradictory policy objectives: protection of the Indians and the need to have a functioning, and more important, decision-making bureaucracy for the regulation of trade. The federal government could not rely on a stable tribal society to regulate itself nor could it pretend that the Indians understood white society with sufficient clarity to protect themselves from unscrupulous people. Vesting the agents with a discretionary power to control the flow of trade, which should have been a function of the free market or of the real needs of the Indians, meant that Congress had become a surrogate for Indian decision making in the important area of cultural and economic relations with the settlers. Once this barrier had collapsed, future policy had to be shaped around the proposition that Indians could not or would not make the proper decisions respecting their best interests.

Congressional policy regarding the ultimate status of Indian tribes, nevertheless, was optimistic. The committee's comments on the criminal jurisdictional provisions of the same act show how starkly at odds the two basic policy objectives actually were. The question facing the House committee concerned the extension of federal criminal law to all persons within Indian country as defined under the Act of March 3, 1817,[8] which the committee believed to need revision and modernization. The report noted:

> It will be seen that we cannot, consistently with the provisions of some of our treaties, and of the territorial act, extend our criminal laws to offences committed by or against Indians of which the tribes have exclusive jurisdiction; and it is *rather of courtesy than of right* that we undertake to publish crimes committed in that territory by and against our own citizens. And this provision is retained principally on the ground that *it may be unsafe to trust to Indian law in the early stages of their Government.* It is not perceived that we can with any justice or propriety extend our laws to offences committed by Indians against Indians, at any place within their own limits.[9]

Presumably Congress believed that Indian tribes would develop their governmental institutions in such a manner that the future administration of justice could be safely entrusted to them, and whites living with them would perceive the justice of their system. Admitting that the United States lacked a legal basis for extending its jurisdiction inside Indian country, the committee justified its tenuous authorization of the imposition of federal law by mentioning that, at that time, the Indians did not possess a sufficiently articulated system of justice to maintain order. The vision of Indian republics performing the judicial function seems well hidden within the committee report, but it is nevertheless present.

Early statutes dealing with Indians revolved around trade and social intercourse on the frontier. With the organization of the Department of Indian Affairs in 1834 the focus shifted from economic concerns to political problems. The federal government began to seek negotiated settlements with the tribes and the majority of important treaties were signed and ratified after 1834. Two major themes emerge in these treaties—land titles and political status. Title to lands east of the Mississippi had basically been clarified in *Johnson* v. *McIntosh,* and this theory had been confirmed in a practical sense by the removal of the tribes to the West. That the removing tribes received a fee simple title to their lands in the western plains is sufficient evidence that the federal government was abiding by the theoretical framework of discovery.

The removal treaties promised that the tribes would never be enclosed within the borders of any state. The major stumbling block that had spelled disaster for the eastern Indians, state claims to civil and criminal jurisdiction, was removed with this provision. Following this format Indian affairs were relatively clear in conception. Tribes would continue to make gradual adaptations to white cultural ways and their governments would approach those of the whites in form and content. Gradually the Indians would become small republics protected by the United States and at some distant future date might be represented in the halls of Congress.

Negotiating with the Cherokees, the Creeks, and the Miamis of the East was not difficult because they had a large segment of mixed-blood leadership in their communities who saw the need for change to make themselves more acceptable to the whites. The western tribes were another matter entirely. Occupying vast tracts of land in the Great Plains and deserts over which they roamed and following a rigid warrior code that saw outsiders as fair game for their depredations, these Indians saw the sedentary life as a form of death and resisted all overtures by the government to change their ways. Most Americans believed that the West was a great desert that could support only small groups of people, certainly not civilized whites, and until the necessity of forging a transcontinental railroad, whites studiously avoided thinking about the possibility of settling the West.

The Plains Indians fought the whites with such ferocity that they became the archetypal Indians in the minds of whites. After it became apparent that extermination was not possible, a peace policy was formulated that sought a military stalemate with the western tribes until their economic base could be destroyed. The president took the initiative in formulating the peace policy, but it was Congress that authorized the formation of the Peace Commission in 1867 and insisted on appointing several members of the body. The treaties of 1867 and 1868 mark a major change of perception of the Indian problem by Congress. First, Congress looked forward to a willing acceptance of settled life by the Indians. Second, and perhaps more important, it provided for the government to educate Indian children as a special benefit.

Congress assumed without much debate that the western Indians wanted the same things that the eastern Indians had desired. The eastern Indians eagerly welcomed missionaries into their villages because they looked forward to intercourse with the whites. They already had a form of allotment in the casual assignment of tribal lands to members. They had been cautiously adopting various institutions more akin to white society than their own traditions. Thus the tribal "Land Book" of the Peace Commission treaties and the provision that for every thirty Indian children who could be induced to attend school, the government would provide a classroom and teacher, were provisions that in congressional minds gave a good bargain to the Indians for their land cessions. The western Indians, unfortunately, rejected both of these provisions out of hand and demonstrated to the federal government that they had not intended to do more than release their claims on peripheral hunting lands and lessen their warfare on neighboring tribes and traditional enemies.

The resistance of the western Indians did not escape the notice of some members of Congress. In 1871, only three years after the Peace Commission had negotiated the most important treaties in the West, a rider was placed on an appropriation act that prohibited any further treaty making with Indian tribes.[10] The significance of this prohibition in tracing the evolution of federal policy making is that it was the act of an individual congressman, taken on his own initiative, and did not provoke the heated debate of the Removal Act, although it had considerably more significance for both Indians and the national honor. Clearly the time had come to begin to include Indians within the domestic body politic, although no one was certain what form this relationship would take. That individuals could exercise congressional courtesy and introduce their own ideas into the administration of Indian affairs without so much as an inquiry on the part of their colleagues was not only an innovation but it distinguished the clearly articulated national Indian policy from the less certain and more practical needs of the federal bureaucracy.

Beginning in 1871 and continuing until 1934 a good deal of the federal trust in resolving the problems of Indian property and political status was blunted by the intrusion into the theoretical policy framework by individual congressmen who believed they had a good idea to force the Indians to conform themselves to congressional beliefs. The most important change in this period was not the General Allotment Act, which only authorized the president to conduct negotiations with the tribes for the allotment of their lands and cession of the surplus to the government for settlement, but the amendments to the Allotment Act, which shifted the theoretical base of allotment from an educative process whereby Indians could learn how to manage private property to an administrative problem in which the federal government was assumed to be the supervisor of how Indian property was to be used. Thus *Lone Wolf* v. *Hitchcock*[11] was really less about the status of Indian treaties or the power of Congress than it was a confirmation of the 1891 amendment to the Allotment Act, which empowered the Bureau of Indian Affairs to act in place of the aged, the young, and the mentally infirm Indians in the use of their property. Since the Bureau of Indian Affairs was already doing more with Indian allotments than Congress sought to do with the lands of the Kiowas and Comanches, the Supreme Court only made clear what had already become a fait accompli.

Many of the amendments attached to Indian legislation during this period reflected the need by the federal bureaucracy to shift its focus from protecting the Indians from white intrusions and, in some instances, from their fellow Indians in a deteriorating tribal social milieu, to a new mission of providing a form of trust for Indian property. Indians became an attachment to their lands rather than owners, and although the avowed policy was that of assimilation, the change in emphasis within the executive branch of the federal government meant that the vested interest of the Interior Department would always work to thwart whatever initiatives Congress might take in resolving the Indian problem. Congress and the Interior Department might work together on a piece of legislation successfully, as with the Omnibus Act of 1910,[12] but the legislation would almost always be supportive of the bureaucratic efforts to tighten Interior's control over the lives and property of Indians. Initiatives wholly derived from Congress, such as the Burke Act of 1906, which attempted to provide broad and more reasonable criteria for issuing patents in fee, were twisted to perform functions the bureaucracy wanted to do, avoiding congressional intent as much as possible.

Indians became a detached third-party observer to the process of policy formulation in every area except claims, where they had to seek special congressionally authorized entrance to the Court of Claims in order to get their complaints heard by the federal judiciary. Claims were not a part of national policy but simply a gratuitous act by a local congressman or a sympathetic senator to quiet Indian resentments. Often the Interior Department sought to block the introduction of claims bills because it felt, and rightly so, that the claim gave evidence of bureaucratic wrong-doing. Claims were not regarded as an important part of federal policy until the events of World War II made them an essential part of America's moral posture in the world.

Until the appointment of Indian Affairs Commissioner John Collier, policy formulation was fundamentally a contest between Congress and the executive branch, represented by the secretary of the interior. The department would allow certain kinds of changes to take place in the structure of Indian affairs, but it zealously protected its established prerogatives in dealing with Indian property. Every initiative that came from the Interior Department sought to enhance its power over Indians' lives and property. The 1926 hearings on tribal courts, for example, saw the Interior Department proposing that the agent perform some functions normally reserved for municipal courts with the then existing courts of Indian offenses made a part of the federal system by congressional fiat. Such a proposal, if passed into law, would have dreadfully perverted the federal judiciary without helping to resolve the problems of law and order on Indian reservations.

Collier's administration can be regarded as the high-water mark of federal bureaucratic supremacy in policy making. Although Senator Wheeler had substantially reduced the powers of self-government that Congress was willing to grant to Indian reservations when he wrote the final version of the Indian Reorganization Act, John Collier proceeded as if his original proposal had been passed intact by Congress. The number of solicitor's opinions issued during the Collier years testify to the propensity of the Bureau of Indian Affairs to make policy in the absence of congressional initiative and perhaps even without congressional knowledge and understanding. That Collier had to continually fend off Indian and congressional efforts to amend or repeal the Indian Reorganization Act, and did so successfully, demonstrates the stark reality of the New Deal's Indian policy. It was, like so many other aspects of that administration, wholly an executive operation with a recalcitrant Congress and the public acquiescing, grateful to receive some largesse from the entrenched liberal establishment.

Much has been written about the termination era and the dominant figure in the creation and promulgation of this policy is always identified as Utah's Senator Arthur Watkins, even though the modern idea of termination appears in the Hoover Commission Report on Indians as early as 1948. Too much is made, however, of the importance of termination and of Watkins, whose high profile and intemperate statements discredited his beliefs soon after he was able to get the first series of termination acts passed by Congress. More important in terms of identifying the status of American Indians in American society was the propensity of Congress to continue the wartime subsidy into the cold war years.

In 1941 the Lanham Act was passed providing for federal subsidies in lieu of property tax payments for those areas of the country in which expanded wartime federal activities might prove a burden.[13] With the realization that the Korean War was only the first shot in a long twilight of cold war, Congress in 1950 passed two additional acts that extended federal aid in construction and maintenance of schools to every school district "impacted" by federal defense activity.[14] Indian reservations were made a part of this federal activity in 1953, and succeeding amendments not only enlarged the pork barrel but placed a national agenda under the funds appropriated for Indian education, which was understood as a subfield of the larger federal presence in the country. After 1953 a substantial amount of federal assistance to Indians came not because of national concern for Indians but because Indians qualified as a part of a national problem and could not be overlooked.

If Watkins, Senator Clinton Anderson of New Mexico, and later Senator Henry Jackson of Washington really advocated separation of Indians from the federal treasury, they did not follow the bouncing ball of national domestic legislation. While they were tediously attempting to terminate a few Indian tribes, the back door to the treasury was being pried open by the Bureau of Indian Affairs and the tribal councils and a good deal of money was transferred to Indian country. The shift in perception of Indians is all-important in this instance. Indians were fading from public view as "domestic dependent" nations, but they were emerging as one of a number of deprived racial minorities who had at least a moral claim on American society. Reservations in the 1960s received massive infusions of money from the poverty programs of the Johnson administration, not because they were Indians but because they were poor. That some tribal officials regarded this financial support as fulfilling previous treaty commitments is all the more tragic because this interpretation of federal assistance gave an artificial boost to the emerging doctrine of tribal sovereignty that distorted the Indian vision of political and economic reality.

The termination policy simply evaporated in the early 1960s because not enough advocates could be found in Congress to make it an important issue. By 1958, Indians were beginning to go to the polls in increasingly larger numbers and could and would retaliate against senators and congressmen who suggested a break in the traditional federal-Indian relationship. Many persons in Congress might have wanted to sever the relationship, but it was a hazardous position to maintain at election time. More appealing was the slogan of the poverty wars—help the poor help themselves by giving them power over the local institutions that touched their lives. Indians then turned the termination policy around to become "self-determination," which, had anyone analyzed it precisely, was more potentially destructive of the traditional relationship than termination, which required all federal debts to be paid before releasing Indians from the tentacles of the national government.

Michael Harrington's famous treatise, *The Other America,* is said to have inspired Lyndon Johnson to undertake the elimination of poverty in America, but the programs of the Office of Economic Opportunity seemed strangely askew when considered in the context of Harrington's thesis. Generally the thrust of the Johnson administration programs emphasized education and training programs, not the transfer of some form of capital to the impoverished. By the late sixties the variety of training and educational opportunities were truly amazing. The Elementary and Secondary Education Act of 1965 and its succeeding amendments recognized "the special educational needs of children of low-income families and the impact that concentrations of low-income families have on the ability of local educational agencies to support adequate educational programs," which was a giant step away from both the Lanham Act and the traditional trust responsibilities of the federal government toward Indians.

The existence and the impact of low-income families could be debated, but no one could deny that the federal government had succeeded in becoming the dominant actor on the American stage. In traditional liberal fashion the identification of a needy group meant its inclusion as an eligible group when the next set of amendments was considered. Need, therefore, depended primarily upon the visibility of a group, and policy seemed to fluctuate between two poles: existing statutes could be interpreted to include needy groups, or amendments could significantly expand the scope of programs to include them. Congress often did not make clear which course of action it wanted, and the press seemed to delight in playing both ends of the political spectrum against each other. A story describing an identifiable need would often be countered by an anecdote illustrating the waste of federal tax monies on undeserving recipients.

It was in this milieu of domestic debate that Indians, through the efforts of a number of Indian organizations and individuals, made a final effort to change federal policy that affected them. President Richard Nixon, at the urging of his White House staff, delivered a ringing denunciation of termination in July, 1970, and this indication from the

White House that Indians were on the national agenda as a distinct item of concern prompted the Democratic opposition to move forward with legislation that could not have passed had a Democratic president been in office. The Indian Education Act of 1972 was the brainchild of Senator Edward Kennedy.[15] Designed to maximize Kennedy's identification with the oppressed, the act opened a Pandora's box of benefits because it failed to describe precisely the Indians who were to be the beneficiaries of an expanded federal effort in Indian education. Title IV of the act simply made school districts with a certain number of Indian students in attendance eligible for grants and subsidies. The act was hardly a law before school districts discovered a multitude of Indians attending classes where no Indians had previously been suspected. The effort to reform Indian education became a national pork barrel and the forward thrust made by Indians in the sixties collapsed from the weight of its own success.

The Indian Self-Determination and Education Act of 1975[16] fared slightly better than the Indian Education Act of 1972. Designed to allow the subcontracting of administrative functions from the Bureau of Indian Affairs to tribal governments, the implementation of the act quickly became entangled with exceptions as career bureaucrats resisted the policy of turning large areas of responsibility over to the Indians. The goal of the act was to reduce the number of federal employees substantially and allow a greater decision-making process to occur at the reservation level. Unfortunately, most of the bureaucrats involved insisted *they* had to oversee tribal decisions because of their role as trustee, and the final product of the Self-Determination Act was simply to duplicate already existing agencies and branches of the government within tribal operations and programs.

The occupation of Wounded Knee, South Dakota, in 1973 provided an opportunity for Indians to demand an accounting from the United States. Tensions between tribal councils and reservation Indians had been increasing since the halcyon days of the poverty programs. Reservation Indians saw their tribal lands and resources used by outside interests, who returned a cash income to the tribal government without significantly improving the Indians' lot. Complaints channeled through the regular administrative levels of the Interior Department were turned aside or ridiculed, leading the more militant Indians to conclude that some kind of violent protest was the only possible way to change their situation. The occupation of the little village had barely ended before Senator James Abourezk of South Dakota introduced a resolution to establish a two-year commission to investigate federal Indian policy and make recommendations for its clarification.

The American Indian Policy Review Commission conducted hearings for two years. Instead of the commission members touring the country to discover for themselves the conditions under which Indians lived, a conglomerate of surrogates, in the form of eleven task forces, wandered aimlessly, with no apparent plan for determining a set of policy priorities for Indian programs. The final report of the Abourezk Commission listed more than two hundred recommendations that were basically housekeeping measures designed to enhance certain privileges of the Indian ruling class while making tribal governments more comfortable in their dealings with the federal bureaucracy. The lot of the reservation Indian was hardly mentioned in the several thousand pages of task force reports that covered a variety of subjects. Following submission of the report, Congress promptly abolished the standing Indian affairs subcommittees in Interior and all thoughts of legislative reform vanished.

Finally, a special Senate Select Committee on Indian Affairs was authorized to try to sort out the various suggestions of the American Indian Policy Review Commission. It was evident, even to the most casual observer, that federal Indian policy objectives had finally run their course and that any future efforts on the federal level to direct the Indian programs would be merely ad hoc instructions designed to placate the natives.

The present posture of Indian policy is not distinguishable from other domestic objectives. Budget cuts by the Carter and the Reagan administrations severely handicapped the progress of tribal programs on the reservation, but they were not a result of any determined effort by either administration to reduce federal responsibilities for Indians. During the 1960s and 1970s tribal governments had significantly expanded their portion of the domestic social program funds and when across-the-board cuts were made in the federal budget, Indians suffered disproportionately. Under both the Carter and the Reagan administrations, the budget for the Bureau of Indian Affairs remained substantially the same. The rhetoric of the Reagan administration was perhaps more harsh regarding federal support because it was coupled with traditional conservative ideology that suggested development of and reliance upon the private sector for continued reservation progress.

In retrospect, an easily defined federal policy designed specifically for American Indians does not presently exist. None has existed since Congress adopted termination as a reachable goal in 1954. Subsequent events have demonstrated that both Indian successes and failures have been connected to the Indian status as an identifiable racial minority within American society, not to the status of Indian tribes as domestic dependent nations. Some efforts have been made by Indians to assert a quasi-nationhood to the exclusion of state and federal jurisdiction and relationships. Bingo games symbolize this expression and demonstrate the desperate need of tribal governments for a large and continuing cash flow to enable them to continue reservation programs. Recently, however, a move has been made in Congress to provide rules and regulations under which tribes can conduct gambling enterprises on their reservations, perhaps forecasting the concluding chapter in the Indian effort to remain as politically distinct communities.

Although the practical fact appears to be that Indians have foresaken their traditional special status for that of a needy minority, untangling the network of federal laws and protections that have been woven around Indians in the past two centuries will not be easy to accomplish. Extensive federal responsibilities attach to Indian properties, and loosening this iron grip without having Indian lands placed in jeopardy will be a major undertaking. Consequently, smaller policy considerations will undoubtedly occupy the attention of Indians and their friends and allies for several generations to come. Instead of broad national policies that speak of directions for programs and services, however, we may discover that constructing small models for stabilization of specific communities or functions more suitable. The Indian "problem," which was derisively labeled a "problem" because of racial and cultural differences a century ago, seems finally to have evolved into a social problem area and may finally be resolved as other such problems have been resolved.

NOTES

1. Cherokee Nation v. Georgia, 30 U.S. (5 Pet.). 1 (1931); Worcester v. Georgia, 31 U.S. (6 Pet.). 515 (1832).
2. 21 U.S. (8 Wheat.) 543 (1823).
3. Among these acts was the first Trade and Intercourse Act, 1 Stat. 329.
4. Wilcomb E. Washburn, ed. *The American Indian and the United States: A Documentary History,* vol. II (New York: Random House, 1973), pp. 1105-1106.
5. 4 Stat. 729; 4 Stat. 735.
6. U.S., Congress, House, Report No. 474, 23rd Cong., 1st Sess., p. 11.
7. Ibid., emphasis added.
8. 3 Stat. 383.
9. House Report, *supra* note 6, pp. 13-14, emphasis added.
10. 16 Stat. 544.
11. 187 U.S. 553 (1903).
12. 36 Stat. 855.
13. 54 Stat. 1125.
14. Pub. L. 81-815 (64 Stat. 967) and Pub. L. 81-874 (64 Stat. 1100) codified at 20 U.S.C. §§ 236-44, 631-47.
15. 86 Stat. 334.
16. Pub. L. 93-638, 25 U.S.C. §§ 455 (1976).

Contributors

Joyotpaul Chaudhuri is Professor of Government and head of the department at New Mexico State University. His interests include democratic theory and American Indian policy.

Vine Deloria, Jr., Professor of Political Science, University of Arizona, and former Executive Director, National Congress of American Indians is a well-known author and an active spokesman and leader in Indian affairs.

Tom Holm is Assistant Professor of Political Science, University of Arizona. He has written a number of articles and a book on different aspects of Indian studies.

Michael G. Lacy is Assistant Professor of Sociology, University of Nebraska at Omaha. His current research interests involve historical and cross-national analyses of energy consumption.

Daniel McCool is Assistant Professor at Texas A&M University. He is the author of several journal articles and a book in his chosen fields of interest, which include western water rights and water development, natural resources policy, bureaucratic behavior, and minority group politics.

Robert A. Nelson is a Ph.D. candidate in the College of Education at the University of Oregon. His research interests include the sociology of organizations and educational policy and management. He is working currently on a study of the policy departments of in-service training programs.

Sharon O'Brien is Assistant Professor, Department of Government and International Studies at the University of Notre Dame.

257

Her research interests include the international protection of human rights and tribal governments. Her recent publications have dealt with Canadian-United States Indian issues under international law.

John F. Petoskey, Staff Attorney for the National Indian Youth Council, Inc., received the Juris Doctor degree from the University of New Mexico School of Law. He is a member of the New Mexico Bar, the Federal District Court for New Mexico, and the 10th Circuit Court of Appeals.

Fred L. Ragsdale, Jr., Professor of Law, the University of New Mexico, is a member of the Chemehuevi tribe in California. He received the Juris Doctor degree from U.C.L.A., and has taught courses in Indian law at several universities and has been a consultant for many Indian tribes and companies on Indian issues. He has served as a Deputy Associate Solicitor for the Department of the Interior and Special Assistant to the Secretary of Energy, and has written many articles in the area of Indian Law.

Joseph F. Sheley is Associate Professor of Sociology at Tulane University. His areas of specialization and research interests include criminology, criminal justice, and the sociology of law.

David L. Vinje is Associate Professor of Economics, Pacific Lutheran University. His research interests include regional economic development and economic analysis and public policy.

Mary Girvin Wallace has received the M.A. degree in Political Science from the University of Arizona, where she is a research assistant. Her research interests include public policy, and Indian policy, with emphasis on negotiated water rights settlements and the leasing of Indian water rights.

Index

259

American Indian Policy in the Twentieth Century,

designed by Bill Cason, was set in various sizes of Times Roman by the University of Oklahoma Press and printed offset on 60-pound Glatfelter B-31 by Cushing-Malloy, Inc., with case binding by John H. Dekker & Sons.